Public Policy and Politics

Series Editors: Colin Fudge and Robin Hambleton

Public policy-making in Western democracies is confronted by new pressures. Central values relating to the role of the state, the role of markets and the role of citizenship are now all contested and the consensus built up around the Keynesian welfare state is under challenge. New social movements are entering the political arena; electronic technologies are transforming the nature of employment; changes in demographic structure are creating heightened demands for public services; unforeseen social and health problems are emerging; and, most disturbing, social and economic inequalities are increasing in many countries.

How governments – at international, national and local levels – respond to this developing agenda is the central focus of the *Public Policy and Politics* series. Aimed at a student, professional, practitioner and academic readership, it aims to provide up-to-date, comprehensive and authoritative analyses of public policy-making in practice.

The series is international and interdisciplinary in scope, and bridges theory and practice by relating the substance of policy to the politics of the policy-making process.

Public Policy and Politics

Series Editors: Colin Fudge and Robin Hambleton

Public Policy and Politics
Series Standing Order
ISBN 0–333–71705–8 hardback
ISBN 0–333–69349–3 paperback
(outside North America only)

You can receive future titles in this series as they are published. To place a standing order please contact your bookseller or, in the case of difficulty, write to us at the address below with your name and address, the title of the series and an ISBN quoted above.

Customer Services Department, Macmillan Distribution Ltd
Houndmills, Basingstoke, Hampshire RG21 6XS, England

Community Care

Policy and Practice

Third Edition

Robin Means
Sally Richards
and
Randall Smith

First edition 1994
Second edition 1998
Third edition 2003

Published 2003 by
PALGRAVE MACMILLAN
Houndmills, Basingstoke, Hampshire RG21 6XS and
175 Fifth Avenue, New York, N.Y. 10010
Companies and representatives throughout the world

PALGRAVE MACMILLAN is the global academic imprint of the Palgrave Macmillan division of St. Martin's Press, LLC and of Palgrave Macmillan Ltd. Macmillan® is a registered trademark in the United States, United Kingdom and other countries. Palgrave is a registered trademark in the European Union and other countries.

ISBN 0–333–98326–2

This book is printed on paper suitable for recycling and made from fully managed and sustained forest sources.

A catalogue record for this book is available from the British Library.

10 9 8 7 6 5 4 3 2
12 11 10 09 08 07 06 05 04

Printed and bound in Great Britain
Creative Print & Design (Wales), Ebbw Vale

To **Deborah Means** and **Jim Malcomson** –
for all their support

To **Brenda Ward** – for a resilient and spirited aunt

Contents

List of Tables, Figures and Boxes

Tables

Figure

Boxes

Preface

Such is the pace of change in the world of health, housing and social policy and practice in Britain that the need for a third edition of this book became apparent within a couple of years after the appearance of the second edition in 1998. Whilst changes have taken place in all parts of Britain, the focus of the book (apart from Chapter 8) is on the impact of change in England. The first chapter of this volume outlines the main issues and concerns that have appeared on the policy agenda in the last years of the twentieth century and the early years of the twenty-first. The two authors of the earlier editions recognised that one of the impacts (on the ground) of the changes introduced in the 1990s was a shift in the relationship between the provider and user of services. The obvious way forward was to recruit a third author who could both complement the experience of the original authors and add a distinctive perspective that enhances the coherence of the book. All three authors have benefited from the new arrangement and they hope that the readers will also find that both the quality and coverage of the book have been enhanced. In agreeing this preface, the authors recognise that the world of community care policy and practice has not settled into a stable state, so it is important for readers to recognise that the 'story' in this volume ends in the last months of 2002.

ROBIN MEANS
SALLY RICHARDS
RANDALL SMITH

Acknowledgements

The production of this book has been greatly helped by advice from a wide range of people. Specifically we would like to thank the following for their very helpful guidance: John Baldock, Sophie Beaumont, Steen Bengtsson, Ingrid Eyers, Hubert Heinelt, Frances Heywood, Andreas Hoff, Rachel Hurst, Anne Jamieson, Hans-Joachim von Kondratowitz, George Leeson, Mark Priestley, Thomas Scharf, Judy Triantafillou and Miguel Angel Verdugo. This has been backed up by support and feedback from our publisher, Steven Kennedy.

Writing a book is a long and arduous business. So is producing a new edition of a book in a rapidly changing policy climate. We would like to thank family and friends for their encouragement and for putting up with bouts of evening and weekend work. Finally our ability to pull the book together has owed much to secretarial support from Claudia Bittencourt, Bernadette Cox, Jan Green and Alanna Ivin.

R.M.
S.R.
R.S.

The authors and publishers wish to thank the following who have kindly given permission for the use of copyright material: The Office of Population Censuses and Surveys for the table from J. Martin, H. Meltzer and D. Elliott, *The Prevalence of Disability Among Adults*, 1988; Basil Blackwell Ltd for a table from J. Higgins, 'Defining Community Care: Realities and Myths', in *Social Policy and Administration*, vol. 23, no. 1, 1989, material from M. Nolan and K. Caldock, 'Assessment: Identifying the Barriers of Good Practice', in *Health and Social Care in the Community*, vol. 4, no. 2, 1996, and from B. Hardy, R. Young and G. Wistow, 'Dimensions of Choice in the Assessment and Care Management Process', in *Health and Social Care in the Community*, vol. 7, no. 6, 1999; Joseph Rowntree Foundation for material from C. Cobbold, *A Cost Benefit Analysis of Lifetime Homes*, 1997, and two tables from P. Leather, *Crumbling Castles? Helping Owners to Repair and Maintain their Homes*, 2000; Ashgate Publishing Ltd for a table from K. Rummery, *Disability, Citizenship and Community Care*, 2002; Personal Social Services Research Unit for a table from M. Knapp,

G. Wistow, J. Forder and B. Hardy, *Markets for Social Care*, 1993; *Community Care* for material from L. Revans, 'Party Politics', in *Community Care*, 27 September–3 October 2001; Centre for Accessible Environments for material from S. Langton-Lockton, 'Centre Forward', in *Access by Design*, no. 75, 1998; The Policy Press for a table from R. Means, M. Brenton, L. Harrison and F. Heywood, *Making Partnerships Work in Community Care*, 1997; and Crown Copyright for permission to use material from the Royal Commission on Long Term Care, *With Respect to Old Age*, 1999; the Office of the Deputy Prime Minister, *Best Value Performance Indicators 2002/2003*, 2002; the Department of Health, *Responsibilities for Meeting Continuing Health Care Needs*, 1995, *The New NHS: Modern, Dependable*, 1997, *Modernising Social Services*, 1998, *A National Service Framework for Mental Health*, 1999, *Valuing People*, 2001, and *A National Services Framework for Older People*, 2001.

1 Introducing Community Care

The second edition of *Community Care: Policy and Practice* was published in 1998 and focused upon progress and problems in the implementation of the far-reaching changes introduced by the National Health Service and Community Care Act 1990. The 1990 Act gave the lead agency role to social services authorities for all the main 'core' groups of service users and required the stimulation of a mixed economy of care through encouraging independent providers. At a strategic level, this was to be achieved through the publication of community care plans on the basis of wide consultation with key agencies and groups, including service users and carers. Care management was to be used at the operational level to ensure service users were offered flexible packages of care which were to draw heavily upon the independent sector.

The second edition concluded with a consideration of the likely impact of a newly elected Labour government upon community care policy and practice in England and Wales. A series of important manifesto commitments were noted:

- A long-term care charter to define the standards of services people should be entitled to receive from health, housing and social services
- A Royal Commission to work out a fair system for funding long-term care for elderly people
- An independent inspection and regulation service for residential and domiciliary care
- Comprehensive civil rights for disabled people.

In addition, the commitment of the new government to collaborative working across health and social care was stressed.

However, these potentially exciting developments were set against the manifesto commitment not to raise tax or exceed the public expenditure plans of the previous administration for two years. They were also set against a judgement about where the energy for health and welfare reform was likely to be found:

> their main thinking has been directed to health care and the NHS, partly because of its great cost but also because of the attachment of the general

public to a universal health care system, free at the point of delivery. Community care for frail elderly and for disabled people does not generate the same response and hence is far lower down the political agenda. (Means and Smith, 1998a, p. 241)

This third edition offers the opportunity to compare these judgements against the reality of a well-established Labour government and its actual impact on the policy and practice of community care.

In a strange way the 1998 judgement has proved both correct and very misguided. It has been correct in that the historical continuity of prioritising acute health care over community care has been more than maintained, as will be repeatedly illustrated throughout the book. However, it was misguided in that the scale of the overall modernisation agenda for the whole of the public sector was not appreciated, nor the willingness of the government to reinvest in the welfare state after the two-year embargo as part of this modernisation strategy.

The overall modernisation agenda for local authorities was set out in *Modern Local Government: In Touch with the People* (Deputy Prime Minister, 1998). This called upon local authorities to think corporately rather than in narrow departmental terms so as to 'promote the economic, environmental and social well-being of their area' (p. 10). Local democracy was to be revitalised through such initiatives as elected mayors, local referenda and new political structures (Leach and Wilson, 2000; Rao, 2000). Economy, efficiency and effectiveness of service provision was to be ensured through the introduction of a new scrutiny system called Best Value. The equivalent White Paper on the health service was called *The New NHS: Modern, Dependable* (Department of Health, 1997b), which outlined far-reaching reforms in clinical governance as well as the need to create a primary care-rather than hospital-driven National Health Service.

The central concern of the third edition of *Community Care: Policy and Practice* is to explore how these modernisation policies are impacting upon the continuing implementation of the community care reforms introduced by the NHS and Community Care Act 1990. Have they pushed forward 'progress' on implementation or undermined the lead agency role for social services? How 'new' is modernisation or are there strong continuities with the past? Is the emphasis upon audit and quality standards improving services for users and carers or creating stifling new bureaucracies? What are the future prospects for community care if present policies are maintained? What alternatives exist? However, before these questions can be tackled, we need to say a little more about what we understand by the term 'community care' and how this relates to the present organisational and legislative framework.

What is community care?

Since the late 1960s, community care has come to be almost universally espoused as a desirable objective for service users and a central pillar of policy for governments and politicians of all persuasions. An obvious starting point is for the authors to offer a clear statement about what they understand by the term 'community care'. Which groups will be covered? Will the book cover unpaid care as well as paid care? Does it include institutional care as well as domiciliary services? Which health care services are included? What does 'community' mean in the context of the term 'community care'? These are simple questions but do not necessarily have simple answers. 'Community care' has long been a contested term used by different people in different ways at different points in time.

The starting point in this definitional quest has to be the loaded power of the word 'community' within the term 'community care'. Titmuss (1968) described community care as 'the everlasting cottage-garden trailer' and went on to remark:

> Does it not conjure up a sense of warmth and human kindness, essentially personal and comforting, as loving as the wild flowers so enchantingly described by Lawrence in *Lady Chatterley's Lover*? (p. 104)

Some 25 years later, in more prosaic language, Baron and Haldane (1992) complained that 'today we are in a period of striking certainties about the value of community care, still strangely combined with silences and absences about the details of what care in the community means, and how it is to operate for the benefit of those with special needs' (p. 3).

But where does the positive power of the term 'community care' come from? Baron and Haldane argue that it flows from the fact that 'community' is what Raymond Williams (1976) called a keyword in the development of culture and society. From the ninth century BC through to the twentieth century AD, Williams traced the use of the term 'community' to grieve for the recent passing of a series of mythical golden ages; each generation perceiving the past as organic and whole compared to the present. As Baron and Haldane point out, the term 'community' thus enables 'the continuous construction of an idyllic past of plenty and social harmony which acts as a critique of contemporary social relations' (p. 4). Thus the call by politicians and policy-makers to replace present systems of provision with community care feeds into this myth by implying that it is possible to recreate what many believe were the harmonious, caring and integrated communities of the past.

Drawing upon Glen (1993) and Purdue *et al.* (2000), Taylor (2003) argues that it is possible to identify three different 'uses' of the term community:

- Descriptive: a group or network of people who share something in common or interact with each other
- Normative: community as a place where solidarity, participation and coherence are found
- Instrumental: (a) community as an agent acting to maintain or change its circumstances; (b) the location or orientation of services and policy interventions. (p. 34)

This perspective helps to explain the popularity of policy initiatives such as community care, community schools and community policing with politicians and policy-makers. Such policies use community in an instrumental way, justified by descriptions of community which stress their assumed normative strengths. Indeed, a strong feature of the modernisation policies of Labour Governments since 1997 has been the stress upon neighbourhood and community renewal from a belief that 'healthy' communities are a prerequisite for a successful society. A key objective of this book is to delve behind the rhetoric of community care and caring communities. For example, several authors have pointed out that individuals and not communities carry out caring work, and that unpaid care is primarily carried out by female relatives (see Chapters 2 and 7). Equally, most people, including the users of community care services, have a highly complex notion of community. For some it is a small number of local streets, and for others their sense of community may come from work or leisure networks which are not geographically based. Indeed research suggests that as many as one in three people have no strong attachment to the 'community' in which they live (Taylor, 2003). Equally the provision of community care services based on local authority boundaries rarely reflects how service users perceive community. A day centre may not seem like a community service to a user if they have to travel three miles by specialist bus to reach it.

An important starting point for this analytical approach to community care is to trace the emergence of the term and its changing use over time. Yet it is very difficult to pin down the exact source. In a 1961 lecture delivered to the National Association of Mental Health, Titmuss (1968) claimed he had tried and failed to discover in any precise form its social origins, but went on to reflect that:

> institutional policies, both before and since the Mental Health Act of 1959, have, and without a doubt, assumed that someone knows what it

means. More and more people suffering from schizophrenia, depressive illnesses and other mental handicaps have been discharged from hospitals, not cured but symptom-treated and labelled 'relieved'. More and more of the mentally subnormal have been placed under statutory supervision in the community. (p. 105)

Titmuss's concern was that the reduced reliance on hospitals would not be balanced by a major expansion of community-based services. In the following year, the then Minister of Health, Enoch Powell, took the 'policy' of community care one stage further with his 1962 Hospital Plan which launched an official closure programme for large mental health and mental handicap hospitals and their replacement by a network of services to be provided in the community by local health and welfare services.

Although the origins of the phrase are obscure, it is clear that the term 'community care' was initially used to refer to a policy shift away from hospitals and towards community-based provision for 'mentally handicapped' people and for people with mental health problems. However, it soon began to be used in reference to the provision of services for elderly people and for physically disabled people. For example, the Chief Welfare Officer at the Ministry of Health was claiming in 1964 that with regard to older people:

the true centre of the picture so far as geriatric services are concerned really has shifted, or is rapidly shifting, to care in the community supported by domiciliary services, and the important thing is to remember that residential homes are in fact a vital and most important part of community service. (Aves, 1964, p. 12)

The context of this quotation was government concern about the cost of long-term hospital care for frail elderly people. The Chief Welfare Officer was justifying a move to a cheaper form of institutional care (local authority residential care) by referring to it as a community service.

The Chief Welfare Officer included the residential home in her definition of community care. But this was increasingly challenged in the 1970s. Residential care was seen by many as an expensive form of provision which consumed resources which needed to be used to fund non-institutional services such as home care, day care and sheltered housing (Bosanquet, 1978). By this definition, community care policies are about keeping people out of expensive hospital *and* residential home provision. But how was this to be achieved? *A Happier Old Age* was published by the then Labour government as a discussion document (Department of Health and Social Security, 1978a) and it asked whether a combination of suitable ordinary housing,

high-quality domiciliary services and more support for informal carers
could keep the majority of frail elderly people out of expensive local authority
residential care.

In the 1980s the definition of community care seemed to have been tight-
ened by central government yet again. The White Paper response, *Growing
Older*, to the discussion document was produced by a Conservative rather
than Labour government. It argued that:

> whatever level of public expenditure proves practicable and however it is
> distributed, the primary sources of support and care for elderly people are
> informal and voluntary ... It is the role of public authorities to sustain
> and, where necessary, develop – but never to displace – such support and
> care. Care in the community must increasingly mean by the community.
> (Department of Health and Social Security, 1981, p. 3)

The overall message was that community care (that is, informal care)
needed to be maximised, partly because it was cheaper than care based on
the provision of state-provided domiciliary services. By this definition,
community care becomes what Abrams (1977, p. 151) called 'the provision
of help, support and protection to others by lay members of societies acting
in everyday domestic and occupational settings'.

In the past, therefore, the term 'community care' has been used to argue
for changes in service emphasis. The positive virtues of community care
have been juxtaposed against expensive, rigid and bureaucratic alternatives,
such as hospitals, residential care and sometimes even domiciliary services.
However, the Wagner Committee (1988) review of residential care found it
very difficult to distinguish between residential care services and care in the
community services because of the growth of sheltered housing schemes,
resettlement hostels and 'core and cluster' schemes which offered a combination of support and housing in non-institutional settings. Equally, the
boundaries between informal care and paid care have become blurred with
the emergence of a variety of payment for caring schemes through tax
allowances, social security benefits and social services payments, which are
designed to increase the willingness of relatives, neighbours and volunteers
to perform caring roles.

Increasingly, 'community care' is used to refer to the full spectrum of
care and services received by certain groups. This was the approach adopted
by the 1989 White Paper on community care, *Caring for People*, which
stated that:

> community care means providing the right level of intervention and sup-
> port to enable people to achieve maximum independence and control

over their own lives. For this aim to become a reality, the development of a wide range of services provided in a variety of settings is essential. These services form part of a spectrum of care, ranging from domiciliary support provided to people in their own homes, strengthened by the availability of respite care and day care for those with more intensive care needs, through sheltered housing, group homes and hostels where increasing levels of care are available, to residential care and nursing homes and long-stay hospital care for those for whom other forms of care are no longer enough. (Department of Health, 1989a, p. 9)

The White Paper explains that its focus is mainly upon the role of the statutory and independent sectors but that 'the reality is that most care is provided by family, friends and neighbours' (ibid.). The statutory and independent sectors are seen as responsible for providing social care (including housing), health care and appropriate social security benefits. This book takes a similarly broad view of what is meant by the term 'community care'. It thus cons ders not only the c   unpaid carers but also the provision of th   full spectrum of   residential and services by the public, pri   ate and voluntar

Having said this, the problematic nature of a   definitional source needs to be recognised. The Act told social services authorities that they were the lead agency in community care and required them to produce community care plans. However, the encouragement for this lead role to involve the development of care management systems, purchaser–provider splits and a mixed economy of social care is to be found mainly in the community care White Paper (Department of Health, 1989a) and subsequent policy guidance (Department of Health, 1990). The development of these tasks required social services to draw upon a patchwork of previous law. Thus, the National Assistance Act 1948 remains the pivotal piece of legislation for residential provision while the legislative underpinning for the provision of domiciliary services is complex with a range of laws affecting entitlement and provision.

Who are the users? Who are the carers?

This book follows the broad definition of the 1989 White Paper *Caring for People: Community Care in the Next Decade and Beyond* in terms of defining who are the potential users of community care services:

> many people need some extra help and support at some stage in their lives, as a result of illness or temporary disability. Some people, as a

result of the effects of old age, of mental illness including dementia, of mental handicap or physical disability or sensory impairment, have a continuing need for care on a longer-term basis. People with drug and alcohol related disorders, people with multiple handicaps and people with progressive illnesses such as AIDS or multiple sclerosis may also need community care at some time. (Department of Health, 1989a, p. 10)

The emphasis of this book is equally broad although it concentrates most of its comments on the traditional main client groups, namely frail older people, physically disabled people, people with mental health problems and people with learning difficulties. However, it does this with a recognition that client groups are really bureaucratic and/or medical labels which rarely reflect how service users and carers perceive their personal assistance needs. Such labels have a number of negative consequences. First, they have the effect of dividing service users against each other in the scramble for resources rather than facilitating and coming together to campaign for the appropriate resourcing for health and welfare systems (see Chapter 7). Second, they fail to recognise that many people cut across the traditional boundaries. For instance, physically disabled people become old as do people with learning difficulties. Many older people experience the physical problems of later life but significant numbers will also have mental health problems such as dementia (Hofman *et al.*, 1991) or depression (Sidell, 1995).

The danger is that social services will respond to only some aspects of the support needs of such individuals and this will be determined by the client focus of their social work team (Rummery, 2002). Thus, Walker *et al.* (1996) in their study of 120 people with learning difficulties in the community found that:

> for the most part, the client group-oriented health and social services culture has not begun to address the emergence of this … user group and as a result, they are falling between services for people with learning difficulties and those for older people. This double jeopardy is resulting in older people with learning difficulties being even more excluded and marginalised than those who fall neatly into the service provision categories. (p. 56)

Similar findings emerged from the more recent study by Daker-White *et al.* (2002) on marginalised groups in dementia care. Younger people with dementia and those from minority ethnic groups were either offered no services or those likely to meet only some of their needs.

Third, much service provision, especially in areas such as supported housing, has traditionally targeted narrowly defined groups such as drug abusers, homeless people or people with mental health problems (Means, 1996). People in need of accommodation and support are thus encouraged to define themselves as drug abusers, homeless people or people with mental health problems rather than as individuals who might face all three challenges. The requirements of many people cut across such narrow administrative categories but they still feel obliged to present themselves as having one particular dominant need if they want to get help. Client group categories encourage service-led rather than user-driven community care provision. Chapter 6 explores whether the *Supporting People* initiative (Department of Transport, Local Government and the Regions, 2001b) will achieve a genuine break from the limitations of this past approach.

In terms of actual numbers of service users, the clearest information is available for those over 65 as a result of the work of the Royal Commission on Long Term Care (Sutherland Report, 1999a) and its associated Research Volume 1 (1999b). Table 1.1 shows that in the late 1990s about 600,000 were receiving home care funded through a local authority while just over 480,000 were in care homes of one kind or another.

TABLE 1.1   Number of people in the UK receiving long-term care services by type of service and funding

	Number of recipients	Total
(a) Domiciliary care		
Home care	610,000	
Community nursing	530,000	
Day care	260,000	
Private help	670,000	
Meals	240,000	
(b) Institutional care		Total
Residential care		
Publicly financed	205,000	
Privately financed	83,750	288,750
Nursing home care		
Publicly financed	115,000	
Privately financed	42,500	157,500
Hospital	34,000	34,000
All institutional residents		480,250

Source: Sutherland Report (1999a) p. 9.

TABLE 1.2   Estimate of numbers of disabled adults in Great Britain with different types of disability (thousands)

Type of disability	In private households	In establishments	Total population
Locomotion	4,005	327	4,332
Reaching and stretching	1,083	147	1,230
Dexterity	1,572	165	1,737
Seeing	1,384	284	1,668
Hearing	2,365	223	2,588
Personal care	2,129	354	2,483
Continence	957	185	1,142
Communication	989	213	1,202
Behaviour	1,172	175	1,347
Intellectual functioning	1,182	293	1,475
Consciousness	188	41	229
Eating, drinking, digesting	210	66	276
Disfigurement	391	*	*

* Data not provided.

Source: Martin *et al.* (1988) p. 25.

However, it needs to be remembered that those 'known' to the community care system are only a small percentage of those with support needs or those providing informal caring services. The Office of Population Censuses and Surveys (OPCS) research in the mid-1980s is still often quoted on the prevalence, range and severity of disability in Britain. The researchers distinguished thirteen different types of disability based on the international classification of impairments, disabilities and handicaps used by the World Health Organisation (see Table 1.2). They also developed a classification system for severity of disability which could be used to classify people with different numbers and types of disabilities. The severity of disability in each of the thirteen areas was established for each individual and the three highest scores were then combined so that people could be allocated to an overall severity category. Category one was for the least severe and category ten was for the most severe.

It was estimated that six million adults in Great Britain had one or more impairments, of which one million were assigned to the lowest severity category. Smaller numbers were identified in each successive category, with 200,000 in category ten. As one might expect, elderly people dominated the two highest categories:

the rate of disability at this level of severity did not rise steeply until age 70, and rose very steeply after 80. Altogether 64% of adults with this degree of severity were aged 70 or over; 41% were aged 80 or over. (Martin *et al.*, 1988, p. 411)

The Sutherland Report (1999b) also looked at the issue of dependency in later life. Drawing upon the concept of activities of daily living, it was 'estimated that 2,470,000 (28%) of the elderly household population have some level of dependency' of which 606,000 (7 per cent) faced difficulties sufficiently severe to mean they could not complete some of these activities without the assistance of another person (p. 6).

There have also been recent prevalence estimates with regard to people with learning difficulties. Drawing upon a range of epidemiological sources, the recent White Paper estimated there were 210,000 people with severe and profound learning difficulties (Department of Health, 2001a) of which 65,000 were children and young people, 120,000 were adults of working age and 35,000 were older people. With regard to people with mental health problems, the National Service Framework (NSF) document noted that one quarter of routine GP consultations were for people with a mental health problem and that around 90 per cent of mental health care is provided solely by primary care (Department of Health, 1999b). The most common mental health problems are depression, eating disorders and anxiety disorders. The NSF pointed out that in any one year one woman in 15 and one man in 30 will be affected by depression and 4,000 suicides are attributed to this cause.

However, the NSF for mental health did not address the issue of dementia. McClatchey (2002) has drawn on the meta-analysis by Hofman *et al.* (1991) of population studies in twelve European countries to develop detailed prevalence figures for a population of 200,000 with an age and sex profile based on that of the whole of England at the 1991 census. His work shows that 1,860 women and 815 men over 70 are likely to suffer from dementia in this size of population.

Finally, there is a need to profile the extent to which people with support needs receive help from informal carers. Estimates of the number of informal carers have been drawn from the regularly repeated General Household Survey (GHS), a large sample of the general population living in private households in Great Britain. In 2000, it was estimated that there were about six–eight million adult carers in five million households (Maher and Green, 2002). Recent research has distinguished between 'informal helping' and 'heavily involved' caring with only the latter likely to lead to any request for public support. Pickard (1999), in her review of research on the 1995 GHS, explains how 'most of the indicators suggest that there were between one and three-quarters and two million heavily involved carers at this time' (p. 18). Phillipson *et al.* (2001), in revisiting three classic community studies in England, compared the present situation for older residents with regard to informal care and social support to the 1950s. They concluded that close kin remained pivotal but that neighbours and friends were playing a growing role in informal helping.

However, it needs to be remembered that there is no agreed methodology for translating prevalence figures for dependency, illness or caring into the need for community care provision. Feminist commentators have long argued that the real need for state-provided services has been suppressed by the encouragement of women to take on this role by government as a mechanism for controlling public expenditure (Finch and Groves, 1983; Dalley, 1996). In a similar vein, disability rights theorists have pointed out how prevalence data stress personal inadequacy requiring a care response when the real problem may be poverty or environmental barriers (Oliver, 1990). For example, Abberley (1991) argued that many of those defined as having major locomotion difficulties in the OPCS disability surveys may simply be disadvantaged by societal failure to build accessible environments. Much of the need for individual community care support would disappear for many if such discrimination was tackled. Chapter 7 explores such critiques of community care policy and practice in more detail.

Introducing social services

The last section looked at the most important stakeholders in any community care system, namely service users and informal carers. However, there is also a need to introduce the reader to the lead agency in community care, namely social services, and some of the other actors and organisations which influence their attempts to fund, co-ordinate and deliver community care provision.

The starting point has to be to stress the complexity and variety of social services departments in England and Wales, or what Challis (1990, p. 2) called 'the dazzling array of problematic characteristics which they exhibit', including accountability to elected members, the wide range of responsibilities, the variety of staff employed and high media interest. However, the exact organisational nature of a social services department has never been precisely defined in law when compared to many NHS agencies and hence there has been a long history of organisational variation even before the 1990 reforms (Means *et al.*, 2002). Individual departments could split their activities by such categories as client group (childcare services and adult services), geography (north and south of the authority) and function (domiciliary services and residential care), and these dimensions could be combined in a variety of complex ways. In more recent years at least three major sources of organisational complexity have emerged. First, the community care reforms introduced by the 1990 Act encouraged social services authorities to split their functions between those with a purchaser/ assessor focus and those concerned with direct service provision (see Chapter 3). Second, a number of local authorities have combined all or some of their social services functions with other statutory responsibilities such as housing or education (Hill, 2000a). Finally, local authorities have begun to explore with the health service a variety of options for establishing joint commissioning and provider functions for particular client groups (Chapter 5) to a point where some have queried the very future of local authority social services (Glendinning and Means, 2002).

Variations in organisational form have long been matched by variations in the range and depth of services provided. For example, a mid-1980s study by the Audit Commission (1985) on services for elderly people in seven different authorities found wide differences, both in terms of residential care places per thousand elderly people and in terms of expenditure on domiciliary services. The following chapters will show how implementation of the community care reforms and the modernisation agenda have done little to reduce such variation despite the growing emphasis by government on performance indicators and league tables.

Such organisational and service variation is partly a reflection of the fact that social services are embedded in local government where councillors from different political parties may have opposing views about what kinds of services should be provided and how best they should be delivered (Clough, 1990; Means *et al.*, 2002). These debates have in the past been played out in the formal policy-making system of the full social services committee but also through more informal meetings and contacts which ensure that many decisions are made prior to full committee meetings (Hill, 2000b). Changes in local government arrangements, such as cabinets and scrutiny committees, have not lessened the force of this comment. Tensions between social services directors and members are common, partly because of the myriad of pressures which have to be faced and balanced (see Figure 1.1). Many of these are top-down pressures from central government, flowing from such factors as the strengths and weaknesses of the legislation and Treasury-driven financial restrictions as well as the service frameworks, practice guidance and performance indicators issued by the Department of Health (Hill, 2000b).

Chapter 4 illustrates how an important element of this pressure is the growing emphasis on audit and inspection through both the Social Services Inspectorate of the Department of Health and the Audit Commission which

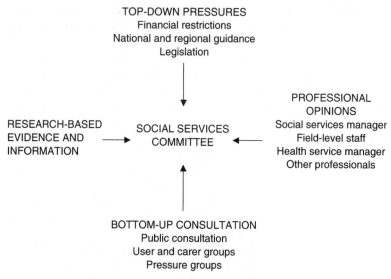

TOP-DOWN PRESSURES
Financial restrictions
National and regional guidance
Legislation

RESEARCH-BASED
EVIDENCE AND
INFORMATION

SOCIAL SERVICES
COMMITTEE

PROFESSIONAL
OPINIONS
Social services manager
Field-level staff
Health service manager
Other professionals

BOTTOM-UP CONSULTATION
Public consultation
User and carer groups
Pressure groups

FIGURE 1.1   Pressures upon social services committees

is a quango with a remit to improve the economy, efficiency and effectiveness of the work of local authorities and the health service. Since July 1996
the Social Services Inspectorate and the Audit Commission have carried out
a rolling programme of joint reviews of social services authorities which are
published and widely reported in the professional press. A bad review can
easily imperil a Director of Social Services.

Against this, councillors have to struggle with a range of professional
opinions and advice from social services managers, health managers and
others about the direction that community care policy should take in their
authority. Both local professionals and those responsible for central government guidance are likely to make reference to research and audit-based
evidence to justify their views. Authoritative sources now include not only
the Audit Commission but also the recently established Social Care Institute
for Excellence (SCIE), a key element of the government's strategy to
encourage evidence-based personal social services (Department of Health,
1998a). Finally, members see themselves as the conduit for the views of
local people in terms of public consultation, a role they are expected to
strengthen as a part of local government reform (Deputy Prime Minister,
1998). In addition, professional staff are also increasingly organising consultation meetings with service users and carers which are now seen as central
to 'Best Value' scrutiny to achieve service improvements (Department of the

Environment, Transport and the Regions, 1998b) while the disability movement continues to call for fundamental changes to the way professionals
engage with the consumers of their service (see Chapter 7).

The impact of these conflicting and ever-strengthening pressures is a
central focus of this book. There is a need to understand to what extent they
help to improve the quality of services available to those with community
care needs or whether the end result is moving close to organisational chaos.
Increasingly, the question has to be asked whether social services will
survive as a definable part of local government, given the intensity of these
pressures.

2 From Institutions to Care in the Community: The History of Neglect

This chapter discusses the historical development of social care and health provision for elderly people and for people with physical impairments, learning difficulties and mental health problems. The response to the perceived needs of all these groups was overwhelmingly institutional in the nineteenth and early twentieth centuries. Current services for these groups carry this institutional legacy, and present community care policies are, at least in part, an attempt to shake off that legacy. Thus the inclusion of this chapter is based on the strong belief that a knowledge and understanding of community care history is of practical value to busy social care managers, field-level staff and students as well as of interest to the community care academic. Those struggling with contemporary policy issues can be supported through a grasp of the way the current situation came about. Undertaking contemporary social history certainly has its own intellectual justification, but it also offers to the practitioner a perspective on the basis of which she or he can understand the dilemmas and the problems of today's agenda. As Parker (1988, p. 3) has argued in the context of residential care, no informed conclusions about the future can be reached without an understanding of key external factors and 'that, in turn, cannot be done satisfactorily without some understanding and appreciation of those forces that have shaped its history'.

The history of community care services is highly complex. Therefore tackling this theme in one chapter of a textbook risks the danger of oversimplifying events and issues. No attempt will be made to provide a detailed history for all services since such accounts exist elsewhere for most of the main care groups. Rather the focus will be on the extent of service neglect in terms of priority for resources and in terms of the quality of what has been provided from the resources made available. In the 1950s and 1960s, critics of this neglect often referred to the 'Cinderella services' or the 'Cinderella groups'. In terms of priority for resources, they were always waiting for a fairy godmother to arrive and get them to the ball. The second half of the chapter goes on to explore the main explanations which have been put forward to account for this neglect.

**The long history of neglect – services for
elderly people and physically impaired people**

Through much of the Victorian period, there was little recognition of a
social group, definable as elderly people, who needed special provision
because of their age. Elderly people, and especially elderly men, were
expected to work until they died. Those elderly people who were unable to
support themselves in the community through the labour market or with the
help of relatives were often forced to enter the workhouse, where no distinction was made between them and other paupers. The stereotype of the
workhouse is one of brutality, although research suggests that regimes were
often more neglectful in terms of boredom and regimentation rather than
anything else (Crowther, 1981) and that there was also considerable local
variation in practice (Digby, 1978).

However, a variety of pressures began to change the role of the Poor Law
in meeting the needs of older people from the late Victorian period onwards.
Technological changes were seen as forcing older workers out of the labour
market through no fault of their own and into dependence upon Poor Law
indoor and outdoor relief. Social researchers such as Booth were chroni-
cling the extent of poverty in old age and calling for the establishment of a
national system of old age pensions. Major pensions legislation was passed
in 1908, 1925, 1940 and 1948. However, it would be wrong to believe that
this was solely a reflection of societal concern about older people.
Increasingly, pension developments were driven by concerns about younger
workers. As Roebuck (1979) explains:

> In the 1920s the demand for the reduction of the pension age was
> supported less by a concern for old age poverty than for the working age
> poverty caused by unemployment. After a brief post-war boom, England
> entered a period of chronic depression and unemployment and there was
> a growing feeling that the pension age should be reduced, partly in the
> interests of the elderly, but mainly in the interest of unemployed younger
> people. All political parties made the lowering of the pension age a major
> election issue in the mid-1920s in the hope that this lowering of the
> pension age would reduce unemployment. (p. 423)

The complex system of contributory and non-contributory pension arrangements which emerged resulted in the gradual removal of older people from
the labour market and the social construction of the concept of retirement
(Phillipson, 1982). Nevertheless, large numbers of elderly people continued
to enter the workhouse, where they became an increasingly dominant group

(Means, 2001). Meanwhile, workhouse provision for older people was itself undergoing change with separate medical provision for the 'chronic sick' gradually emerging as well as a more general segregation of older people from other inmates in some institutions. Major organisational change of the Poor Law system was introduced by the Local Government Act 1929, through which the best Poor Law hospitals were retitled 'public health hospitals' and became the responsibility of local authority health committees, and hence no longer part of the Poor Law system. However, these hospitals were almost entirely focused on the acute sick, rather than medical provision for older people, who were usually seen as chronic cases.

The remaining medical provision together with other workhouse provision also ceased to be the responsibility of the 62 Poor Law boards, and was transferred to 145 counties and county boroughs, each of which was required to establish a public assistance committee. The workhouse was retitled the public assistance institution (PAI). However, the 1929 Act made little attempt to abolish the taint of pauperism. For example, entry to a PAI meant that the new elderly 'inmate' was disqualified from receiving a pension unless he or she was admitted specifically for medical treatment and even then pension rights were lost after three months. Equally, the principle of family responsibility for destitute people was maintained. The Poor Law Act 1930 stated:

> It should be the duty of the father, grandfather, mother, grandmother, husband or child, of a poor, old, blind, lame or impotent person, or other poor person, not able to work, if possessed of sufficient means, to relieve and maintain that person not able to work.

In other words, an application for relief involved an assessment of the means of near relatives, who were also expected to make a contribution to those in institutional care.

Restrictive regulations remained in force about different elements of the institutional regime such as clothing, the retention of personal possessions, visiting rights and the ability to take days out. As Roberts (1970, p. 26) put it, most elderly inmates continued to sleep 'in large dormitories, sat on hard chairs, looked out on cabbage patches diversified by concrete, were separated by sex and, except on one day a week, could not pass the gates without permission'. Disquiet about this situation developed in the late 1930s. For example, Matthews (undated) called for more colour to be brought into the lives of elderly people in institutions 'through contact with visitors from the outside world, by providing occupations as well as entertainments and by introducing more variety into their food, clothing and surroundings' (p. 13). A campaign emerged calling for the introduction of pocket money for inmates. Some public assistance committees developed small homes with more liberal regimes, although they were usually reserved for 'women of the more gentle type' or men of 'the merit class' (quoted in Means and Smith, 1998a, p. 19).

A more detailed picture of life in the medical and non-medical parts of public assistance institutions emerged during and just after the Second World War. It was a portrait of extensive neglect (Titmuss, 1976; Means and Smith, 1998b, Chapters 2 and 3). With regard to the so-called 'elderly chronic sick', there seems to have been a shortage of both beds and high-quality care. Writing in the late 1940s, McEwan and Laverty (1949) argued that the 1929 Act had a disastrous impact upon people with long-term health care needs since 'many of the new and aspiring municipal hospitals got rid of their undesirable chronic sick ... sending them to Public Assistance Institutions to upgrade their own medical services' (p. 9). This placed added pressure upon the medical wards of public assistance institutions, many of which could not cope with the increased demand for beds, and so elderly patients often had to be 'housed' elsewhere in the institutions. For example, in Bradford:

> In the Public Assistance Hospitals (The Park and Thornton View) ... patients are discharged or returned from the chronic sick wards to the ambulant or 'house' section ... In The Park, where the chronic sick wards were overcrowded, the most fit (but often frail) patients had to be sent to the ambulant wards to make room for admissions to the hospital section. There was, in consequence, a proportion of sick or disabled people in the ambulant section, where they had to remain, often confined to bed, there being no room for them in hospital. (p. 8)

The overall situation was further worsened by the creation of a 300,000-bed Emergency Medical Service at the outbreak of the Second World War since this involved the discharge of 140,000 patients in just two days. Many of the reserved beds were in PAIs and one commentator of the time claimed that:

> the people who fared worst of all were the chronically sick, the bed-ridden, the paralysed, the aged, people suffering from advanced cancer or from tuberculosis who were discharged in their hundreds from public institutions to their own homes, where they could get little, if any, care, where in all too many cases they were regarded as an intolerable burden on their relatives, and even to houses from which all their relatives had been evacuated to the country. (Morris, 1940, p. 189)

As the war progressed, further problems emerged. Many elderly patients who remained in PAI hospitals were in danger from bombing raids but there was government reluctance to move them. The ability to manage outside the hospital was undermined by the disruptions of war and so 'thousands who had formerly been nursed at home were clamouring for admission to hospitals when families were split up, when homes were damaged or destroyed, and when the nightly trek to the shelter became a part of normal life for Londoners' (Titmuss, 1976, p. 448). Some of these problems eased, but the extent to which such hospitals continued to fail to offer effective treatment to their 'chronic sick' patients was underlined by the government hospital surveys of the 1940s. Ten survey teams were appointed in 1941, some by the Minister of Health and some in conjunction with the Nuffield Provincial Hospitals Trust, to cover both voluntary and public hospitals. The aim of the surveys was to gather information about existing hospital facilities as a basis for future planning for a possible National Health Service. The findings were drawn together in *The Domesday Book of the Hospital Services* which stressed how the surveys outlined the haphazard growth and lack of planning within existing hospital services. *The Domesday Book* showed how care for the 'chronic sick' received the bitterest comments from the investigators:

> All are agreed that 'the reproach of the masses of undiagnosed and untreated cases of chronic type which litter our Public Assistance Institutions must be removed'. Without proper classification and investigation, at present young children and senile dements are 'banded together' in these institutions, along with many elderly patients whom earlier diagnosis and treatment might have enabled to return to their homes ... 'The great essential is that every patient should be thoroughly examined and treated with a view to restoration to a maximum degree of activity. Only if treatment is unsuccessful or is clearly useless, should he be regarded as chronically sick', and 'even then [he] should be subject to periodic review'. (Nuffield Provincial Hospitals Trust, 1946, p. 16)

All the investigators called for hospital services and accommodation to be completely divorced from public assistance institutions.

The subsequent establishment of the National Health Service in 1946 did bring the PAI hospitals under the same administrative system as other types of hospital provision. *The Domesday Book* did generate government awareness of the cost of blocked hospital beds from the failure both to tackle the acute illnesses of elderly patients and to provide them with appropriate rehabilitation services. Elements of the medical profession also began to argue the need to develop the specialism of geriatric medicine so as to transform the quality of medical care available to elderly patients (Martin, 1995). There is not the space in this chapter to trace the development of hospital-based geriatric medicine after the Second World War. However, it remained a low-status route for medical graduates and a low priority for health care expenditure. Some impressive initiatives did emerge but many elderly people were classified as non-curable and placed in long-stay annexes and supervised by visiting GPs. Martin has argued that these annexes were little better than the overcrowded chronic wards of the inter-war years.

The Second World War also had a negative impact on the ability of elderly people to remain in their own homes even when they had no major health problems. Support from children was reduced. Others were made homeless as a result of bombing raids. One consequence was that 'respectable' elderly people were being pushed towards PAIs, as were many elderly people definable as war victims or casualties. Many felt that regimes of PAIs and their continued association with pauperism were inappropriate for such people. A campaign around these issues emerged in spring 1943 as a result of a letter which appeared in the *Manchester Guardian*. The letter was entitled 'A Workhouse Visit' and spoke of 'a frail, sensitive, refined old woman' of 84 who was forced to live in the regime described in the following extract:

> But down each side of the ward were ten beds, facing one another. Between each bed and its neighbour was a small locker and a straight-backed, wooden uncushioned chair. On each chair sat an old woman in workhouse dress, upright, unoccupied. No library books or wireless. Central heating, but no open fire. No easy chairs. No pictures on the walls ... There were three exceptions to the upright old women. None was allowed to lie on her bed at any time throughout the day, although breakfast is at 7 a.m., but these three, unable any longer to endure their physical and mental weariness, had crashed forward, face downwards, on to their immaculate bedspreads and were asleep. (Quoted in Samson, 1944, p. 47)

The subsequent Nuffield survey committee on the problems of ageing and the care of old people which was chaired by Seebohm Rowntree indicated that poor conditions and restrictive regimes were not unusual:

> Day-rooms in such institutions are usually large and cheerless with wooden Windsor armchairs placed around the walls. Floors are mainly bare boards with brick floors in lavatories, bathrooms, kitchens and

corridors. In large urban areas such institutions may accommodate as many as 1,500 residents of various types, including more than a thousand aged persons. (Rowntree, 1980, p. 64)

The survey committee confirmed that rules in these large institutions were often harsh or harshly administered, while apathy was widespread among the residents.

The National Assistance Act 1948 was presented to Parliament as the solution to these problems. Section 21 of the Act stated that 'it should be the duty of every local authority ... to provide residential accommodation for persons who are by reasons of age, infirmity or any other circumstances in need of care and attention which is not otherwise available to them'. Townsend (1964) argued in *The Last Refuge* that changing the names of PAIs to residential homes and transferring responsibility for running them from public assistance committees to health/welfare committees had achieved little. This is perhaps a little unfair. The old system of family responsibility for maintenance was abolished and users were now perceived as residents who contributed to their keep through their pension, although they were allowed to retain five shillings for pocket money (Means, 2001). However, in many respects, the tradition of neglect continued. For example, Townsend (1964) reported that ex-PAIs 'accounted for just over half the accommodation used by county and county borough councils, for just under half the residents and for probably over three-fifths of the old people actually admitted in the course of a year' (p. 190). With regard to the 39 former PAIs visited by Townsend, 57 per cent of the accommodation was in rooms with at least ten beds. Basic amenities such as handbasins, toilets and baths were not only insufficient, but were often difficult to reach, badly distributed and of poor quality. With regard to staff, Townsend found that many were middle-aged and elderly persons who had given 'a lifetime's service under the old Poor Law as well as the new administration' (p. 39). Townsend felt:

> it would be idle to pretend that many of them were imbued with the more progressive standards of personal care encouraged by the Ministry of Health, geriatricians, social workers and others since the war ... Some were unsuitable, by any standards, for the tasks they performed, men and women with authoritarian attitudes inherited from Poor Law days who provoked resentment and even terror among infirm people. (p. 39)

In conclusion, Townsend argued that the main shortcoming was not the failure to improve the quality of residential buildings and staff, but rather the failure to develop community-based services so as to reduce the need for people to enter institutional care.

The legislative power to provide social care services in the community was very slow to develop and is a further indication of neglect, especially towards elderly people. Section 29 of the National Assistance Act 1948 did empower local authorities 'to promote the welfare of persons who are blind, deaf or dumb and others, who are substantially and permanently handi-capped by illness, injury or congenital deformity'. Nevertheless, it remained *ultra vires* for local authorities to develop preventive services for most frail elderly people, with the exception of home care, where legal empowerment was provided through the National Health Service Act 1946. Under the 1948 Act, local authorities could not develop their own meals-on-wheels services, chiropody facilities, laundry services, visiting schemes or coun-selling services for elderly people, a situation which led Parker (1965) to remark:

> The concern to maintain and foster family life evident in the Children Act was completely lacking in the National Assistance Act. The latter made no attempt to provide any sort of substitute family life for old people who could no longer be supported by their own relatives. Institutional provision was accepted without question. (p. 106)

The belief of the legislators behind the 1948 Act was that domiciliary services were an 'extra frill' and so could be left to voluntary organisations, such as old people's welfare committees (now Age Concern), the Women's (Royal) Voluntary Service and the Red Cross to develop. A complex patch-work of visiting services, day centres, meals services and chiropody did emerge but much of this provision was not easily available or was unevenly spread geographically, despite attempts by central government to develop the planning role of local authorities (Sumner and Smith, 1969). For exam-ple, Harris (1961) carried out a survey of 453 meals-on-wheels schemes and found that 40 per cent had difficulties finding enough volunteers, 40 per cent of recipients received a meal on only one day a week and 162 schemes closed completely for part of the year.

However, legislative change to empower local authorities occurred very slowly despite growing research evidence of the paucity of services being provided through the voluntary sector (Means and Smith, 1998b, Chapter 6). The National Assistance (Amendment) Act 1962 allowed local authorities to provide meals services directly for the first time, whereas previously they could only provide a grant to enable a voluntary organisation to do so. The Health Services and Public Health Act 1968 gave local authorities the general power to promote the welfare of elderly people, while the National Health Service Act 1977 made home care a mandatory responsibility rather than a discretionary power as had hitherto been the case. The implementation of the 1968 Act was delayed until April 1971 to coincide with the creation of unified social services departments. These new departments were soon dominated by childcare concerns, especially after the death of Maria Colwell in January 1973 (Parton, 1991). Research studies confirmed that social services departments maintained client group hierarchies with elderly people at the bottom so that elderly clients were usually allocated to unqualified staff on the grounds that intervention was perceived as likely to be routine and unglamorous (Bowl, 1986). Hopes of a major expansion of domiciliary services were further hit by the first tremors on the public expenditure front in the mid-1970s with the oil crisis. Increasingly, debate shifted away from the need for overall increases in social care expenditure towards arguments about the need for a shift of priorities between domiciliary and residential provision (Means *et al.*, 2002).

Less detailed contemporary research has been carried out on the historical development of health and welfare services for physically disabled people. However, several authors have claimed that 'with the Industrial Revolution and the advent of machinery designed to be operated by the able-bodied, disabled people were progressively excluded from the workplace' (Drake, 1996, p. 150). Thus, the combination of new work patterns and the breakdown of traditional community support systems imposed dependency upon many disabled people and made them heavily reliant upon welfare services. This was not very different from the experience of elderly people. Large numbers of physically disabled people were forced to live in institutions.

At first glance, Section 29 of the National Assistance Act 1948 seemed to ensure that people with physical, visual and sensory impairments were not neglected in the post-war period especially when compared with frail elderly people, since this section gave local authorities the power to develop domiciliary services for these groups. However, this was largely illusory, for reasons pointed out by Eyden (1965):

> It is clear ... that if local authorities implement to the full this legislation in close co-operation with voluntary organisations, all groups of the handicapped or their families should have a comprehensive service to which they can turn to meet any of their specialized needs. Unfortunately, this has not been the case. The duty of providing services was continued under the National Assistance Act only for the blind. Guidance to local authorities on the provision of welfare services for other classes of

handicapped persons was issued by the Ministry of Health in Circular 32/51 in August 1951, and local authorities were invited to submit schemes and their subsequent implementation was not made compulsory until 1960 ... As a result, the development of services for the deaf and other categories of handicapped persons over the past sixteen years has been patchy and inadequate. (p. 171)

Even the 1960 deadline had little meaning since local authorities were able to offer minimal provision yet still meet the requirements of the Act. This situation meant that the main community-based service available to physically disabled people and their families was the home care service (Topliss, 1979).

These inadequacies led Alf Morris MP to introduce a private member's bill designed to compel local authorities to develop comprehensive welfare and support services for disabled people and this subsequently became the Chronically Sick and Disabled Persons Act 1970. This Act imposed duties but it was not paralleled by the allocation of sufficient extra resources to local authorities. Topliss claims that 'this has meant that the claims of the disabled have had to compete with the claims on the local authority budget of all other sections of the community' and that 'the sort of massive reallocation of expenditure needed to implement the ... Act fully, in the absence of special earmarked funds, has apparently proved politically impossible for local authorities' (p. 114).

On residential care for physically disabled people, the National Assistance Act 1948 did make reference to the specific needs of younger physically disabled people as being different from those of frail elderly people. However, most local authorities continued to place physically disabled people in residential homes for older people. Only a minority of local authorities developed separate homes in the 1950s and 1960s, despite the growing awareness that the overall number of younger disabled people had increased because of a number of factors, including the war, the 1950s polio epidemic and increased life expectancy from medical advances. Detailed figures in the balance of provision are difficult to come by, although Leat (1988, p. 206) shows that in 1972 'there were 8,000 younger people in homes also housing elderly people although more than half of these younger people were in their early sixties'. She also draws upon a survey by Harrison (1986) to show that by the mid-1980s only 54 of the 115 local authorities in England and Wales had set up homes catering specifically for younger physically disabled people, but she points out that many of the others may have been making use of specialist voluntary and private homes. By far the most influential of these independent sector providers of residential care was Cheshire Homes, which was founded in 1948 and developed the concept of a 'family home' which claimed to meet the needs of younger physically disabled people.

The most detailed survey of residential provision in the early post-war period was carried out by Miller and Gwynne (1972) who revealed many of the same inadequacies found by Townsend (1964) for elderly people, but with the added concern that many of those surveyed were being offered residential care as their only accommodation option for the whole of their adult life course and not just for the last part of it. They lamented that 'by the very fact of committing people to institutions of this type, society is defining them as, in effect, socially dead' because 'society has effectively washed its hands of the inmates as significant social beings' (p. 89). By the early 1980s, some of these 'inmates' had decided to organise their own housing and support solutions outside such residential institutions. Integrated living and independent living models began to emerge. However, most commentators point out that this was the response of disabled people to the neglect they had received from able-bodied professionals and policy-makers in terms of developing service responses which enable disabled people to be fully integrated within society (Finkelstein, 1993).

Services for people with mental health problems and learning difficulties

Having looked at the development of provision for elderly and physically impaired people, it is now appropriate to consider the growth of services for people with mental health problems and learning difficulties. Does the same pattern of neglect emerge? Several authors have charted the growth of asylums for 'lunatics' (people with mental health problems) and 'idiots' (people with learning difficulties) from a community care perspective (see, for example, Malin *et al.*, 1980; Murphy, 1991; Jones, 1993) while others have studied asylums from a more general sociological interest in madness (Scull, 1993). More recently, Bartlett and Wright (1999) have produced a detailed account of the care in the community from 1750 to 2000 which has always existed outside the walls of the asylum.

Murphy (1991) has argued that asylum growth from the late 1840s onwards was initially a development to be welcomed, since previous workhouse provision was failing to cope. She argues that the social reformers had a vision of a therapeutic community in which 'insanity ... might be healed by a gentle system of rewards and punishments, amusements, occupation and kindly but firm discipline' (p. 34) although she accepts that the reality proved far inferior to the vision. Others have been far less sanguine. Scull (1993) saw the asylums as a mechanism by which the community and individual families could shed their responsibilities for troublesome and unwanted people. Certainly the legislative framework was draconian up to 1930, since admission depended on certification as 'a lunatic, an idiot or a person of unsound mind', which involved an order to be detained by a judicial authority. As Parker (1988, p. 12) points out:

> Such a requirement imposed a stigma additional to any that was associ- ated with being in an asylum. Not only was admission dependent upon certification, but the order for commitment carried with it the prospect of its irrevocability. De-certification and release were not easily obtained.

The majority of such inmates were also certified as paupers unless they or their relatives could pay privately for their detention.

The numbers of people with mental health problems detained in asylums (renamed mental health hospitals in 1930) grew spectacularly. Gibbons (1988, p. 161) talks of a situation where

> by 1890 there were sixty-six county and borough asylums in England and Wales with an average 802 inmates and 86,067 officially certified cases of insanity in England and Wales, more than four times as many as forty- five years earlier. By 1930 there were nearly 120,000 patients in public asylums and by 1954 at the peak in numbers, there were over 148,000.

Gibbons sums up this situation as being one in which there were 'ever larger numbers of chronic cases in institutions of increasing size, with ever fewer therapeutic pretensions' (p. 160). Scull (1993) argues forcibly that such growth reflected how these 'warehouses of the unwanted' covered a dis- parate collection of individuals whom the community were keen to be rid of, such as the alcohol-dependent with delirium tremens, people with epilepsy, women depressed and exhausted by multiple pregnancies and older people with dementia.

Murphy (1991) provides a glimpse of life in the typical Victorian asylum. She claims that:

> life … was governed by a rigid timetabled regime of sleep, work, eat. Whitewashed walls; plain brick, stone or wooden floors; deal benches and tables; and two WCs for thirty or forty patients provided a fairly cheerless though roomy environment. Windows were generally barred and many wards were locked, although the better asylums gave consider- able internal freedom to the inmates. (p. 38)

Such asylums had few trained doctors, perhaps three or four for every thousand patients. Hence, much of the day-to-day work was performed by low paid nursing attendants who often worked a 90-hour week.

In many respects, the situation was just as alarming for people with learning difficulties in the pre-war period. The term 'neglect' is probably misleading since services for this group have often been influenced by moral panics about the need to protect the genetic stock of the country by discouraging those of 'low' intelligence from 'breeding'. Gladstone (1996) indicates that the Victorian period was often a period of optimism about the potential for training and educating people with learning difficulties, even if this was often in the context of their removal to an institution under the Idiots Act 1886. However, Ryan and Thomas (1980) point out that the growth of such institutionalised provision reflected pressures upon families as a result of the Industrial Revolution which undermined the capacity of families to care for those with long-term dependency needs.

In any case, optimism about the potential of institutions to help those with learning difficulties was undermined by the new science of genetics with its tendency to perceive 'mental defectives' as less than human. Most geneticists believed that intelligence was innate. They were alarmed by high birth rates amongst the poorest and by implication the least intelligent members of society, since such a trend could undermine the overall genetic stock of the nation and hence the capacity to remain a dominant colonial power. Mental defectiveness was seen as genetically inherited and hence the segregation of 'mental defectives' from the rest of society was essential.

Several authors have charted how this led to calls for the establishment of farm and industrial colonies, together with the prohibition of marriages involving those labelled as 'moral defectives' who were seen as often on the borderline of 'mental defectiveness' (Malin *et al.*, 1980, Chapter 4; Abbott and Sapsford, 1987). Such views had a major impact upon the thinking of the 1908 Royal Commission on the Care and Control of the Feeble-Minded and on the legislative details of the Mental Deficiency Act 1913. This Act made reference to idiots, imbeciles and the feeble-minded, categories based on the extent of the learning difficulty, while the term 'moral imbecile' was introduced to cover what was seen as a more generalised social problem group whose low intelligence made them prone to 'loose morals'. Section 2 of the Act specified the circumstances under which a 'defective' from these groups might be dealt with by being sent to an institution or placed under guardianship:

- At the insistence of his parent or guardian
- If in addition to being a defective he was a person (i) who was found neglected, abandoned, or without visible means of support, or cruelly treated

or ... in need of care or training which could not be provided in his home; or (ii) who was found guilty of any criminal offence, or who was ordered to be sent to an approved school; or (iii) who was undergoing imprisonment, or was in an approved school; or (iv) who was an habitual drunkard; or (v) who had been found incapable of receiving education at school, or that by reason of a disability of mind required supervision after leaving school. (quoted in Malin *et al.*, 1980, p. 41)

Once a person had been admitted to an institution on these grounds, the Board of Control was in a position to block the discharge of anyone they considered unfit to live in the community. Certain safeguards were built into this draconian system. Parents and guardians needed two medical certificates, one of which had to be approved for such purposes by the local health authority or the Minister of Health. Section 2(b), quoted above, used the phrase 'in addition to being a defective'. However, in practice, it was relatively easy to place any person with learning disability in an institution using this Act, while others experiencing social difficulties such as homelessness were equally vulnerable irrespective of their mental abilities. Once they were committed, 'the term "certification" had a permanence about it, probably enhanced by the prevailing views of invariance of intellectual abilities and certainly compounded by the essentially subjective nature of the definitions of the Act' (Malin *et al.*, 1980, p. 42).

Ryan and Thomas (1980, p. 107) summed up the overall situation in the following way:

This Act established the basis of a separate and unified service, which would exclude mental defective people from other welfare and social agencies as well as from the general education system.

The total number of 'defectives' under the care and control of the mental deficiency legislation rose rapidly. Figures supplied by Tredgold (1952) and quoted by Malin *et al.* (1980, p. 43) show that numbers rose from 12,000 in 1920 to 90,000 by 1939. Most of them were placed in large isolated 'colonies', whose regime was outlined in the Report of the Mental Deficiency Committee (1929):

The modern institution, generally a large one, preferably built on a colony plan, takes defectives of all grades of defect and all ages. All, of course, are probably classified according to their mental capacity and age. The Local Mental Deficiency Authority has to provide for all grades of defect, all types of case and all ages, and an institution that cannot, or will not, take this case for one reason and that case for another is of no use to the Authority. An institution which takes all types and ages is economical because the high-grade patients do the work and make everything necessary, not only for themselves, but also for the lower grade. In an institution taking only lower grades, the whole of the work has to be done by paid staff, in one taking only high grades the output of work is greater than is required for the institution itself and there is difficulty in disposing of it. In the all-grade institution, on the other hand, the high-grade patients are the skilled workmen of the colony, those who do all the higher processes of manufacture, those on whom there is a considerable measure of responsibility; the medium-grade patients are the labourers, who do the more simple routine work in the training shops and about the institution; the rest of the lower-grade patients fetch and carry or do the very simple work. (Quoted in Malin *et al.*, 1980, p. 43)

How was the situation changed for people with learning difficulties and mental health problems by the establishment of a National Health Service and other related reforms? The National Health Service saw provision for those with mental health problems and learning difficulties brought more into mainstream health care provision. Asylums were redesignated as hospitals and became the responsibility of regional hospital boards. Local authorities became responsible for the following range of services under Section 28 of the National Health Service Act 1946:

- The initial care and removal to hospital of persons dealt with under the Lunacy and Mental Treatment Acts
- The ascertainment and (where necessary) removal to institutions of mental defectives, and the supervision, guardianship, training and occupation of those in the community, under the Mental Deficiency Acts
- The prevention, care and after-care of all types of patients, so far as this was not otherwise provided for.

However, the first two were statutory responsibilities, while the third represented a permissive power. Local authorities showed little enthusiasm for using their permissive powers and in 1958/9 overall local authority expenditure on people with mental health problems was only £4.1 million (Goodwin, 1990, p. 68).

Expenditure on hospital-based provision was not much more impressive. Drawing upon a number of sources, Goodwin (1990, p. 67) found that in the early 1950s, mental and mental deficiency hospitals contained 40 per cent of in-patient beds in the NHS but received only 20 per cent of the hospital budget. He also pointed out that the average cost of treating a mentally distressed in-patient was £3 15 s 11 d in 1950/1 compared with £4 13 s 11 d in 1959/60 (at 1950/1 prices) but that far more dramatic price rises had occurred for other groups in the same period. For example, the cost of in-patient maternity care rose from £6 9 s 5 d to £16 11 s 3 d. Goodwin claims 'these figures clearly underline why the mental health services have earned the tag of a "Cinderella" service' (p. 67).

At first glance, the Cinderella tag appears to have been removed as a result of the Royal Commission on Mental Illness and Mental Deficiency which sat from 1954 to 1957, and the subsequent Mental Health Act 1959. The latter reformed the legislative framework of constraint and envisaged the development of a complex infrastructure of local authority-provided services such as hostels, day care, social work support and sheltered employment schemes.

However, not only did these services fail to materialise (Welshman, 1999), but in 1961, Enoch Powell, the then Minister of Health, informed the annual conference of the National Association for Mental Health that:

> I have intimated to the hospital authorities who will be producing the constituent elements of the plan that in fifteen years time, there may be needed not more than half as many places in hospitals for mental illness as there are today. (Quoted in Jones, 1993, p. 160)

As a result, Murphy (1991, p. 60) describes 1962–90 as 'the disaster years' for people with mental health problems. She explains that 'by 1974 there were 60,000 fewer residents in large mental hospitals than there had been in 1954, but very few services at all existed in the community', while Payne (1999) points out how this situation encouraged the 'revolving door' syndrome of admission, discharge and readmission for those with enduring mental health problems. In a similar vein, Atkinson (1988) notes the failure of local authorities to develop services for children and adults with learning difficulties. She indicates that 'a few residential homes, or hostels, appeared here and there' while 'local authorities developed some training facilities in the community and appointed Mental Welfare Officers to make routine visits to the family homes' (p. 128). Provision remained based on hospitals. Institutional and treatment regimes remained controversial. For people with mental health problems, the emphasis was now on treatment not custody. However, the introduction of anti-psychotic drugs and new treatments such as ECT were seen to raise major issues about civil liberties. There were also numerous exposés of physical and mental cruelty by staff over patients. Such practices with regard to psycho-geriatric patients were outlined by

Robb (1967) in *Sans Everything: A Case to Answer*, while Morris (1969) in *Put Away* provided evidence of the generally poor conditions in many long-stay mental handicap hospitals. Against this, Jones (1972) lamented how the popular press of the late 1960s began to exaggerate such stories and to imply that the worst abuses were the norm rather than the exception.

Governments continued to take initiatives in the 1970s to promote community-based provision and to reduce hospital provision for both people with learning difficulties (*Better Services for the Mentally Handicapped*, Department of Health and Social Security, 1971) and for people with mental health problems (*Better Services for the Mentally Ill*, Department of Health and Social Security, 1975). Yet the pivotal report of the Audit Commission (1986), *Making a Reality of Community Care*, found limited movement on the hospital front and virtually no progress in terms of developing adequate community services. Both groups continued to be treated as a low priority for service developments.

As a result it is impossible to be certain about the overall standard of provision and how this varied in the 40-year period from the establishment of the National Health Service in 1946 to the publication of *Making a Reality of Community Care* (Audit Commission, 1986). However, Frank Thomas's diary of everyday life in the ward of a large mental handicap hospital in the late 1970s perhaps captures how 'patients' become treated as less than fully human through mundane everyday actions rather than through spectacular examples of abuse. Here are two examples:

1. Tea mixed with milk and sugar to save time, mess and trouble. How many lumps, say when with the milk? You must be joking. (Thomas, 1980, p. 35)
2. Bad habit I picked up from the other nurses. Fitting out someone for his trip to the workshop and muttering 'That'll do', as if the guy's appearance meant nothing to him, just a neat reproduction of my own preferences or lack of them. Not asking the guy if he was all right, whether it'll do. If a person is not allowed a say in what he looks like, then what is the point? Haircuts en masse – short back and sides, no one is allowed to refuse. Choice of raincoat from a communal pile, communal underwear and socks. Communal combs and brushes. One tube of toothpaste and a couple of tooth mugs for twenty-five patients. (p. 43)

Throughout this section on the long history of neglect of community care services for all the main care groups, one cannot but be struck by the continuity of the images of institutional regimes over the last hundred years, and the persistent failure to develop alternative community-based systems of provision.

Explanations of neglect

How can we explain the long history of neglect of services for these 'Cinderella' groups? This chapter makes no pretence that there is a single simple answer to this question, but rather identifies a number of strands. Four different explanations will be addressed. First, we will look at the political economy approach which explains social policy developments (or lack of them) by reference to the changing needs of the capitalist mode of production. Second, the complex role of institutions in social control will be considered, and third, we will outline the central concern of governments to encourage informal care and the knock-on consequences of this for the neglect of community-based services. The fourth and final explanation looks at cultural stereotypes about ageing and disability.

The political economy perspective

The main tenets of the political economy approach to disability have been clearly summarised by Oliver (1990):

> Changes in the organisation of work from a rural-based, cooperative system where individuals contributed what they could to the production process, to an urban, factory-based one organised around the individual waged labourer, had profound consequences ... As a result of this, disabled people came to be regarded as a social and educational problem and more and more were segregated in institutions of all kinds including workhouses, asylums, colonies and special schools, and out of the mainstream of social life. (p. 28)

Oliver points out that this is a major simplification of some highly complex processes but stresses that the key insight is the need to search for linkages between changes in public policy and changes in the sphere of production. In a similar vein, Scull (1993) argues that the asylum became a convenient dumping ground for a wide range of individuals who could not cope in the community and hence contribute to the economy.

Perhaps the clearest example of this relationship concerns the emergence of a system of retirement pensions in the early twentieth century as part of a process of removing elderly people from the labour market during a period of high unemployment (Phillipson, 1982). The effect of such initiatives has been to minimise opportunities for elderly and disabled people in the labour market and this has ensured their 'structured dependency' on the state (Townsend, 1981). At the same time, elderly people form a reserve army of labour which can be drawn back into work during periods of labour shortage. Research has provided graphic illustrations of the way retirement from work was painted as encouraging physical decline and death in the labour market shortage years of the 1950s so as to draw older people back into employment (Phillipson, 1982). Against this, in the recession years of the 1980s, older workers were encouraged to make way for younger workers by retiring as early as possible. In a similar way, it could be argued that Conservative Governments in the 1980s encouraged disabled people on to invalidity benefit so as to reduce unemployment rates, only to reverse this trend when their primary concern switched from unemployment to levels of social security expenditure, a policy emphasis very much reinforced by Labour Governments since 1997. Structured dependency has taken a number of forms. First, it has involved dependence on state benefits which keep many elderly and disabled people trapped within poverty (Oliver, 1996; Tregaskis, 2002). Second, it has encouraged an outlook in which health and community care services for disabled people are seen as a low resource priority compared with service developments for children, since the latter have a clear future role in production and reproduction. During the Second World War there was early support for the evacuation of children and mothers from areas under threat from bombing raids, but a great reluctance to extend this provision to frail elderly people because they were not, in the government jargon of the day, 'potential effectives' (Means and Smith, 1998b, Chapter 2). Equally, the overall cost of providing health and social care services for elderly and disabled people can be seen as a public expenditure burden which inhibits economic growth. Such concerns have appeared in official reports. For example, *The Rising Tide* from the Health Advisory Service (1983) explained that the number of people with dementia would rise rapidly because of the growth of the very old and that 'the flood is likely to overwhelm the entire health care system' (p. 1). Godsell (2002) has argued how a key driver for deinstitutionalisation was the high cost of specialist hospital-based care rather than the limitations of such provision.

There are several criticisms which can be levelled at the political economy approach, although, in fairness to most of its proponents, they recognise that its value lies in providing a very broad grasp of the link between changes in the means of production and changes in public policy (Phillipson, 1998). In Chapter 1, it was shown how some people misuse history to manufacture a fictitious golden past based on mythical values. Prior to the Industrial Revolution, all frail elderly people were *not* supported in the 'bosom' of their extended families, local villages did *not* 'support' every person with a learning difficulty, and appropriate work was *not* found for all those with physical impairments and mental health problems. However, this is recognised by Oliver (1990, p. 28), who indicates that the Industrial Revolution had a major impact on disabled people but that it is impossible 'to assess whether these changes affected the quality of the experience of disability negatively or positively, largely because history is silent on the experience of disability'.

Another linked criticism is the argument that the emergence of state benefits represented a major 'gain' for elderly and disabled people compared with their previous reliance on the workhouse, Poor Law relief, the family and low-paid employment (Johnson, 1987). Pensions are provided as a right. They protect elderly people from the vagaries of the labour market and hence provide many of them with the option of a fairly comfortable retirement which they are likely to prefer to continued employment in unattractive work. However, such views can be challenged on the grounds that they deflect attention away from the extent of benefit-based poverty amongst elderly and disabled people. They can also be challenged on the grounds that many elderly and disabled people wish to work. Indeed, Oliver (1996) quotes from the fundamental principles of disability as laid out by the Union of the Physically Impaired Against Segregation which included the need to fight for jobs rather than improved benefits. This is because 'in the final analysis the particular form of poverty principally associated with physical impairment is caused by our exclusion from the ability to earn an income on a par with our able-bodied peers, due to the way employment is organised' (p. 23).

A third criticism is that the concept of structured dependency can easily drift into an acceptance of structural determinism which treats elderly and disabled people as 'cultural dopes' who lack any autonomy or capacity for self-determination (Gilleard and Higgs, 2000). It is crucial to recognise the frequent imbalance of power between elderly and disabled people and the providers of state services. However, the consequent 'dependency' should not be perceived as a static, determined phenomenon, but rather recognised as a component of social processes in which elderly and disabled people continue to struggle to influence the form of their lives even in situations where they have only limited power (Tulle and Mooney, 2002).

Institutions and service neglect

There is a rich and complex literature on institutions and their role in social control. A frequent theme in the literature on institutions is that many were designed to impose stigma upon residents, and that one function of the institution was to provide a warning to others. Here are two quotations reflecting this perspective:

> Residential homes for the elderly serve functions for the wider society and not only for their inmates. While accommodating only a tiny percentage of the elderly population, they symbolise the dependence of the elderly and legitimate their lack of access to equality of status. (Townsend, 1986, p. 32)

> The workhouse represented the ultimate sanction. The fact that comparatively few people came to be admitted did not detract from the power of its negative image, an image that was sustained by the accounts that circulated about the harsh treatment and separation of families that admission entailed. The success of 'less eligibility' in deterring the able-bodied and others from seeking relief relied heavily on the currency of such images. (Parker, 1988, p. 9)

From this perspective, neglect within institutions can be understood in terms of the need to generate a negative image to those outside their walls. This negative image, in turn, helps to persuade people into accepting the lack of sufficient public expenditure on benefits, health care services and social care services which would enable people to remain in the community with comfort. Instead, the choice is between discomfort in the community, and discomfort and stigma in the institution.

Not everyone has been satisfied with this approach to understanding institutions. Jones and Fowles (1984) argue that the classic literature on 'total institutions', 'institutional neurosis' and 'carceral power' associated with Goffman (1968), Foucault (1967) and others contained 'sweeping statements, massive generalisations, and some fairly shoddy reasoning; but also disturbing insight, sound scholarship and lively argument' (p. 1). Not all institutional regimes are totally oppressive, and this was true of workhouses (Digby, 1978) as well as more recent institutions. Not all institutions have a negative impact upon potential users. Jones (1993) has argued that the rundown of mental health hospitals has itself been a form of neglect with negative consequences for many with severe mental health problems. Nevertheless, the critical literature on institutions does provide insights into the neglect of health and social care services for elderly and disabled people.

Finally, it is quite clear that the increasing cost of institutional provision has been a factor in the growing emphasis of governments in both the UK and other countries in arguing for a need to switch resources from institutional provision to the development of care in the community (Goodwin, 1990; Pynos and Liebig, 1995; Godsell, 2002). What had started as a low-cost form of provision had become an increasingly expensive response to the needs of disabled people. However, to understand the slow government response to the growing criticisms of institutions on grounds of both cost and quality of care, it is necessary to consider the politics of informal care.

Informal care and service neglect

Most disabled people have always lived in the community rather than in institutions, and the majority of them have received enormous support from their families and relatives, and in particular from female kin (Phillipson *et al.*, 2001). There is an extensive literature which argues that the reluctance of government to fund the development of domiciliary services springs from a fear that such services will undermine the willingness of families (that is, female kin) to continue their caring role. This would have the effect of both increasing public expenditure and undermining the family as an institution (Means and Smith, 1998b).

Detailed information about the extent of informal care and the pressures that this places upon carers has been available for a long time. For example, Sheldon (1948) studied 600 elderly people from Wolverhampton and found that the management of illness was carried out by wives and daughters, so that 'whereas the wives do most of the nursing of the men, the strain when the mother is ill is yet to fall on the daughter, who may have to stay at home as much to run the household as to nurse her mother' (p. 164). Sheldon felt the burden upon such women needed to be shared with the rest of the community through the establishment of a national home help service. Sheldon's findings were subsequently backed up by a number of other studies, which emphasised not only the willingness of families to care but also the costs this imposed upon them (Townsend, 1957; Shanas *et al.*, 1968).

However, such evidence was being generated at a time of concern that the welfare state reforms of the 1940s might undermine the willingness of families to carry out their traditional obligations, one of which was to provide care and support for disabled members. Thompson (1949) was involved in the surveys of chronic sick patients after the NHS reforms and he argued that:

> the power of the group-maintaining instincts will suffer if the provision of a home, the training of children, and the care of disabled members are no longer the ambition of a family but the duty of a local or central authority. (p. 250)

Ten years later, a consultant physician from a geriatric unit was putting forward a similar argument:

> The feeling that the State ought to solve every inconvenient domestic situation is merely another factor in producing a snowball expansion on demands in the National Health (and Welfare) Service. Close observation on domestic strains makes one thing very clear. This is that where an old

person has a family who have a sound feeling of moral responsibility, serious problems do not arise, however much difficulty may be met. (Rudd, 1958, p. 348)

From such a perspective it was essential for the state to avoid the development of domiciliary services if families were not, in turn, to avoid their domestic responsibilities towards elderly and disabled people. The failure to expand home care services and the heavy reliance upon the voluntary sector for the provision of other domiciliary services is a consequence of this point of view.

Such views were heavily challenged by those involved in research on caring:

The health and welfare services for the aged, as presently developing, are a necessary concomitant of social organisation, and therefore, possibly of economic growth. The services do not undermine self-help, because they are concentrated overwhelmingly among those who have neither the capacities nor the resources to undertake the relevant functions alone. Nor, broadly, do the services conflict with the interest of the family as a social institution, because they tend to reach people who lack a family or whose family resources are slender, or they provide specialised services the family is not equipped or qualified to undertake. (Townsend, in Shanas *et al.*, 1968, p. 129)

Rather than being restricted from a fear of undermining the family, domiciliary services needed to be rapidly expanded to support families and help the isolated.

This argument was gradually accepted by central government. However, this was achieved by emphasising the capacity of domiciliary services to persuade family members to continue to care for disabled relatives rather than their capacity to offer such members real choices about whether or not to continue such care. Moroney (1976) put the argument for more services quite bluntly:

By not offering support, existing social policy might actually force many families to give up this function prematurely, given the evidence of the severe strain many families are experiencing. If this were to happen, the family and the state would not be sharing the responsibility through an interdependent relationship and it is conceivable that eventually the social welfare system would be pressured with demands to provide even greater amounts of care, to become the family for more and more elderly persons. (p. 59)

In this respect, service neglect continues to the present day. All governments assume that if you care about someone you should be willing to care for them (Dalley, 1996).

This has always been the assumption about frail elders but it is also now the basis of policy with regard to people with learning difficulties and mental health problems. The family is assumed to exist and expected to cope. Informal carers may be offered more support from the state than was once the case and this is a positive development where both the service user and informal carer wish the latter to take on the primary caring responsibilities. However, there is little sign of policies emerging which enable service users and family members to make choices about who should carry out such personal assistance roles. In this respect, Morris (2002) asserts that disabled people have a right not to be made dependent upon family members and other close relatives in order to have such needs met.

Cultural stereotypes about ageing and disability

Most western societies possess negative stereotypes about old age and disability (Phillipson, 1998). Wilson (1991) has argued that most western views of the life course are pyramidal, in which 'ageing is seen as an inevitable or irreversible slide downwards into dependency' (p. 43). Or as Johnson (1990) has put it:

> Dependency is one of the words closely associated in the public mind with old age. The image of older people becoming like children – dependent on able-bodied adults – and the loss of mental faculties, are other stereotypes which have wide currency. Even my children, long schooled in the rejection of ageism, like to remind me of the epigram 'old professors never die, they only lose their faculties'. (p. 209)

Similarly negative images and stereotypes are often associated with the term 'disability'. Morris (1990, p. 22), for example, bluntly states that 'just as the issue for black people is racism rather than being black so the issue for disabled people is the fear and hostility that our physical difference and limitations raise for non-disabled people'. Barnes (1996), although sympathetic to this view, points out that not all societies and cultures are universally hostile to disabled people. However, 'the importance and desirability of bodily perfection is endemic to western culture' (p. 56), resulting in the oppression of disabled people through such mechanisms as genetic engineering, prenatal screening, denial of medical treatments, misrepresentation in the media, and institutional discrimination in education, employment, housing, welfare and leisure.

Such everyday cultural attitudes to elderly and disabled people will be part of the assumptive worlds of many of those who develop community care policies and by many of those who deliver community care services. Certainly, Rowlings (1981) has argued that this helps to explain the oft-remarked reluctance of social workers to develop their careers in community care rather than childcare:

> Old age confronts us not just with death (which is inevitable) but with decline (which is probable, at least to some degree) ... It is the prospect of loss in old age – impairment in mental and/or physical function, loss of spouse and family and loss of independence – which is more frightening to contemplate than loss of life itself ... Social workers may well be faced with clients whose experience of and response to ageing represent those very aspects of old age which they, the social workers, fear most for their future selves. (pp. 25–6)

Although this quotation is from a book on *Social Work with Elderly People*, similar comments could be made about the fear of many professionals about working with physically impaired people and people with learning difficulties and mental health problems.

Such fear may provide a partial explanation of service neglect, especially if combined with an appreciation of the low status of work with these groups rather than in childcare (for social workers) or acute medicine (for doctors). Neglect can also result from pessimism about what can be achieved in terms of improving lives through health and social care intervention. This pessimism has deep roots. Haber (1983), for example, found in her study of medical models of growing old in the late nineteenth and early twentieth centuries that:

> most European clinicians seemed to imply that illness and old age were inseparably intertwined, if not quite synonymous. At best the division between the two was extremely subjective. A large proportion of the diseases of old age are attributed to natural intractable changes in the organism. (p. 62)

The term 'chronic sick' sums up this attitude of mind within the medical profession. Illness in old age was chronic, inevitable and barely treatable since 'the organic difficulties that increased with age made the hope of corrective treatment illusory' (p. 72).

However, such arguments do have their limitations. To say that older people and disabled people are oppressed by the negative stereotypes generated by the young and non-disabled does little to help us understand how such stereotypes emerge from a complex interplay of cultural, political, economic and social factors. For example, how do such stereotypes relate to the process of removal from the labour force associated with the Industrial Revolution? Are these stereotypes and their implications the same for disabled men as for disabled women (Shakespeare, 1996; Thomas, 1999)? And are negative attitudes to frail elderly people connected not just to issues of age but also to the fact that the majority of them are women rather than men (Arber and Ginn, 1995)? These issues are addressed further in Chapter 7.

Concluding comments

The focus of this chapter has been upon the neglect of services for elderly and disabled people and the different ways in which this can be explained. However, as we warned at the outset, there is a real danger that a compressed chapter on the complex history of services is likely to oversimplify policy developments. More specifically, the thematic focus on neglect risks obscuring the fact that social care and health provision for these groups have achieved a high visibility on political and policy agendas from time to time.

At least three main strands to such periodic increased interest can be identified. First, wars can generate concern about the quality of health and welfare provision for members of the armed forces and/or civilians. For example, the emergence of blind welfare legislation in 1920 was a response to the perceived needs of blind and partially sighted ex-servicemen from the First World War. With regard to civilians, this chapter has illustrated the lack of priority allocated to older people in terms of evacuation places and with regard to access to health care services. However, the second half of the Second World War saw the debate on reconstruction driven by the Beveridge Report (1942). This period saw elderly citizens being increasingly defined as war victims and deserving of state support. This helps to explain the *Manchester Guardian* campaign about workhouse conditions in the 1940s (see earlier discussion) as well as the emergence of home care and meals-on-wheels services for older people in the same period.

Second, the ideology of family and family care means that there are great sensitivities about the 'abandonment' of elderly and disabled people to the state, especially if this is low-quality provision where staff abuse inmates. The history of institutional provision is one of periodic scandals, taken up by pressure groups and the media, and then responded to with campaigning energy by politicians. However, such energy rarely lasts and the Cinderella groups return to being the concern of the committed few at the margins of political and policy influence. Despite this periodic determination to improve and humanise institutional regimes, one is struck by the continuity of the institutional descriptions in this chapter from the Victorian period to the present day. This tradition of scandals about individuals in institutions is now in the process of being transformed into media stories of people being abandoned in the community with inadequate support services. For example, the early 1990s saw high-profile coverage of a young man with mental health problems who was mauled by a lion after entering its cage at London Zoo (Jones, 1993, pp. 228–34). In the mid-1990s there was enormous press interest in the killings of Jonathan Zito and Jonathan Newby by people with severe mental health problems (Timmins, 1996).

Third, policy-makers raise the visibility of community care debates when they become concerned about the cost of existing, usually institutional, provision because of demographic and other trends. This became the case in the mid-1980s when concern grew about both the projected growth in the old old (those over 75 years), the mushrooming cost of social security payments to residential and nursing homes, and the failure to run down expensive mental health and mental handicap hospitals. The development of disquiet about this situation and how this eventually fed into *Caring for People*, the 1989 White Paper on community care, is the initial focus of the next chapter. A central concern of the rest of the book is whether or not the Cinderella tag of service neglect has become outdated.

3 Implementing the Community Care Reforms

The focus of the last chapter was on the historical neglect of service provision for older and disabled people and for people with mental health problems and learning difficulties. By the late 1980s the pressures for reform had built up and the then Conservative government commissioned Sir Roy Griffiths to review the funding and organisation of community care. His report, *Community Care: An Agenda for Action* (Griffiths Report, 1988), proposed a radical strategy for reform that reflected the government's commitment to increasing choice and efficiency through the development of welfare markets. There would be an increased role for the private and voluntary sectors in residential and domiciliary services, but with social services authorities assuming the lead role in purchasing and organising care. His recommendations fed into the White Paper *Caring for People* (Department of Health, 1989a) and the National Health Service and Community Care Act 1990.

This and the following chapter look at the development of community care policy and practice since the implementation in April 1993 of the main community care changes required by the 1990 Act. This chapter looks at the implementation of the reforms by social services departments in their new lead agency role. It starts with a discussion of the White Paper and of subsequent legislation enacted under the Conservative government of 1992–7. It moves on to consider the political and organisational context within which social services authorities were operating in the mid-1990s, as any judgement about their performance needs to be set against an awareness of the difficult climate they faced in this period, since key elements of the modernisation agenda for social services are based on a critique of their community care performance (see next two chapters). Implementation required fundamental changes not only in the organisation of care but in departments themselves. Evidence from research is used to examine three such changes in detail from 1993 through to the time of writing: the development of care management and assessment; the introduction of purchaser–provider splits; and the mixed economy of care. The chapter ends with an assessment of the impact on service users and carers and of the strengths and weaknesses of the reforms.

Chapter 4 takes the analysis one stage further by outlining the main community care changes brought in by Labour Governments since 1997 as part of their modernisation agenda. It explores the likely implications of the growing emphasis of audit, national standards, performance indicators and league tables on aspirations to achieve user control and flexible approaches to service delivery.

The community care reforms

The Griffiths Report was published in March 1988 and yet the White Paper on community care did not appear until November 1989. During that period, central government examined several alternatives to the proposals made by Griffiths, but in the end decided that none of them were implementable. The White Paper therefore followed the main recommendations of the Griffiths Report, but with some notable exceptions.

Despite the reported reluctance of several cabinet ministers, social services authorities were given the lead agency role and it was stressed that the government 'endorses Sir Roy's vision of authorities as arrangers and purchasers of care services rather than as monopolistic providers' (Department of Health, 1989a, p. 17). The White Paper went on to list the main responsibilities for this lead agency role:

- Carrying out an appropriate assessment of an individual's need for social care (including residential and nursing home care), in collaboration as necessary with medical, nursing and other caring agencies, before deciding what services should be provided
- Designing packages of services tailored to meet the assessed needs of individuals and their carers. The appointment of a 'case manager' may facilitate this
- Securing the delivery of services, not simply by acting as direct providers, but by developing their purchasing and contracting role to become 'enabling authorities'. (p. 17)

The implied critique of past approaches was that they involved slotting people into a limited number of inflexible and traditional services which often did not meet their needs or which were organised to meet the requirements of service providers rather than service users and carers. Now, at the operational level, social services authorities were to develop case management (soon to be called care management) as a way to deliver needs-led rather than service-led systems of assessment and care delivery. At the strategic level, social services were to be responsible for producing community care plans based on an assessment of need for the whole community. These plans

were to be consistent with the plans of health authorities and other relev
agencies, and were to be submitted on an annual basis to the Social Services
Inspectorate of the Department of Health. They were to be the basis for
developing a wide spectrum of services, many of them contracted out,
which could be drawn on as appropriate by care managers. Care managers
would be responsible for client assessment and then for delivering flexible
packages of care for individual clients. The White Paper was quite clear that
such packages should 'make use wherever possible of services from voluntary, "not for profit" and private providers insofar as this represents a cost-
effective care choice' (p. 22). In other words, social services authorities
were expected 'to take all reasonable steps to secure diversity of provision'
(p. 22) and 'in particular, they should consider how they will encourage
diversification into the non-residential care sector' (p. 23).

The White Paper indicated that 'the government ... favours giving local
authorities an opportunity to make greater use of service specifications,
agency agreements and contracts in an evolutionary way' (p. 23) as the best
way to achieve such a mixed economy of care. It also suggested that this
required local authorities to separate their purchaser functions from their
provider functions. Through this mechanism, purchasing staff within social
services could be encouraged to assess objectively the contribution of 'in
house' service providers, such as the home care service, against what the
independent sector might be able to provide.

The position of social services as purchasers of social care would be
secured through a new funding structure for those seeking public support
for residential and nursing home care. Local authorities would take over
responsibility for the financial support of people in private and voluntary
homes, over and above their entitlement to general social security benefits.
This was to be funded primarily through a transfer of money, currently used
as payment for residents with low incomes and resources in private and
voluntary residential care, from the social security budget to local authorities. Local authorities would have discretion to use this money to fund
domiciliary services, which might reduce the need for so many people to
enter residential care.

Most of these proposals were very close to those of the Griffiths Report.
However, the White Paper did not propose a Minister of Community Care
and it did not offer a new system of earmarked funds for social care along
the lines advocated by Griffiths. Apart from a limited scheme to fund community services for those with severe mental health problems and another to
fund alcohol and drug services, the extra funds to meet the increased social
care responsibilities of local authorities were to be channelled through the
revenue support grant system.

Two other important changes were announced in the White Paper. Local authorities were required to establish procedures for receiving comments and complaints from service users and a new system of inspection was to be developed for residential care in all sectors. Each authority would have an inspection unit 'at arm's-length' from the management of services and accountable to the Director of Social Services.

The NHS and Community Care Act was passed by Parliament in the summer of 1990, only for the government to announce major delays in the implementation timetable. Proposals on the inspection of residential homes, the new complaints procedure and the earmarked mental health grant proceeded as scheduled on 1 April 1991, but community care plans did not become a statutory requirement until twelve months later and the new funding regime was not introduced until April 1993.

Further legislation intended to strengthen particular aspects of the reforms soon followed. The Carers (Recognition of Services) Act 1995, passed as a result of a private member's bill, received wide political backing. It gave a right to a separate assessment for people providing informal care on a regular basis to ill, elderly or disabled friends or relatives who were seeking help from social services departments. The latter were required to take the results of the assessment into account when deciding what services to provide to the person being cared for. The White Paper had acknowledged 'that the great bulk of community care is provided by friends, family and neighbours' and 'that carers need help and support if they are to continue to carry out their role' (Department of Health, 1989a, p. 4). The proponents of the Carers Act argued that this required a right to a separate assessment so as (i) to recognise the pivotal role of carers in many care packages; (ii) to encourage social services to think about carers' support needs; and (iii) to discourage social services from exploiting carers, especially where they are young.

The Community Care (Direct Payments) Act 1996 gave physically disabled people and people with learning difficulties, below the age of 65, the possibility of receiving a payment to arrange their own care services rather than receiving services arranged for them by the local authority. Previously, such direct payment, personal assistance or independent living schemes were legal only if social services gave a grant for a third party (usually a well-established voluntary organisation) to run such schemes on behalf of others. This private member's bill was advocated by the British Council of Organisations of Disabled People and the Independent Living Movement because it would enable many more people to arrange their own personal assistance, employ their own workers and manage their own care. It received cautious government support because it was seen as consistent with their self-help/mixed economy philosophy so long as it was not extended to older people who might 'open the floodgates' in terms of public expenditure (House of Lords Library, 1995). Direct payments were eventually extended to older people by the Labour government, from February 2000.

The social services authorities were given only a permissive power to develop direct payment schemes and hence there would be no guarantee of local availability. The Act also gave service users the right to refuse this option and placed on social services the duty to establish that the recipient could manage a direct payment (with support or through an agent if necessary). The money could not be used to pay for residential care.

The history of neglect associated with social care services in England and Wales was described in the previous chapter. As a result, social services authorities were not only being asked to implement a complex reform package, but were doing this in a context where existing service provision was often woefully inadequate. They were soon warned by the Audit Commission (1992) that they faced 'a cascade of change' with the clear implication that they risked being swept away if the pace and timing of changes were not thought through by individual departments. Social services were being asked to tackle this massive implementation challenge in the mid-1990s in a context of considerable uncertainty in terms of national politics, financial stringency, dependency upon others and organisational uncertainty as already outlined in Chapter 1.

Political uncertainty seemed initially to have been overcome with the return of a Conservative government after the 1992 general election. The possibility of a Labour government, less committed to the development of social care markets, had encouraged some Labour-controlled local authorities to delay their thinking on future structures until the outcome of the election was known. However, the result did little to resolve or reduce overall tensions between central and local government. In many Labour and Liberal Democrat authorities, in particular, these tensions created an immensely stressful climate for senior managers as they attempted to respond to the often conflicting advice and instructions from central government and from local politicians (Hoyes *et al.*, 1994). Uncertainty continued right through to the 1997 general election, fuelled by the early and extensive lead for the Labour Party in national opinion polls combined with their ambiguity about which elements of the reforms they would change.

Closely linked to political uncertainty was the issue of *financial stringency*, both in terms of local government finance overall and community care funds in particular. The funding system for community care was highly complex (Lunt *et al.*, 1996), with the money available to social services drawing upon such diverse elements as the revenue support grant, the council tax, specific grants and income generated through charges. All of these components were mediated through the budgetary process of individual authorities to produce an agreed budget for each new financial year. The squeeze from central government on all forms of public expenditure in this period meant that local authorities often had to cut services, withdraw grants, increase service charges or freeze posts in order to stay within agreed budgets.

The third area of pressure concerned *dependence upon others* in that social services could only be successful in implementing the community care reforms with the co-operation of a wide range of other organisations with local purchasing and providing responsibilities. This included both health agencies (health authorities and trusts) and housing agencies (housing associations, housing authorities). It also included a dependence on the rules and regulations of the social security and housing benefit systems in terms of the financial viability of various housing and support arrangements (hostels, sheltered housing, group homes) for service users (Griffiths, 1997a).

This links into the final area of pressure, namely *organisational uncertainty*. A review of local government boundaries was initiated in the early 1990s with an initial emphasis from central government on the desirability of abolishing those authorities which were seen as somehow artificial entities (for example 'newer' counties such as Avon, Cleveland and Humberside), together with the need to extend the number of single-tier arrangements whereby all local authority services are provided by a single unit of administration (unitary authorities). In Wales 22 unitary authorities were established in April 1996 out of the previous eight county councils and 37 districts. Local government reorganisation (LGR) in England, completed in 1998, involved a wider mix of new unitary authorities, in urban and rural areas, with the retention of some two-tier counties and districts.

The resultant disruption to social services was enormous. Each new unitary authority had to appoint a new Director of Social Services (or equivalent) and management team which in turn needed to review with councillors the most appropriate approach of the new authority to the implementation of the community care reforms. Craig and Manthorpe's research on the impact of LGR on community care suggested that 'the process of transition' generated 'uncertainty, political tension, service planning blight and disruption to working arrangements' (1996, p. 32). This was not only amongst social services staff but also within those voluntary agencies whose very survival depended upon grants and contracts from social services.

Developing care management and assessment

The White Paper stressed that a primary objective of the community care reforms was 'to make proper assessment of need and good case management the cornerstone of high quality care' (Department of Health, 1989a, p. 5).

Subsequent policy guidance outlined the three stages of a proper care management system, namely:

- Assessment of the circumstances of the user, including any support required by carers
- Negotiation of a care package in agreement with users, carers and relevant agencies, designed to meet identified need within available resources
- Implementation and monitoring of the agreed package, together with a review of outcomes and any necessary revision of services provided. (Department of Health, 1990, p. 24)

By identifying individual needs and securing services to meet those needs, the new system of assessment and care management would achieve no less than six major objectives:

- Ensuring that the resources available (including resources transferred from the social security system) are used in the most effective way to meet individual care needs
- Restoring and maintaining independence by enabling people to live in the community wherever possible
- Working to prevent or to minimise the effects of disability and illness in people of all ages
- Treating those who need services with respect and providing equal opportunities for all
- Promoting individual choice and self-determination, and building on existing strengths and care resources
- Promoting partnership between users, carers and service providers in all sectors, together with organisations of and for each group. (Department of Health, 1990, p. 23)

So far, it might appear that care management is like 'mum's apple pie', an uncontroversial positive development for users, carers and professionals alike. However, the implementation of care management strategies proved far from straightforward and continued to generate concerns, as well as improvements, for all three groups. To appreciate some of the reasons for this, we need to understand the background and some of the disputes about the way care management should be organised, whom it should be aimed at and what it might be able to achieve.

The approach of the Department of Health to care management was heavily influenced by the research findings of the Personal Social Services Research Unit (PSSRU) at the University of Kent in their evaluation of care management pilot projects in Thanet (Kent) and Gateshead (Davies and

Challis, 1986; Challis *et al.*, 1988). Both were aimed at frail elderly people at risk of entering residential or nursing home care. The emphasis was on giving social workers with considerable experience of work with elderly people, and with smaller caseloads than usual, access to a decentralised budget. This money could be used to bring in a variety of services not normally available through the social services system. Just under 100 frail elderly people were supported through this care management service in Thanet and their experiences were compared to a matched group receiving services in the conventional way from a neighbouring area in Kent. The results were overwhelmingly positive (as they were in the subsequent Gateshead experiment). The probability of death within one year and of admission to long-term care within one year was halved and the probability of continuing to live at home was doubled. Informal carers felt less exploited and more supported, while perceptions of well-being on the part of service users were improved. All of this was achieved at lower cost than if residential care had been the main option.

However, at least three complications arose in interpreting these results in terms of their general implications for the reform of community care in England and Wales. First, queries were raised about the robustness of the methodology in terms of whether or not too many problematic clients were filtered out from the experimental group. Fisher (1990–1) pointed out that 110 of the originally identified cases were excluded by using criteria such as clients keen to enter care, carers being unwilling to share care and so on, leading him to suggest that some key practice dilemmas were not addressed. A second linked point was whether or not 'success' with frail elderly people wishing to avoid residential care could be translated into 'success' for a much wider range of elderly people and also for the other main user groups. Indeed, the PSSRU research team have warned repeatedly that this is an approach which can benefit certain types of users in certain types of situations, rather than an approach which should be applied to all users, or even to all users with the most complex needs. Hence, their justification for screening large numbers of elderly people from their original samples is that they have known all along that care management cannot keep everyone in the community and out of residential care at low cost and within tolerable levels of burden for carers. Therefore, Davies (1992, p. 20) is unapologetic about the fact that the Thanet experiment was based on the principle of offering 'case-managed care for selected users', who were essentially people who were 'at high risk of *inappropriate* and *avoidable* admissions to institutions for long-term care' (our emphasis).

The third complication facing local authorities as they considered their care management implementation strategy was that available care management models were much wider than just the Thanet/Gateshead approach. One reason for this was that the Department of Health and Social Security (DHSS) established in 1983 28 pilot 'care in the community' projects designed to help long-stay hospital residents move to community settings. These pilot projects covered people with learning difficulties, mental health problems and physical impairments as well as people with age-related problems. Cambridge (1992) stressed the enormous variety of service delivery arrangements which emerged from this initiative with one key dimension of variation being whether the care management pilots were based in social services, in a health setting or within multidisciplinary teams. Also, several of the models chosen stressed the need for care managers to act as advocates or brokers on behalf of clients. They should not be constrained by the resource dilemmas of the statutory agencies, but rather should be based in independent or semi-independent organisations.

Thus, local authorities found themselves facing considerable uncertainty and disagreement about what care management was and how it might be able to help within the new community care arrangements. Was care management something to be applied to all clients, all clients with complex needs or clients in very specific situations? Should care managers be located inside or outside social services? Are they advocates on behalf of clients, rationers on behalf of social services, or both? Should assessment be carried out just by social workers, or also by other professional groups such as home care organisers, community nurses and occupational therapists? Further policy guidance, on assessment and care management, only confirmed the complexity of the choices facing local authorities (Department of Health/Social Services Inspectorate, 1991a, b and c).

The full extent of the implementation challenge was perhaps best summarised by the Audit Commission's (1992) report on *Community Care: Managing the Cascade of Change*. This report opened by outlining how, under previous systems, the user was expected to fit in with existing service requirements, and the service received was often more dependent on which professional received the initial request for help rather than on actual needs, even for people in very similar situations. Hence, an occupational therapist referral would be assessed as requiring an occupational therapy service, whilst the same person, if referred to home care, might be defined as requiring a home help. However, the simple decision to place user and carer needs first had sparked off a cascade of change. The central point was not only the scale of change required, but also the order in which the changes might have to be tackled. Key strategic decisions had to be made about how to stimulate a mixed economy of care, and whether or not to develop an internal split within social services between purchasers and providers. These decisions then had to be underpinned by new and appropriate financial, structural and procedural arrangements. Social services authorities also needed to develop new assessment systems which were needs-driven and which were acceptable to a wide range of agencies. Decisions had to be made about who would be a priority for services in the light of scarce resource levels. And thought would have to be given as to how wide a range of staff within and outside social services might perform the role of care manager. All this had to be tackled before a needs-led assessment and care management system could be put into operation. As the Audit Commission (1992) explained, 'a process of change has been set in motion which will turn organisations upside down' (p. 19).

Under these circumstances, it is perhaps not surprising that most authorities took some considerable time to establish assessment and care management systems. Early research by Hoyes *et al.* (1994) into the initial approach by four authorities found wide variations in the resultant systems, which were often closely linked to different approaches to the implementation of an internal purchaser–provider split. For example, the split could be at district level, with the purchasing function allocated to care management teams as distinct from provider units, or at team level, with team members retaining a mixture of purchaser and provider functions. A similar spread of approaches to the development of care management was identified by Lewis and Glennerster (1996) from their study of five local authorities. The feasibility of applying care management to all client groups and the difficulties in meshing care management into the broader purchasing and enabling strategy of each of the authorities studied were among the major problems reported.

It was not only managers who faced significant challenges. Front-line staff also had to adapt to new ways of working although most welcomed the opportunity to work with service users in ways that were more responsive to their needs. From the earliest days of implementation, examples of creative and flexible responses to the needs of service users were in evidence:

> A young [disabled] woman ... had been enabled to take part in swimming, relaxation and Tai Chi groups, using local facilities and volunteers where necessary. This reflected the authority's aim to move from a model of day provision dominated by more traditional, statutory day centres. These activities had become such a part of this woman's life that she no longer regarded them as part of her package. (Hoyes *et al.*, 1994, p. 19)

This kind of imaginative care package depended not only on well-designed care management systems but on the development of assessment skills in care managers. A growing consensus began to emerge on what the benchmarks of good assessment practice needed to be (see Box 3.1). However, it was one thing to agree these benchmarks but another to create an environment in which they could flourish.

Good assessment, as defined in Box 3.1, requires highly developed communications and interpersonal skills and a capacity for reflective practice. However, evidence from research suggests that although good practice exists, the way in which assessment and care management systems have been implemented may have restricted the use and development of such skills.

BOX 3.1   Benchmarks for assessment practice

1. Empower both the user and carer – inform fully, clarify their understanding of the situation and of the role of the assessor before going ahead;
2. involve, rather than just inform, the user and carer, make them feel that they are full partners in the assessment;
3. shed their 'professional' perspective – have an open mind and be prepared to learn;
4. start from where the user and carer are, establish their existing level of knowledge and what hopes and expectations they have;
5. be interested in the user and carer as people;
6. establish a suitable environment for the assessment, which ensures there is privacy, quiet and sufficient time;
7. take time – build trust and rapport, and overcome the brief visitor syndrome; this will usually take more than one visit;
8. be sensitive, imaginative and creative in responding – users and carers may not know what is possible, or available. For carers in particular, guilt and reticence may have to be overcome;
9. avoid value judgements whenever possible – if such judgements are needed, make them explicit;
10. consider social, emotional, relationship needs, as well as just practical needs and difficulties. Pay particular attention to the quality of the relationship between user and carer;
11. listen to and value the user's and carer's expertise or opinions, even if these run counter to the assessor's own values;
12. present honest, realistic service options, identifying advantages and disadvantages and providing an indication of any delay or limitations in service delivery;
13. not make assessment a 'battle' in which users and carers feel they have to fight for services;
14. balance all perspectives; and
15. clarify understanding at the end of the assessment, agree objectives and the nature of the review process.

Source: Nolan and Caldock (1996) pp. 83–4.

From the earliest days two contrasting approaches to care management were apparent (Challis, 1993). An *administrative* approach rests on an interpretation of the core care management tasks as essentially administrative activities. Potentially, different individuals, employed in a variety of roles, may take responsibility at different stages of the process. A *clinical* approach emphasises human relations skills and assumes the involvement of a single care manager throughout. Each requires a different understanding of the purchaser–provider split. An administrative approach tends towards a rigid separation between purchaser and provider functions; a clinical approach depends on interpreting this divide in a way that permits the care manager to integrate traditional social work skills with the organisation of service provision. From the outset local authorities tended towards an administrative approach, with care managers spending increasing time on administrative tasks at the expense of direct contact with service users and with the balance shifting firmly away from counselling (Lewis and Glennerster, 1996). Within this overall trend there is evidence of considerable variation in practice. A longitudinal study of care management in ten local authorities found that only one in three care managers, interviewed in relation to individual cases, reported time spent on counselling and that counselling was most likely when a principal informal carer was involved (Bauld *et al.*, 2000). However, the same study also found evidence of continuity of involvement with the original care manager present at the review in two-thirds of cases where a review had taken place. An in-depth study of care management in two teams (Postle, 2001a) found that care managers employed a variety of strategies to cope with the changed nature of their work, with the result that different approaches to care management coexisted within the teams. Some practitioners seemed willing to follow procedural methods of working and had adapted to a *client-processing* role. Others tried, with some success, to incorporate social work skills into the care management task, whilst others again were confused or demoralised about their role.

Faced with continuing financial stringency and organisational turbulence, it is scarcely surprising that local authorities have focused on the administrative aspects of the care management task (Rummery, 2002). The extent of this has been confirmed by the PSSRU mapping and evaluation study of care management systems which commenced in 1997. Challis (1999) has indicated how:

> nearly two-thirds of local authorities defined care management as an organisational process, one-fifth as a specific job role and the rest as both. This indicates the variability in definition employed for care management

and also the probability that it is employed as a means of describing how people are processed through the assessment process. (p. 76)

It is difficult to provide a highly personalised service and continuing contact between care manager and service user, through the ongoing cycle of assessment, care planning, monitoring and review, in circumstances where high caseloads and high staff turnover are the norm.

TABLE 3.1   Eligibility criteria in local authority

Who is eligible for an assessment?	People who are vulnerable or are asking for an assessment under the 1986 Disabled Person's Act
When is this decided?	During 'screening' undertaken by a duty social worker or welfare assistant
Are there different levels of assessment?	Yes – 3 levels of assessment according to the level of risk and whether or not applicants have complex needs

Source: Rummery (2002) p. 49.

Instead, care management systems were soon dominated by debates about which types of client should be a priority for a care package, as social services authorities sought to target scarce resources by bureaucratic means. Eligibility criteria and priority matrices abounded as devices for defining ever more narrowly the number of people likely to receive services. The twin concepts of risk and dependency were widely used to determine eligibility (see Table 3.1) and to create priority bands, although the significance of these bandings differed widely between authorities. For example, in some authorities only users deemed to fall within the highest banding are eligible for services; in others the 'acceptable' cost of a care package may be reduced according to the band to which the user has been allocated.

Buckinghamshire Social Services Department is adopting a risk/dependency approach, as part of a 'banding' system, around high, medium and low levels, attaching cost ceilings for care within each band. The authority has carried out an option appraisal of banding methods. A dependency risk model has been tested by staff. Feedback has been very positive and encouraging, with staff finding the method straightforward to use. It provides an effective way of placing people into high, medium and low categories. Each band is assigned a maximum spend per case, as follows:

● High priority – the average net cost of residential care plus 20 per cent premium if spent on community services, enabling people to stay in their own homes

- Medium priority – 60 per cent of the average net cost of residential care
- Low priority – 30 per cent of the average net cost of residential care.
  (Quoted in Audit Commission, 1996, p. 12)

The end product of this has been numerous highly complex assessment forms in which 'criteria that define those needing care with sufficient precision to limit expenditure in a predictable way may well be too complicated for people to understand or operate on a day-to-day basis' (Audit Commission, 1996, p. 11).

Such forms have been a generator of much ill will amongst those expected to use them, especially when linked to the collection of information about the personal resources of clients in order to estimate service charges. Field-level staff have felt care management has meant more paperwork and more bureaucracy or, as one third-tier manager told Lewis and Glennerster (1996):

> I think people have felt weighed down by paperwork ... and they feel the department wants to turn them into administrators and financial processors. All the emphasis is on filling out forms, and a lot of staff are saying 'That isn't what I was trained to do ...' (p. 140)

The emphasis on form filling has also impacted on interactions with service users and carers. Richards (2000) found that the process of completing assessment forms could help all the parties involved to develop a clear picture of the difficulties to be addressed. However, there was also a real danger that structuring the interview around an assessment schedule could distort the process of communication and impede the development of understanding. By pre-determining the areas of investigation and focussing on routine information required by the agency, this approach to assessment risked marginalising the concerns of users and carers. Time and energy could be wasted through exhaustive questioning that ultimately failed to capture the subtlety and complexity of individual needs.

Another factor frustrating the development of a creative user-centred care management system has been the lack of computer-based information systems to underpin the purchasing of complex care packages and their subsequent monitoring. There is much talk of the contract economy and spot purchasing, but the harsh reality is that numerous social services authorities have developed care management systems based on the devolved purchase of services with completely inadequate IT and information system back-up (Bovell *et al.*, 1997; Postle, 2001a). Inadequate IT systems also continue to pose substantial barriers to the exchange of information between agencies,

---

BOX 3.2   Review of care management by the Department of Health

- There is continuing acknowledgement by SSDs [social services departments] that older people usually prefer to remain in their own homes as long as is feasible.
- Assessment has become more needs-led, but assessment arrangements need to match the complexity and needs of individual cases better than they do.
- While there is a more planned approach to the care of older people, often care plans are not sufficiently focussed on outcomes nor agreed by users.
- Many SSDs continue to give insufficient attention to monitoring and reviewing cases.
- Older people and family carers feel more involved in assessment and care planning.
- Despite considerable investment in public information, many leaflets do not reach the public and users, and some are not particularly helpful.

Source: Warburton and McCracken (1999) p. 28.

---

a point highlighted by the Chief Inspector of Social Services (Department of Health/Social Services Inspectorate, 2000).

The view of the Department is that real progress has been made with regard to care management and older/disabled people despite the problems discussed above (see Box 3.2). However, there has been much less satisfaction with regard to people with mental health problems relating to the parallel/overlapping system of the Care Programme Approach (Department of Health/Social Services Inspectorate, 1995, 1999). Shaw (2000) explains how the Care Programme Approach was introduced in 1991 and required social services authorities and health to collaborate in a new co-ordinated framework of care. Chapter 5 looks in more detail at attempts to mesh this with the care management system.

Closely linked to care management and assessment was the need for social services authorities to establish clear purchaser–provider splits as a starting point for generating markets in social care. The next section traces the initially hesitant progress of a concept that, by the end of the 1990s, had become an everyday feature of the social care landscape.

Establishing purchaser–provider splits

The importance of establishing purchaser–provider splits within social services departments (SSDs) was emphasised in the White Paper on community care (Department of Health, 1989a) and in the subsequent policy guidance (Department of Health, 1990), with the latter stressing that

> In practical terms in developing the enabling role authorities will need to distinguish between aspects of work in SSDs concerned with
>
> - the assessment of individuals' needs, the arrangement and purchase of services to meet them
> - direct service provision. It will be important that this distinction is reflected within the SSD's management structure at both the 'macro' level (involving plans to meet strategic priorities as a whole) and at the 'micro' level (where services are being arranged for individuals). (Department of Health, 1990, pp. 37–8)

It can be argued that the purpose of this proposed split was twofold. First, it would ensure equality of treatment for alternative suppliers and the authorities' own services in terms of the identification of service costs. Second, it would increase the fairness of consumer choice, since the care manager would feel distanced from in-house provision and hence under no pressure to recommend its take-up in preference to those services available from alternative suppliers.

The Department of Health subsequently commissioned the consultants, Price Waterhouse, to produce a report which offered advice on options and implementation strategies. This report identified three different approaches to developing a purchaser–provider split (Price Waterhouse/Department of Health, 1991). These were:

- Separation of purchaser/commissioner and provider functions at strategic level only. Here the split is very much at the macro level with headquarters staff contracting with area offices to provide assessment, care management and direct services, within a block contract. The contract would be at a high level of generality even though targets might be set for unit prices and activity levels. The report felt that this was only a transitional option since it did not fully meet the policy objectives
- Separation of purchaser/commissioner and provider functions at senior management team level. In this approach, the Director of Social Services would be the only post combining both purchaser/commissioner and provider functions. Assistant Directors would head separate hierarchies including fieldwork teams (on the purchaser side) and establishments (on the provider side). Purchasers would agree which services were to be supplied by providers to individual clients so that service agreements or contracts would be at the micro level

- Separation of purchaser/commissioner and provider functions at the local level. This model involves a series of separate purchaser/commissioner and provider teams operating under a combined management structure at the area level, an approach likely to appeal to those authorities which have already undergone considerable decentralisation of budgets and decision-making. Care management teams would take new referrals, assess need and put together packages of care, taking account of resource limitations. They would purchase appropriate care packages from in-house providers or independent suppliers.

The report recognised that all three models posed major implementation challenges and that all three models had major strengths and weaknesses. For example, the first model minimised disruption but failed to separate assessment from provision. The second model achieved a much clearer separation but the purchasers were very centralised and there was a danger of managerial duplication. Model three was potentially the most responsive to local needs, yet was highly complex, placing high demands on middle managers and on information systems. With regard to the latter, it should be noted that as late as 1999 the Department of Health was still recognising that most social services 'continue to lack adequate management information to help them commission and develop services' (Warburton and McCracken, 1999, p. 25).

Faced with these choices and the restructuring implied, local authorities were initially slow to respond to the challenge. The 25 authorities studied by Wistow *et al.* (1992) from April 1990 to May 1992 had made little progress on clarifying their position in relation to the purchaser–provider split. In their follow-up study of the same authorities, based on 1993 data, Wistow *et al.* (1996) found that there was still a reluctance to go for the most radical purchaser–provider split options because, as one Assistant Director put it, 'the last thing we wanted to do was to chuck the organisation up into the air ... and go through a massive organisational change' (p. 76). However, what had been happening was a devolving of purchasing power down social services departments so that team managers and/or care managers were now the most likely staff to make purchasing decisions both from internal/in-house providers and from external independent sector providers of social care services. However, only one of the case studies ran the in-house provision through a full trading account and just four had shadow trading accounts.

It seemed that social services authorities had been selective in the way they had embraced the philosophy of the White Paper with regard to purchaser–provider splits. They were keen for their own services to become more responsive to the needs of clients through placing purchasing power in the hands of team managers and care managers. At the same time, they seemed reluctant to fully expose their in-house services to unprotected competition from the private and voluntary sectors in the belief that this could undermine existing high-quality provision.

By the late 1990s attention had shifted away from the purchaser–provider split to focus instead on the further development of the commissioning role of local authorities. In part this reflected the recognition that local authorities were not simply purchasers of care but were also charged with the strategic role of planning and developing resources in the most effective way to meet the needs identified in their communities. Chapter 5 looks in detail at the growth of joint commissioning between health and social services, especially in the area of mental health services (Peck *et al.*, 2002). However, this focus on commissioning was also a consequence of the steady withdrawal by local authorities from their role as direct service providers, despite their anxieties about maintaining high-quality provision. By March 2001 the independent sector was providing 85 per cent of places in residential care homes (Department of Health, 2001g). Some authorities had ceased in-house provision altogether in particular services (Knapp *et al.*, 2001). To understand the reasons for this, it is necessary to take a detailed look at the role of local authorities in developing a mixed economy of care.

Developing a mixed economy of social care

Caring for People (Department of Health, 1989a) placed emphasis on the need for local authorities to develop their lead agency role through the skills of enabling rather than through service delivery. Local authorities were to stimulate markets in social care through maximising the service delivery role of the voluntary and private sectors. As we saw in Chapter 2, a mixed economy of care had always existed but the inherited market structure varied enormously between residential and day and domiciliary services and between authorities and geographical areas. Thus social services departments faced very different starting points with regard to the further development of social care markets in their areas.

The social security system had funded a major growth in the private residential and nursing home sector in the 1980s. This provision was unevenly distributed with a concentration in seaside resorts (Audit Commission, 1986). However, if future services were to be based on individual packages of care for people in their own homes, domiciliary and day services were bound to assume greater importance. The independent market in these services was far less developed in nearly all authorities, with voluntary sector organisations playing a significant role as providers, usually with the aid of grants from the local authority or through joint finance monies. Table 3.2 illustrates not only the extent of social services funding of non-statutory organisations in the late 1980s, but also the great variation in the extent of that funding between different local authorities and between different user groups.

The role of social services departments as a purchaser of social care services would substantially increase with the transfer of funding from social security. To ensure that this money was used to develop the independent sector, and not simply to support or increase local authority provision, the government stipulated that 85 per cent of the funding was to be used in that sector.

However, stimulating new and diversified markets proved to be difficult. The voluntary sector expressed fears about losing autonomy and flexibility and about compromising its advocacy and campaigning roles. Smaller groups in particular did not always feel up to the demands of bidding for and fulfilling contracts (Deakin, 1995; Taylor *et al.*, 1995; Means *et al.*, 2002). The government recognised the need for authorities to continue to provide core grant funding to voluntary organisations to underpin administrative infrastructure and development work, but it was questionable whether social services authorities would choose to spend their limited resources on this

TABLE 3.2   **Local authority social services department funding of non-statutory organisations as percentage of total expenditure, 1988–9[1]**

	General contributions to voluntary organisations			Contracts with private and voluntary organisations		
	ELD[2]	MH/LD[3]	ALL[4]	ELD[2]	MH/LD[3]	ALL[4]
Inner London mean	2.6	1.1	3.2	7.1	27.2	8.0
Outer London mean	0.6	1.0	1.1	5.0	16.9	7.1
Metropolitan district mean	0.3	0.7	1.1	1.4	4.1	3.0
Shire county mean	0.8	1.5	1.4	2.8	10.0	3.8
All authorities mean	0.8	1.1	1.4	3.2	11.2	4.6

Notes
1. Allocations expressed as percentages of relevant total client group expenditure.
2. Services for elderly people.
3. Services for people with mental health problems or learning disabilities.
4. All personal social services.

Source: Taken from Knapp *et al.* (1993) p. 8.

rather than the purchase of particular services. Diversification from residential provision appeared to be a logical step for many suppliers, especially if demand was shrinking. However, it would not necessarily be a straightforward move for small, or even larger, organisations whose experience was limited to providing care in an institutional setting (Wistow *et al.*, 1996).

If a local authority was to stimulate a market, it would need to do more than contract out its own residential care. Interventions required on the supply side included help with business development grants; subsidies and credit for start-up and working capital; training; and licensing and regulation. Local authorities could attempt to influence the market by the way in which they related to service providers. For example, to what extent were local authorities willing to draw upon the rhetoric of user-centred services and the mixed economy to support the growth of voluntary organisations 'where services are provided for minorities by minorities' (Atkin, 1996, p. 150)? For conventional markets to operate efficiently, perfect competition required that there should be neither a monopoly (one or few providers) nor a monopsony (one or few purchasers). It was likely that in some areas, for some services, the social services department would be the only purchaser. Whilst this might make it easier for the authority to dictate terms, it might also deter potential providers from entering a market where they would be dependent on a single buyer. On the other hand, if an authority, for the sake of administrative convenience or economy, chose to enter into block contracts with one or two providers, they risked squeezing out other smaller providers and could find themselves faced with a monopoly and in a very weak position. Authorities needed to consider to what extent they were able and would wish to guard against these situations by, for example, operating care management systems which devolved responsibility and resources to many purchasers, and by encouraging many suppliers by undertaking the interventionist strategies of the kind described above.

Early research studies indicated that implementation strategies were being pursued with some caution in terms of developing internal purchaser–provider splits, tendering out services and stimulating markets in social care (Hoyes and Means, 1993; Wistow *et al.*, 1994). However findings from the continued monitoring of progress by Wistow *et al.* in 25 local authorities suggests that by 1993, although a majority of authorities wished to continue in their role as service providers, they were increasingly convinced of the opportunities offered by a more mixed economy system (Wistow *et al.*, 1996).

The second phase of the research also pointed to local authorities beginning to increase their knowledge and information about both need and supply, whilst also increasing in confidence in terms of their individual purchasing strategies (Wistow *et al.*, 1996, Chapters 4 and 5). However, their ability to map the market might have improved but the research conclusion remained that 'areas of ignorance still exceeded the areas of knowledge' (p. 69). This was not surprising given what was said above about the inadequate IT systems available in most social services departments. On the need side, key gaps tended to include the lack of work on projected future need across client groups and the paucity of information on client groups other than older people. On the supply side, much more was known about residential and nursing home care provision compared to the providers of other services.

Despite these continuing weaknesses a mixed economy of social care continued to develop and to include domiciliary services as well as residential and nursing home care. The desire of local authorities to contract out some of their home care work to the independent sector stimulated a mushrooming of small agencies. By 2001, the independent sector was providing 60 per cent of home care contact hours compared with 2 per cent in 1992 (Department of Health, 2002e). A survey of independent sector providers of home care services, affiliated to the United Kingdom Home Care Association (UKHCA), gives an insight into this rapidly expanding market. Replies were received from 266 organisations or 26 per cent of the membership, the vast majority of whom were small recently established for-profit organisations:

> Sixty per cent of organisations are providing services to less than 100 clients and just five per cent had more than 500 clients on their books. Only 4 per cent of respondents were providing more than 25,000 hours of service per month and 74 per cent fewer than 5,000 hours. Around 6 per cent of providers had been in business for less than one year, 23 per cent for between one and two years and just 10 per cent for more than ten years. (Young and Wistow, 1996, p. 18)

Most of these small providers found such business to be sporadic with no clear flow of cases and that small profit margins were being offered for working with often complex cases. The resultant high turnover of staff risked undermining the quality of provision and caused many of these providers to be pessimistic about the future of their organisations. The difficulties of entering the domiciliary care market are further illustrated in the findings of a survey of private residential homes in Devon (Andrews and Phillips, 2000). Twenty-three per cent of proprietors had diversified their business into new services, with the encouragement of the local authority. However, of these new services, 35 per cent were for respite care, an easier and cheaper option than, for example, meals on wheels, which accounted for only 14 per cent of the new provision.

The pressures to diversify in the residential care sector reflected not only rising demand for domiciliary services but also increasing difficulties in the market for residential care (Laing and Saper, 1999). By 2001 85 per cent of all residential care home places for adults were in the independent sector (Department of Health, 2001g), but this was no longer an expanding market. From 1998 onwards there is clear evidence of a rising number of closures, with 141 nursing homes closing that year and 215 closing in 1999 (Player and Pollock, 2001). In part the problems are attributed to falling occupancy rates. A majority (84 per cent) of the residential care home proprietors surveyed in Devon in 1994 claimed that they had had no vacancies immediately before the local authorities took over the purchasing of care. By 1997 only 25 per cent claimed to have no vacancies and a further 25 per cent of proprietors claimed that their homes were barely breaking even or were operating at a loss (Andrews and Phillips, 2000).

This illustrates one of the key tensions faced by social services authorities as they have attempted to develop a mixed economy of social care. The emphasis of many authorities on placing purchasing decisions at the level of the care manager, and their team leaders, encourages a system of spot contracts or purchase which may be user-centred but which can have the effect of undermining the financial viability of small independent sector providers. Against this, agreements from social services to block purchase services from established providers can have the effect of limiting the extent of the services available for the care manager to draw upon. Senior managers with overall strategic responsibilities for purchasing have been learning how to develop and work with local (quasi) markets, not only in terms of the block versus spot contract debate but also in terms of how detailed to make contract conditions so as to ensure they develop in a way which generates high-quality appropriate responses to the needs of local service users (Forder *et al.*, 1996).

Future directions are unclear. A survey of eleven local authorities and their domiciliary providers indicated that whilst some were seeking to reduce the number of providers, others were still seeking new providers to meet demand. Overall, there had been a move away from the spot contracts to contracts with an element of guaranteed hours (Ware *et al.*, 2001). Laing and Saper (1999) argue that consolidation of the independent sector is inevitable since 'only larger scale operators will be able to offer local authorities the systems, management skills and financial strength that local authorities will increasingly require' (p. 100). Against this, the rapid growth of direct payment schemes (Glasby and Littlechild, 2002) and their popularity with government (Department of Health, 1998a) may encourage the opposite trend. Large numbers of direct payment clients will employ their carer(s) but others may spot purchase the required help from a myriad of small providers.

Impact on service users and carers

A central objective of the community care reforms, emphasised throughout the White Paper, was to improve choice and independence for service users and carers. This was to be achieved through the provision of:

- Services that respond flexibly and sensitively to the needs of individuals and their carers
- Services that allow a range of options for consumers
- Services that intervene no more than is necessary to foster independence
- Services that concentrate on those with the greatest needs. (Department of Health, 1989a, p. 4)

To what extent has this vision for community care services become a reality and what has been the impact of the reforms on the lives of service users and carers?

The impetus for the community care reforms lay in government concerns about the spiralling cost of care provision and its consequences for public expenditure. Provision was to be targeted on those in greatest need with what counted as need defined by the local authorities (Department of Health/ Social Services Inspectorate, 1991b). The way in which local authorities have gone about this difficult task has had profound consequences for service users and carers and for those seeking access to services.

Across all user groups, priority for services has been given to individuals with complex needs who are considered at risk of admission to residential care (see Table 3.1). In the period since the reforms clear evidence of such targeting has emerged. For example, in 1992 the average number of contact hours a week for households receiving home help/home care services was 3.2. By 2001 this had more than doubled to an average of 7.6 hours and the number of households receiving six or more visits a week had increased from 16 per cent in 1992 to around half in 2001. At the same time the number of households receiving home help/care in 2001, approximately 398,000 during a survey week in September, had declined by 28 per cent compared to the same week in 1992 (Department of Health, 2002e).

This suggests that a growing number of individuals have been able to stay in their own homes, instead of entering residential care. This is indeed confirmed by the research findings from Bauld *et al.* (2000) in a 'before' and 'after' the community care reforms study of 419 service users. They concluded that the reforms resulted 'in scarce resources being targeted more effectively than hitherto towards those older people with the greatest need and there is clear evidence that this resulted in tangible benefits' (p. 388). However, this increase in intensive care packages, which typically involve help with personal care, has been accompanied by a withdrawal of low-level support services, mainly help with housework and shopping, to those deemed at only medium or low risk (Raynes *et al.*, 2001; Help the Aged, 2002). As a consequence, this latter group may be left to struggle on alone, or become increasingly dependent on family members and other informal carers, with a reduced quality of life. Research by Clark *et al.* (1998) reveals the importance of domestic help, especially for older women whose self-esteem is often closely linked to the appearance of their home:

> Well you go down if you let the house go down, don't you? If you're not troubled about the house, you're not troubled about yourself are you? No you must keep over plimsoll line, dear, keep yourself up regardless. (Mrs George, 82 years, quoted in Clark *et al.*, 1998, p. 19)

Left without support, older people may face increased risks to their physical and mental well-being and thus to their ability to remain in their own homes:

> Mrs Smith, a widow aged 81, became tearful as she explained that her curtains 'were filthy'. Following a fall two weeks before our first meeting no housework had been done. She explained to the researcher during the second visit that the curtains 'have never been that colour in my life' and that before her fall, they had been 'religiously done'. She used to, she said, 'drag the steps upstairs', stepping from them onto a blanket box under the window to change her nets: 'It took a time but I did it'. (Clark *et al.*, 1998 p. 27)

The priority given to personal care needs has meant that other needs may be ignored or meet with only a limited service response. Social contact and company, for example, may be perceived by service users as central to their quality of life but be rated as wants rather than needs by social services (Vernon and Qureshi, 2000). The social needs of older service users and people with learning disabilities have been addressed through segregated day centre provision rather than through individual support that is tailored to their needs and preferences. When individual support for social activities is available this may transform the quality of life of younger and older disabled people:

> I've a very good social life now ... I go for drinks, go to friends' houses, they come to me, go out to have a bite and I have a mobile phone so I can phone my PA for her to be here when I want to come back. (Vernon and Qureshi, 2000, p. 264)

When people are denied access to particular services, or to services in general, they have no choice. But has choice increased for those in receipt of services? The number of care providers, particularly of domiciliary services, has substantially increased with the growth of the independent sector. However, from the perspective of service users and carers, choice is about much more than just the range of service providers. Accessing and organising services is likely to involve not only major decisions, for example, whether a person with learning disabilities should move into independent accomodation or an older person into residential care, but also numerous micro-level choices. Box 3.3 illustrates the potential dimensions of choice at each stage in the assessment and care management process.

Hardy *et al.* (1999) investigated the parameters and types of choice for older service users in four local authorities. Care managers, service users and carers were interviewed for the study, which also explored the extent to which users and carers perceived themselves as 'able to make genuinely informed choices at each stage of the process' (p. 487). Their findings suggest that the scope for choice was exceedingly limited:

> Even if encouraged to participate in their assessment, domiciliary care users and carers were being restricted to choosing from an increasingly limited range of options; and those with the most complex needs often felt under pressure to enter residential care because it was 'too expensive' to maintain them in their own home. (p. 488)

They concluded that although the growth of provider numbers represented an increase in choice, in practice this was more significant for purchasers than for service users and carers. The latter were more concerned with the day-to-day workings of their care package than with who provided it and, at this level, there was no guarantee that users would automatically receive either the provider, the care worker or the service of their choice. It is also extremely difficult for service users to exercise choice if they have difficulty in understanding the process and when professionals behave in a disempowering way. Although the majority of users and carers interviewed for

---

BOX 3.3   Dimensions of choice in the assessment and care management process

Assessment and definition of needs

Choices about what services

- Choice between residential or nursing care and remaining at home with domiciliary support
- Choice over the type and range of support provided within the categories of residential, nursing or domiciliary care.

Care planning and implementation

Choices about what services and when to receive them

- Choice over the timing, duration and components of the care package
- Choice over level and method of client contribution for different elements of formal support.

Choices about from whom to receive services

- Choice between local authority 'in-house' provision and the independent sector (including voluntary, not-for-profit and private sector organisations)
- Choice between individual providers of residential, nursing or domiciliary care
- Choice of care worker to deliver the different elements of the care package
- Choice over the balance between the formal and informal support (paid and unpaid).

Monitoring and review

Choices about what, when and from whom to receive services

- Choice over the nature of the response to changing user and carer needs
- Choice in terms of when and how the case is reviewed.

Note: Assessment and care management is not the strictly linear process implied here.

Source: Hardy *et al.* (1999) p. 485.

---

this study were satisfied with the outcome of the assessment, this did not necessarily mean that they had defined their own needs or been asked if the package offered was what they thought they needed. Older people in crisis situations are particularly likely to be marginalised in the assessment process if the care manager fails to establish the problem as perceived by the older person and their preferred solutions (Richards, 2000).

Rigorous targeting does not necessarily mean that all those with high levels of need receive services. Concerns have continued to emerge about particular groups who may fall through the net. Sometimes the problem relates to the way in which need is defined. For example, the emphasis on need for help with personal care, as a primary indicator of high dependency/ risk, has made it more difficult for people with severe visual impairments to access support services (Lovelock *et al.*, 1995). The lack of flexible home-based care is also highlighted as a problem for older people with mental health problems in a report by the Audit Commission (2000b). This report points to failures in joint working between health and social services and between primary health care teams and specialist services. A study of provision for people with Parkinson's disease showed a similar picture. Despite having complex needs which made them obvious candidates for community care services, only 9 per cent of respondents with the disease were certain that they had had a community care assessment (M. Lloyd, 2000). Lloyd reports high levels of unmet need amongst users and carers, with only a minority referred to social services by their neurologist or general practitioner. Not only users and carers but also the specialist services for Parkinson's disease seemed unaware of what social services might have to offer.

Strengths and weaknesses of the reforms

Despite the many changes in local authority social services in the wake of the community care reforms, by May 1997 and the election of a Labour government it was clear that there had been at best only partial success in meeting the aims set out in the White Paper, *Caring for People*. The underlying objective of the reforms, to cap public expenditure on independent sector residential and nursing home care, had been achieved with the establishment of a needs-based yet cash-limited system. Local authorities had transformed themselves into commissioners and purchasers of care with decreasing involvement in direct care provision; and there was continuing growth in the independent sector provision of day and domiciliary services. For some users at least there was increased choice. Funding and services were now available to support frail older people in their homes as an alternative to residential care. Younger people with severe disabilities could now access a wider range of services and, through direct payments schemes, exercise greater control over the organisation and delivery of support. However, concerns about the organisation and quality of care continued to appear in the media and were confirmed in reports by the Social Services Inspectorate and the newly established joint review teams (see Chapter 4), and by organisations representing users and carers (Frazer and Glick, 2000; Social Policy Ageing Information Network, 2001). A wide range of difficulties could be identified.

There have been problems with the funding arrangements for community care. The local authorities consistently argued that the system is undermined by chronic underfunding and is liable to collapse, especially in winter months when demand increases. Independent sector providers complain that the level of fees paid by local authorities make it impossible to provide high-quality care and threaten their businesses with closure. Social services routinely spend more on care costs than the amount allocated to them by central government through the standard spending assessment. This has consequences for their ability to develop and improve their services and for the resourcing of other local services. On average local authorities spent 8.9 per cent more than allowed for by the standard spending assessment in 2000/1 and typically entered the following financial year with their budget overspent (Social Policy Ageing Information Network, 2001, p. 15). However, the decision to channel the funding for community care through the revenue support grant system, rather than to create earmarked funding as proposed by the Griffiths Report, has meant that social services can divert money intended for community care into services where the priority and pressures for improvement are greater. The Local Government Association estimates that 64 per cent of overspend is on children's services and 21 per cent on services for older people (p. 16).

Whatever the reasons for the funding problems, the lack of resources for social care has increased the emphasis on rationing and targeting. Inevitably, therefore, the pressures on care managers to restrict access to services, in their role as gatekeepers for the local authority, make it more difficult for them to promote individual choice and self-determination (Rummery, 2002). The need for advocacy that is independent of the local authority, albeit in limited circumstances, is recognised in the policy guidance (Department of Health/Social Services Inspectorate, 1991c) but with little acknowledgement of the fundamental contradictions in the care management role (Richards, 1994). From the user perspective, the priority given to particular types of need, such as the need for personal care, in the framing of eligibility criteria may mean that they have little choice in deciding which of their needs are met.

The restructuring of social services was intended to achieve a system of care that put the needs of services users and carers first. However, in responding to this fundamental shift in thinking, authorities concentrated from the outset on developing structures and procedures (Lewis and Glennerster, 1996). Much less attention was paid to processes and outcomes and to how these are experienced by practitioners and by service users. A growing number of research studies have revealed the difficulties faced by users and carers when gaining access to services and in making sense of the systems and procedures they encounter and the information they receive (Rummery and Glendinning, 1999; Richards, 2000; Vernon and Qureshi, 2000). There is also continuing evidence that efforts are focused on the critical phases of the care management process, assessment and care planning, with a relative neglect of monitoring and review. The longitudinal study of care management by Bauld *et al.* (2000) found that only 60 per cent of cases were reviewed within the timescale of the study.

Workforce issues have been a further cause for concern. The lack of formal training for much of the social care workforce has raised doubts about its capacity to deliver high-quality care. The problem is compounded by difficulties in recruiting staff in both the statutory and independent sectors. These difficulties are attributed to the low rates of pay for work that is often challenging and demanding. Low morale and high staff turnover have been reported not only amongst basic-grade staff but also amongst managers in all sectors (Hadley and Clough, 1996; Andrews and Phillips, 2000).

Conclusion

This chapter has looked at the strategy for the reform of community care set out in the 1989 White Paper *Caring for People* and at the way in which these reforms were implemented by social services. As the lead agency for community care, departments were expected to develop a needs-based system of care in which their role was to be commissioners and purchasers of care rather than direct providers. This involved the development of care management systems, promoting a mixed economy of social care and introducing purchaser–provider splits. By the end of the 1990s it seemed that they had been only partially successful in their task, given the growing concern about the quality of services and about the failures in inter-agency working, particularly in the relationship with health. These issues are explored in depth in the next two chapters.

4   Community Care and the Modernisation Agenda

The last chapter focused on the reforms of the 1990s and the implementation challenge facing local authorities as the lead agency for community care. Continuing upheaval and uncertainty followed the election of a Labour government in May 1997. The incoming government planned to 'lay the foundations of a modern welfare state in pensions and community care' (Labour Party, 1997) but gave little indication of an alternative vision for community care to set against the market-orientated approach of its predecessors. Nevertheless, by the time Labour was returned for a second term, in June 2001, potentially radical changes affecting all the agencies involved in community care were under way. This chapter stays with the local authorities to look at the development of a complex and interlocking set of reforms, intended to transform the regulatory framework for social care and to improve performance in every sector. These initiatives form part of a wider New Labour agenda for 'modernising' public services and local government and represent a significant increase in the involvement of central government in the management and delivery of services.

The chapter begins with the move towards greater central regulation and control which developed under the previous Conservative administration. This is followed by an overview of the White Paper *Modernising Social Services* (Department of Health, 1998a) as a starting point for Labour's programme of reform. Different elements in this programme are examined, beginning with the cluster of initiatives intended to raise standards and improve consistency in care services and to protect vulnerable groups: the Long Term Care Charter; guidance on Fair Access to Care; the Best Value regime; and the National Care Standards Commission. The standards and skills of the workforce are addressed through the creation of the General Social Care Council (GSCC), working in conjunction with the Training Organisation for the Personal Social Services (TOPSS), and the Social Care Institute for Excellence (SCIE). Measures to improve services for specific groups include a White Paper on learning disability, *Valuing People* (Department of Health, 2001a), which is examined in this chapter, and a series of National Service Frameworks which are discussed in the following chapter. Finally, we look briefly at changes in the organisation and decision-making structures of social services as a consequence of wider local government reforms. The chapter ends with a brief assessment of the progress and likely impact of the programme for modernising social care.

The growth of inspection and regulation

The process of welfare restructuring, begun under Conservative Governments in the 1980s, involved significant changes in the role of the state (Clarke and Newman, 1997). The partial withdrawal of the state from direct welfare provision, and the delegation of responsibilities to private and voluntary organisations, has been accompanied by a substantial growth in the mechanisms for regulation and control over an increasingly fragmented welfare sector (Hood *et al.*, 2000). The implications of this are far-reaching with the move to regulation through contracting, monitoring and inspection seen as symptomatic of wider cultural changes and the development of *an audit society*, in which accountability is achieved through constant checking and verification (Power, 1997). Within the state itself there has been a shift in power towards the centre as successive governments have sought to restrict the autonomy of local government by increasing control over local expenditure and services.

In the case of the social services this process was already well under way before the Labour government took office in 1997. Local authorities had closed or reduced their in-house care services for adults and assumed responsibility for inspection and regulation of the independent sector. As concerns about care standards grew, central government agencies became increasingly involved in reviewing and inspecting performance at local level. After 1985, the national Social Services Inspectorate (SSI) became responsible for a national programme of inspections to evaluate the quality of services, which was supplemented in 1996 with a system of joint reviews conducted by the SSI with the Audit Commission over a seven-year cycle (reduced, at the time of writing, to five years). Besides assessing performance and identifying how services might be improved, these reviews are intended to help local authorities achieve better value for money. Since 1997 failing authorities have been placed on 'special measures' by the Department of Health and monitored closely until improvements are achieved.

In the final months of the last Conservative government the publication of a White Paper, *Social Services: Achievement and Challenge* (Department of Health, 1997a), confirmed the government's determination to consolidate further the process of reform. Local authorities were to withdraw more or less completely from adult care provision and there was to be a new regulatory framework for the registration and inspection of care facilities undertaken by consortia of local and health authorities.

Modernising Social Services – the White Paper

The Labour victory in the general election of May 1997 meant the scrapping of Conservative plans for reform, but the new government's intentions remained unclear. Would it broadly continue the policies of its predecessor or choose a path of radical reform? Specific commitments in the Labour manifesto (Labour Party, 1997) included the introduction of a long-term care charter, an independent inspection and registration service for residential and domiciliary care and a Royal Commission on the funding of long-term care (see Chapter 5), but there was no indication of any overall strategy for social care. However, the key manifesto commitments, not to raise the basic rate of income tax or to exceed the previous administration's plans for public expenditure for the first two years, meant there was little prospect of any immediate increase in funding for social care, despite the pleas from local authorities and from independent sector providers.

What soon became clear was that the reform of social care would be closely linked to the reform of the health service. A White Paper, *The New NHS* (Department of Health, 1997b), published within months of the election, signalled the government's intention for a closer integration between health and social care through proposals that included the involvement of social services in primary care groups (see Chapter 5). This was followed, in September 1998, by the publication of the first *National Priorities Guidance* (Department of Health, 1998b), which set out the key priorities for health and social services for the years 1999/2000–2001/2. Social services were assigned the lead in three of the ten priority areas: children's welfare, inter-agency working and regulation. In three more areas, cutting health inequalities, mental health and promoting independence, they were assigned a joint lead with health.

A White Paper, *Modernising Social Services* (Department of Health, 1998a), finally appeared in November 1998 trailing in the wake of *The New NHS* and of another White Paper, *Modern Local Government: In Touch with the People* (Deputy Prime Minister, 1998) which was published in July 1998. The proposals in *Modernising Social Services* link closely with the earlier White Papers and all three form part of an ambitious programme for modernising public services, the overall aims of which were later set out in yet another White Paper, *Modernising Government* (Cabinet Office, 1999):

- Ensuring that policy is more *joined up and strategic*
- Making sure that *public service users*, not providers, are the focus, by matching services more closely to people's lives

- Delivering public services that are *high quality and efficient*. (p. 6, emphasis in original)

Note that issues of interdepartmental and inter-agency working are now seen as central to public sector reform. Tackling them requires the development of new ways of working and a willingness to collaborate in every area of policy-making and implementation at all levels of government and the public services. Acknowledging the complexity of this task and the challenge of raising standards overall, *Modernising Government* outlines principles to guide the process of reform. These have become hallmarks of the New Labour approach to modernisation and distinguish it not only from its Conservative predecessors but also from previous Labour administrations. These principles include:

- A focus on outcomes to enable working across organisational structures
- The promotion of partnership between different areas of government and with the voluntary and private sectors
- Greater use of evidence and research
- Consultation with service users
- The use of targets and performance monitoring to secure quality and continuous improvement in public services
- Additional investment to be conditional on improved results
- A greater valuing of public services by developing skills and rewarding results
- The development of information technology throughout government. (Cabinet Office, 1999)

Modernising Social Services provided the first clear indication of how this agenda for change would be translated within the context of social care services. In his foreword, the Secretary of State makes the government's aspirations clear:

We are determined to have a system of health and social care which is convenient to use, can respond quickly to emergencies and provides top quality services. We haven't got that at present. (Department of Health, 1998a, p. 2)

The White Paper begins by identifying six areas of difficulty:

- *Protection*: the lack of effective safeguards to protect children and vulnerable adults from neglect and abuse

- *Co-ordination*: the failure of various agencies to work together to support people in need
- *Inflexibility*: provision that suits social services rather than the needs of the individual and that may increase dependency and exclusion
- *Clarity of role*: a lack of clear objectives and standards has meant that noone has a clear understanding of which services are or should be provided, or what standards can reasonably be expected
- *Consistency*: a problem of inconsistency in the quality of and access to services between and even within areas and perceived unfairness in the operation of charging policies
- *Inefficiency*: evidence from joint reviews that there are wide variations in costs between similar authorities providing the same services in the same parts of the country. (pp. 5–7)

The clear implication of this is that, despite a decade of reform, little progress had been made in tackling many of the problems identified in the Griffiths Report and elsewhere (see Chapter 2). So who or what is responsible? The White Paper attributes part of the blame to the social services themselves, on the basis of evidence from SSI inspections and from joint reviews. However, they are not solely responsible as 'the law and the central framework within which social services operate' are also flawed (p. 7). Stephen Mitchell, the civil servant with overall responsibility for the production of the White Paper, explains the problem as follows:

> The Conservative governments of the 1980s and 1990s never really succeeded in providing an overall policy and strategy for the personal social services, in which the role of local authorities could be clearly, and positively, located. This lack of a clear strategy with which all concerned in central and local government could identify, was compounded by continuing evidence (not least from Social Services Inspectorate reports) of serious deficiencies in the quality, effectiveness and efficiency of social services. (Mitchell, 2000, p. 182)

He acknowledges that the major policy implementation challenges of the 1990s, the community care reforms and the reform of childcare services following the Children Act 1989, were, for the most part, successfully tackled. But, in doing so, he highlights the active role taken by the Department of Health in 'prescribing, monitoring and supporting the implementation' (p. 182).

Accordingly, the proposals for reform in the White Paper involve a significant increase in the mechanisms for directing and controlling the social services at a national level. The problems in social services, it stated, require a new approach, one that contrasts with the previous government's 'devotion to privatisation of care provision' which 'put dogma before users' interests and threatened a fragmentation of vital services' (Department of Health, 1998a, p. 8). The White Paper is equally clear that there can be no return to earlier times and the monolithic model of service provision where 'users were expected to accommodate themselves to the services that existed' (p. 8). Instead, the reforms should focus on the quality of services and their outcomes for users and carers, not on who provides the service. This 'third way for social care' is to be based on seven key principles as a foundation for high-quality effective services:

- Care should be provided to people in a way that supports their independence and respects their dignity. People should be able to receive the care they need without their life having to be taken over by the social services system
- Services should meet each individual's specific needs, pulling together social services, health, housing, education or any others needed. And people should have a say in what services they get and how they are delivered
- Care services should be organised, accessed, provided and financed in a fair, open and consistent way in every part of the country
- Children who for whatever reason need to be looked after by local author- ities should get a decent start in life, with the same opportunities to make a success of their lives as any child. In particular they should be assured of a decent education
- Every person – child or adult – should be safeguarded against abuse, neglect or poor treatment whilst receiving care. Where abuse does take place, the system should take firm action to put a stop to it
- People who receive social services should have an assurance that the staff they deal with are sufficiently trained and skilled for the work they are doing. And staff themselves should feel included within a framework which recognises their commitment, assures high-quality training standards and oversees standards of practice
- People should be able to have confidence in their local social services, knowing that they work to clear and acceptable standards, and that if those standards are not met, action can be taken to improve things. (pp. 8–9)

It is interesting to compare these principles with the objectives for service delivery set out a decade earlier in *Caring for People*:

- To promote the development of domiciliary, day and respite services to enable people to live in their own homes wherever feasible and sensible

- To ensure that service providers make practical support for carers a high priority
- To make proper assessment of need and good case management the cornerstone of high-quality care
- To promote the development of a flourishing independent sector alongside good quality public services
- To clarify the responsibilities of agencies and so make it easier to hold them to account for their performance
- To secure better value for taxpayers' money by introducing a new funding structure for social care. (Department of Health, 1989a, p. 5)

There is considerable overlap here. Both are concerned with promoting independence, ensuring that services are responsive to the needs of individual users and with holding agencies to account for their performance. However, where *Caring for People* promotes the role of the independent sector, *Modernising Social Services* emphasises the protection of vulnerable service users, consistency in provision and in access to services, and the need to raise standards and to monitor them more effectively.

The Labour government's proposals for change are complex and engage with the details of service provision at an operational level to a far greater extent than in the earlier White Paper. They include a mixture of new initiatives, most of which had already been announced elsewhere, and of adjustments to existing systems and structures at both local and national levels. These are considered here under four main headings: improving standards and protection; improving the workforce; improving services for specific groups; and local government changes.

Improving standards and protection

Variations between local authorities in the quality and efficiency of care provision and in access to services are seen, in the White Paper, as symptomatic of the fundamental lack of clarity about the role and expectations of the social services, described by Mitchell. Ten years earlier, Sir Roy Griffiths had reached similar conclusions in his report on the state of community care when he observed:

the imperative is that policy and resources should come into reasonable relationship so that we are clear about what community care services are trying to achieve and so that leadership and direction to those providing service can be given. (Griffiths, 1988, p. iv)

He had recommended the appointment of a Minister of State for Community Care with responsibilities that included:

- Preparing and publishing a clear, short statement of government's community care objectives and priorities
- Deciding on those areas in which government wishes to lay down standards of service delivery
- Making arrangements for reviewing local social services authority plans, against national objectives, and for linking that process with the allocation of resources. (p. 1)

There was to be no Minister for Community Care and arguably these responsibilities survived in the community care reforms only in an attenuated form, as in the arrangements for the monitoring of community care plans, or not at all, as in standards for service delivery.

The influence of Griffiths may be detected in the White Paper's call for a more prescriptive approach that provides direction to local authorities and requires explicit linkage between national and local policies. It is to be achieved through the creation of a coherent framework for social services, which will establish service objectives and an expectation of the outcomes they are to deliver, set targets for performance, provide resources to support change and include effective systems to monitor and manage performance (p. 109).

The first plank in this framework is the set of national objectives which lays out the Government's expectations for the social services in order to guide and focus their efforts. There are separate objectives for adult and children's services and a set of common objectives. The adult and common objectives are listed in Box 4.1. There is little that is surprising here. The objectives relate directly to the problems identified at the beginning of the White Paper and to the principles for social care provision that followed. They are, however, only a starting point. A more detailed steer to the local authorities is given with two further initiatives, the Long Term Care Charter and Fair Access to Care.

The Long Term Care Charter and Fair Access to Care

The purpose of the Long Term Care Charter is 'to set out more clearly at national level what people – both users and carers – can expect if they need support from health, housing and social services; and also what individuals' own responsibilities are in their dealings with the agencies' (Department of Health, 1998a, p. 32). A draft charter drawing on discussions with service

---

BOX 4.1   National objectives for social services

Adult services

- To promote the independence of adults assessed as needing social care support arranged by the local authority, respecting their dignity and furthering their social and economic participation
- To enable adults assessed as needing social care support to live as safe, full and as normal a life as possible, in their own home wherever feasible
- To ensure that people of working age who have been assessed as requiring community care services, are provided with these services in ways which take account of and, as far as possible, maximise their and their carers' capacity to take up, remain in or return to employment
- To work with the NHS, users, carers and other agencies to avoid unnecessary admission to hospital, and inappropriate placement on leaving hospital; and to maximise the health status and thus independence of those they support
- To enable informal carers to care or continue to care for as long as they and the service user wish
- To plan, commission, purchase and monitor an adequate supply of appropriate, cost-effective and safe social care provision for those eligible for local authority support
- To identify individuals with social care needs who are eligible for public support, to assess those needs accurately and consistently, and to review care packages as necessary to ensure that they continue to be appropriate and effective.

Common objectives

- To actively involve users and carers in planning services and in tailoring individual packages of care; and to ensure effective mechanisms are in place to handle complaints
- To ensure through regulatory powers and duties that adults and children in regulated services are protected from harm and poor care standards
- To ensure that social care workers are appropriately skilled, trained and qualified, and to promote the uptake of training at all levels
- To maximise the benefit to service users for the resources available, and to demonstrate the effectiveness and value for money of the care and support provided, and allow for choice and different responses for different needs and circumstances. For adult services, to operate a charging regime which is transparent, consistent and equitable; and which maximises revenue while not providing distortions or disincentives which would affect the outcomes of care for individuals.

Source: Department of Health (1998a) p. 111.

---

users and carers, and with front-line staff, was published for consultation in January 1999 (Department of Health, 1999a) and finally appeared in December 1999 under the title *Better Care, Higher Standards* (Department of Health, 1999e). Local authorities and health services were required to work in partnership with users, carers, voluntary organisations and others on the publication of joint local *Better Care, Higher Standards* charters by the end of June 2000. These local charters were to follow both the principles and values set out in the national charter and to set local standards in six prescribed areas:

- Helping users and carers to find out about services
- Understanding and responding to the needs of users and carers
- Finding a suitable place to live
- Helping people to stay independent
- Getting the right health care
- Helping carers to care. (Department of Health, 1999e, p. 4)

The sentiments of the Charter were generally welcomed, but with considerable scepticism about its likely impact (Valios, 1999). Without a significant increase in the resources available to the long-term care sector, local authorities would be unable to set and maintain high standards or provide access to the range of services required to meet diverse individual needs.

Disparities in access to services, as a result of differing eligibility criteria in local authorities, are addressed through a related initiative, Fair Access to Care. This provides guidance to local authorities on the principles to follow when devising and applying eligibility criteria and other procedures relating to access. Local authorities will be required to show:

- **consistency** in the way that every person's needs are assessed, with fair and transparent procedures and criteria followed in every case
- clear **objectives**, based on the overriding need to promote independence, which should apply at all stages in the process, from initial screening, through to assessment, devising a care package, and monitoring it
- a common understanding of **risk assessment** on which to base decisions about services – what kind of risk someone faces, how serious, its cause, how likely, and so on. Most authorities already assess risk, but in different ways
- **regular reviews**. There needs to be more consistency not only about people accessing services for the first time, but about people already receiving services, to ensure that the services continue to meet objectives. (Department of Health, 1998a, p. 26)

The final version of the guidance, *Fair Access to Care Services*, was published in May 2002 after a process of consultation. Its centrepiece is a framework for determining eligibility, which councils are directed to use. The framework is divided into four bands, critical, substantial, moderate and low, 'which describe the seriousness of the risk to independence or other consequences if needs are not addressed' (Department of Health, 2002a, p. 4). Within each band the risk to independence is broadly defined to include not only physical safety and well-being but a range of factors seen as essential to maintaining independence over time, such as employment and the fulfilment of family and social roles and responsibilities. Any impression that this may extend the services available to particular groups is short-lived. It is firmly stated that there are only limited resource consequences as, for the most part, the guidance only confirms and consolidates the earlier policy guidance that accompanied the community care reforms (Department of Health, 1990; Department of Health/Social Services Inspectorate, 1991a, 1991b).

Providing national direction for the social services is only the first step. The next is to monitor standards and progress towards achievement of the national objectives in each local authority. This is to be done through the Best Value regime, a key element in the government's plans for the reform of local government as set out in the White Paper *Modern Local Government: In Touch with the People* (Deputy Prime Minister, 1998).

Best Value

Best Value had been announced in June 1997, soon after the election, as a replacement for compulsory competitive tendering (CCT). CCT, which was first introduced under the Local Government, Planning and Land Act 1980, was a mechanism for reducing costs in specified, mostly blue-collar, services. It had forced local authority direct labour organisations to compete with external providers for the provision of particular services and, by 1997, a wide range of services, including highway maintenance, refuse collection and ancillary services such as catering and cleaning, had been contracted out to the independent sector. Best Value goes far beyond CCT in scope and ambition, as a performance regime that extends to every aspect of local authority activity, including social services. It imposes on local authorities a 'duty to deliver services to clear standards – covering both quality and cost – by the most effective, economic and efficient means available' (Department of Health, 1998a, p. 113). The Best Value process is intended to ensure that authorities 'achieve continuous improvement in all their services' whilst the 'poorest performing authorities are to reach the performance of the best within five years' (Audit Commission, 2001, p. 4).

The principles of Best Value were piloted in projects in 40 English authorities and from April 2000 all local authorities have had a statutory duty to provide Best Value under the Local Government Act 1999. This involves two main activities:

- Best Value performance planning (BVPP) monitors and reports performance against national and locally defined standards and targets. It sets out future priorities and targets for improvement
- Fundamental Best Value reviews (BVRs) of all services must identify what needs to be improved, and how to do it. (Audit Commission, 2001, p. 4)

Authorities were expected to publish annual Best Value performance plans and to review all their functions over a five-year cycle, although this requirement was relaxed in February 2002. Fundamental to the Best Value process are 'the four Cs', which must be applied to each service under review:

- *Challenging* why and how a service is being provided
- *Comparing* their performance with others (including organisations in the private and voluntary sectors)
- embracing fair *competition* as a means of securing efficient and effective services
- *Consulting* with local taxpayers, customers and the wider business community. (Audit Commission, 2000a, p. 1)

In addition to the process of internal review, local authorities are also subject to external inspection by the Audit Commission's Best Value work service, or by the existing inspectorates whose work now incorporates Best Value issues. Each inspection focuses on six questions:

- Are the authority's aims clear and challenging?
- Does the service meet the aims?
- How does its performance compare?
- Does the BV review drive improvement?
- How good is the improvement plan?
- Will the authority deliver the improvements? (Audit Commission, 2000a, p. 1)

The answers to these questions form the basis for judging the quality of the service (excellent, good, fair, poor) and its potential for improvement.

A battery of performance indicators and associated performance targets, which enable local authority performance to be measured and compared against specified outcomes, underpins the Best Value regime. For social services managers this proliferation of indicators and targets has become the most tangible aspect of the New Labour strategy for modernising public services. The first performance assessment framework for the personal social services, containing 50 performance indicators related to the national objectives for the social services, appeared in 1999. It is revised annually in line with changing objectives and after consultation with interested parties, as the selection of indicators and targets, and the ways in which they are defined and measured, may be contested. The framework covers five domains and is illustrated by the social services Best Value performance indicators for adults for 2002/3 (see Table 4.1).

TABLE 4.1 **Social services Best Value performance indicators for adults for 2002/3**

Domain	Indicator
National priorities and strategic objectives	None
Cost and efficiency	Average gross weekly expenditure per person on supporting adults and older people in residential and nursing care and providing intensive home care
Effectiveness of service delivery and outcomes	Households receiving intensive home care per 1,000 population aged 65 or over Older people helped to live at home per 1,000 population aged 65 or over
Quality of services for users and carers	Adults and older clients receiving a review as a percentage of those receiving a service Percentage of items of equipment costing less than £1,000 delivered within three weeks The percentage of adults and older people receiving a statement of their needs and how they will be met Users who said they were satisfied with the help they received from social services Users who said that if they asked for changes to services those changes were made
Fair access	None

Source: Office of the Deputy Prime Minister (2002).

The initiatives described so far focus on three of the areas of difficulty in the organisation and provision of care identified in *Modernising Social Services*: clarity of role, consistency and inefficiency. Another area of concern identified in the White Paper was protection and specifically the problem of safeguarding children and vulnerable adults who are receiving care services from neglect and abuse.

The National Care Standards Commission

Since 1991 local authority inspection units, 'at arm's length' from the commissioning and management of services, had been responsible for the registration and inspection of care homes in both the independent and statutory sectors. Responsibility for the registration and inspection of nursing homes lay with local health authorities. Significant weaknesses in these arrangements, including evidence of inconsistency between local authorities, and between local and health authorities, in the application of their regulatory regimes, were identified in *Moving Forward*, a consultation document from the Department of Health (1995e). There were also concerns, despite the 'arm's length' arrangement, about a potential conflict of interest between the regulatory and service commissioning roles of local authorities. Also, the burgeoning number of day and domiciliary care providers lay outside the regulatory framework. The Burgner Report (1996) that followed recommended a fundamental revision of the entire framework for the regulation and inspection of care services. The report was welcomed by the Labour Party in opposition and a commitment to establish an independent inspection and registration service for residential and domiciliary care was included in their election manifesto (Labour Party, 1997).

Modernising Social Services proposed the creation of eight Regional Commissions for care standards based on the boundaries of the NHS and Social Care Regions. Each would be an independent statutory body with its own chair, appointed by the Secretary of State, and a management board made up of representatives from local and health authorities and from user and provider interests. The commissions would be self-financing, through the fees paid by regulated providers (Department of Health, 1998a, pp. 67–9).

There was some opposition to these proposals from the local authorities, who feared that local knowledge and links would be lost, and from the independent care sector who argued for the appointment of new inspectors instead of the transfer of existing staff (Hunter, 1998). Nevertheless, the government went ahead with its plans and a National Care Standards Commission, in place of the Regional Commissions originally proposed, was established under the Care Standards Act 2000. The Commission started work on 1 April 2002 with headquarters in Newcastle and a network of regional and area offices staffed by inspectors, most of whom had transferred from local and health authorities. The Commission has responsibility for regulating (and inspecting):

- care homes
- children's homes
- domiciliary care agencies
- residential family centres
- voluntary adoption agencies

and for inspecting:

- independent fostering agencies
- private and voluntary hospitals and clinics
- nurses' agencies
- day centres
- local authority fostering
- local authority adoption
- welfare aspects of boarding schools. (Department of Health, 2002b)

The inspection of adult day care centres, specifically excluded in *Modernising Social Services*, was subsequently included and provisions in the Care Standards Act enable other services to be added in future, if required.

The Commission is required to regulate and inspect the services against national minimum standards. These standards are published initially in draft form to enable consultation with user and provider interests. The first set of standards, *Fit for the Future? National Required Standards for Residential and Nursing Homes for Older People* (Department of Health, 1999c), was drafted by the Centre for Policy on Ageing. Although generally welcomed by social services departments, health authorities and organisations representing service users, they were greeted with consternation by care home owners (Department of Health, 2001b). In response to their concerns, publication of the final version in March 2001 was accompanied by an announcement that the deadline for reaching many of the standards would be extended by five years to April 2007 (Department of Health, 2001c). Despite this concession, the National Care Homes Association and other provider organisations continued to argue that implementation of the proposed minimum standards for room size and for staffing ratios would force many homes to close unless there was a significant increase in the fees paid by local authorities (Revans, 2001a). Faced with continuing care home closures, the government responded again the following year, this time with the publication of amended proposals, which exempted care homes open before April 2002 from meeting some of the environmental standards, including those for room size (Department of Health, 2002c). Although welcomed by provider organisations, there were concerns from various quarters that this would compromise standards but with no guarantee, without an increase in funding, that it would enable homes to remain open (Leason, 2002). Further care standards, covering all the services inspected by the Care Standards Commission, have been published but so far these have proved relatively non-controversial.

Improving the workforce

Improving the quality of social care depends crucially on the quality of the workforce and *Modernising Social Services* devotes a whole chapter to this issue. It identifies three serious problems in a workforce numbering around one million people, two-thirds of whom work in the independent sector, mostly in residential homes:

- 80 per cent of this large workforce which works directly with very vulnerable people have no recognised qualifications or training
- There are no national mechanisms to set and enforce standards of practice and conduct
- The standards and suitability of some education and training in social care do not enjoy general confidence. (Department of Health, 1998a, pp. 84–5)

The General Social Care Council and the Training Organisation for the Personal Social Services

The strategy for tackling these problems has two main elements. The first is the creation of a new regulatory body, a General Social Care Council (GSCC) and equivalent bodies in Scotland, Wales and Northern Ireland. Formally an independent statutory body, the Council members are appointed by the Secretary of State with a lay person in the chair. Although all key interests are to be represented, service users and lay people form a majority on the Council (Department of Health, 1998a, p. 86), an indication of the government's concern to avoid any perception of the Council as a self-regulating professional body.

The GSCC has been given three main areas of responsibility. First, it is responsible for setting conduct and practice standards for all social services staff. Enforceable standards of conduct and practice are to be published as codes, which staff will be required to sign up to as a condition of their employment. Second, the Council has responsibility for registering individuals in those groups where a suitable form of training exists, initially qualified social workers and residential childcare workers, qualified at NVQ Level 3. The heads of adult care homes will be the next priority group for registration and further groups will be added as training is extended. Breaches of codes of conduct and practice may lead to suspension from the register and to deregistration, after a full hearing of the issues by the GSCC. Finally, the Council becomes the regulatory body for social work education in place of the Central Council for Education and Training in Social Work (CCETSW), which had undertaken this role since 1971. The GSCC became fully operational in October 2001.

The responsibility for developing and promoting training at every level of the social care workforce is given to another body, the Training Organisation for the Personal Social Services (TOPSS). TOPSS had been licensed prior to the publication of the White Paper as a National Training Organisation (NTO), one of a series of employment-led bodies each of which is responsible for a different sector of the workforce. The functions of TOPSS are:

- To maintain the occupational standards underpinning the qualifications recognised by social care staff and employers
- To carry out workforce analysis
- To identify training needs and ensure they are met. (Department of Health, 1998a, p. 94)

The development of national occupational standards for each section of the social care workforce requires TOPSS to work in close conjunction not only with employers but also with the General Social Care Council.

'A Quality Strategy for Social Care'

The proposals in the White Paper left pressing concerns unresolved. In particular *Modernising Social Services* had little to say about the future of social work, as distinct from other aspects of social care, leading many in the profession to fear that the government's modernising agenda included no specific role for social work as such (Orme, 2001a). The absence of clear plans for the future of social work training gave weight to such fears, as academics and practitioners had long argued that the standard two-year qualifying programme did not prepare student social workers adequately for the demands and increasing complexity of their role. The situation was unfavourably compared with that in other OECD countries where qualifying programmes are set at graduate level for a minimum of three years. A related issue, the widespread concern of academics and practitioners about the failure of research to influence policy and the development of practice, had also been neglected. A lack of systematic and easily accessible accounts of the evidence from research and its relevance to practice and continuing barriers to the effective dissemination of research findings meant that practitioners were often unaware of potentially relevant research. Although *Modernising Social Services* emphasised the importance of practice that is based 'on the best evidence of what works for clients' and that is 'responsive to new ideas from research' (p. 93), there were no specific suggestions for how this might be fostered. Most glaring of all, the White Paper had also failed to mention the growing crisis in recruitment for training courses and to jobs in all areas of social care, particularly in London and other inner cities (Douglas, 1998).

The government returned to the problem of the social care workforce with the publication, two years later, of *A Quality Strategy for Social Care* (Department of Health, 2000a). This detailed paper proposed a series of further reforms to address shortcomings in training, inconsistencies in practice and other workforce-related issues, and sought the views of interested parties. Its centrepiece was the announcement of the creation of a Social Care Institute for Excellence (SCIE), which would address the perceived lack of reliable evidence about what works best in social care by:

- Establishing and developing a rigorous knowledge base founded on the views and experiences of users, research evidence, Social Services Inspectorate and Audit Commission reports and the experiences of managers and practitioners
- Producing authoritative and accessible guidelines on effective social care practice and service delivery
- Ensuring dissemination through creative partnerships across the diverse range of organisations involved in the research, monitoring, regulation, commissioning and provision of social care. (Department of Health, 2000b)

This suggests an inclusive approach to the vexed question of what constitutes knowledge in social care. However, one of the difficulties for SCIE, which started work in October 2001, is the shortage of research in key areas and the lack of funding for research programmes in social care at a national level. It is as yet uncertain to what extent SCIE will be able to address these problems and whether, as a not-for-profit company limited by guarantee, it will be able to preserve its independence from government.

A *Quality Strategy for Social Care* also addresses the concerns of the social work profession about its future with the statement that:

> social work has a specific contribution to make to the government's modernising agenda, with its emphasis on rights and responsibilities, citizenship and participation. (p. 37)

It goes on to call for 'a clear definition of the future role of social work' and for 'a radical consideration of the future structure and content of social work training' (p. 38). Views were then sought on how best to proceed with the reform of social work education, a move that was widely seen as delaying any firm commitment to an extension of social work training. Back in 1998 the Department of Health had commissioned a review of social work education from independent consultants who recommended that social work qualifying courses should be extended from two to three years and be set at degree level (JM Consulting Ltd, 1999a, 1999b), but nothing had happened since. Moving towards an all-graduate profession would necessarily involve an increase in costs and it was feared that a reduction in the supply of newly qualified social workers could also accompany such changes (Department of Health, 2000a). After a further period of delay the government finally announced, in March 2001, that the basic social work qualification would be upgraded to a three-year honours degree, with integrated academic and practice learning. This would be followed by a probationary year in employment prior to full registration with the GSCC. The changes are to take effect from the start of the academic year 2003–4.

Improving services for specific groups

Modernising Social Services announced an extension of the direct payment scheme to people aged 65 and over (p. 18). Otherwise, the White Paper contained little that was targeted at specific groups, as these initiatives were to follow. The health White Paper, *The New NHS*, (Department of Health, 1997b), had already announced the development of National Service Frameworks which would set national standards and define service models for specific services, for example mental health, or care groups, for example older people. These frameworks, each with associated performance targets, bring a further increase in the level of monitoring for both health and social services (see Chapter 5).

'Valuing People: A New Strategy for Learning Disability for the 21st Century'

The publication in March 2001 of *Valuing People* (Department of Health, 2001a), a White Paper on services for people with learning disabilities, was seen as long overdue. In the thirty years since the last White Paper, *Better Services for the Mentally Handicapped* (Department of Health and Social Security, 1971), the context within which people with learning disabilities live their lives had changed dramatically. In addition to the changes brought about by the closure of large long-stay institutions and the development of services in the community, the growth of the disability rights movement had led to a general questioning of the position of people with learning disabilities in society by service users and their families and by service providers (see Chapter 7).

Valuing People takes as its starting point the position of people with learning disabilities as 'amongst the most vulnerable and excluded in Britain today' (p. 14). Most lack independence and choice throughout their lives and their views are rarely heard. The extent of the consultation process which informed the White Paper signalled the importance of challenging that exclusion at every level. Service users and carers served alongside policy-makers and service providers on working groups and contributed through other consultative processes. Their views were presented in the White Paper itself and in three reports published alongside (Department of Health, 2001d, 2001e, 2001f).

The White Paper identified a wide range of problems affecting people with learning disabilities and carers. They include:

- Poorly co-ordinated services for **families with disabled children especially for those with severely disabled children**
- Poor planning for **young disabled people at the point of transition into adulthood**
- Insufficient support for **carers, particularly for those caring for people with complex needs**
- People with learning disabilities often have little **choice or control** over many aspects of their lives

- Substantial **health care** needs of people with learning disabilities are often unmet
- **Housing choice** is limited
- **Day services** are often not tailored to the needs and abilities of the individual
- Limited opportunities for **employment**
- The needs of **people from minority ethnic communities** are often overlooked
- **Inconsistency in expenditure and service delivery**
- Few examples of real **partnership** between health and social care or involving people with learning disabilities and carers. (Department of Health 2001a, pp. 2–3, emphasis in original)

Addressing these problems requires radical change, but of a kind that is consistent with the government's wider modernisation agenda. Echoing *Modernising Social Services*, the proposals in *Valuing People* are intended to:

- Tackle social exclusion and achieve better life chances
- Ensure value for money from the large public investment in learning disability services
- Reduce variation and promote consistency and equity of services across the country
- Promote effective partnership working at all levels to ensure a really person-centred approach to delivering quality services
- Drive up standards by encouraging an evidence-based approach to service provision and practice. (p. 22)

As in the 1998 White Paper, *Valuing People* is explicit about the principles, four in number, on which the proposals are based. People with learning disabilities are to have enforceable *civil and legal rights* in order to eradicate discrimination and to ensure the full protection of the law. They will be supported in exercising these rights by the Disability Rights Commission established in April 2000 (see Chapter 7). Second, the aim of services for people with learning disabilities will be to promote *independence* rather than dependence. Third, people with learning disabilities, including those with severe and profound disabilities, should be enabled to make *choices* and express preferences in daily living. Finally, they should be able to use mainstream services and be fully *included* in their local community (pp. 23–4).

Valuing People goes on to set out eleven national objectives for services for people with learning disabilities, the purpose of which is to provide a clear direction for local agencies and to achieve greater consistency and equity in services. The first eight focus on outcomes for people and the last three on improvements to the systems intended to deliver those outcomes. The objectives are listed in Box 4.2. Each objective has a set of associated sub-objectives, and the targets and performance indicators through which progress is to be monitored are specified. A strong national lead is to be provided through the establishment of a Learning Disability Task Force, with a membership including people with learning disabilities and carers, and a national Implementation Support Team. Responsibility for ensuring implementation of the programme at local level will lie with Learning Disability Partnership Boards.

Funding to support the key priorities of the White Paper, the development and improvement of community services, will be provided through a new Learning Disability Development Fund of up to £50 million per annum from April 2002. The revenue element of this funding (up to £30 million) will come from the release of old long-stay health funding, as the pro-gramme of hospital closure moves towards completion by April 2004. In addition to this, an Implementation Support Fund of £2.3 million a year for three years will be used to establish (i) a National Citizen Advocacy Network and support for the promotion of self-advocacy in partnership with the voluntary sector; and (ii) a National Learning Disability Information Centre and Helpline in partnership with Mencap.

Valuing People was generally welcomed for its person-centred approach, which focuses on the rights of people with learning disabilities, and for its emphasis on partnership working, but there were also widespread concerns about the lack of long-term funding to support the major changes required (Gates, 2001; Revans, 2001b). Rob Grieg, who was later appointed as Director of the Implementation Support Team, indicated the extent of these changes by identifying three substantial challenges for those in manage-ment and leadership roles (Grieg, 2001). The first is to listen to and engage with people with learning disabilities in order to prioritise their interests. Grieg anticipates that the development of direct payment schemes for peo-ple with learning disabilities will secure a shift in power away from service providers towards service users and carers. Second, ensuring that main-stream government initiatives are inclusive of people with learning disabil-ities will require specialist learning disability and mainstream services to work closely together. The specialist services will have to become aware of wider agendas, whilst the mainstream services will need to 'understand a) the particular needs that people with learning disabilities have in relation to their sphere of responsibility, b) how to communicate effectively with people with learning disabilities and c) the links available into specialist learning disability services to help them in their task of including people

BOX 4.2   Government objectives for learning disability services

Objective 1: Maximising Opportunities for Disabled Children
To ensure that disabled children gain maximum life chance benefits from educational opportunities, health care and social care, while living with their families or in other appropriate settings in the community where their assessed needs are adequately met and reviewed.

Objective 2: Transition into Adult Life
As young people with learning disabilities move into adulthood, to ensure continuity of care and support for the young person and their family and to provide equality of opportunity in order to enable as many disabled young people as possible to participate in education, training or employment.

Objective 3: Enabling People to Have More Control Over Their Own Lives
To enable people with learning disabilities to have as much choice and control as possible over their lives through advocacy and a person-centred approach to planning the services they need.

Objective 4: Supporting Carers
To increase the help and support carers receive from all local agencies in order to fulfil their family and caring roles effectively.

Objective 5: Good Health
To enable people with learning disabilities to access a health service designed around their individual needs, with fast and convenient care delivered to a consistently high standard, and with additional support where necessary.

Objective 6: Housing
To enable people with learning disabilities and their families to have greater choice over where and how they live.

Objective 7: Fulfilling Lives
To enable people with learning disabilities to lead full and purposeful lives in their communities and to develop a range of friendships, activities and relationships.

Objective 8: Moving into Employment
To enable more people with learning disabilities to participate in all forms of employment, wherever possible in paid work and to make a valued contribution to the world of work.

Objective 9: Quality
To ensure that all agencies commission and provide high quality, evidence-based and continuously improving services which promote both good outcomes and best value.

Objective 10: Workforce Training and Planning
To ensure that social and health care staff working with people with learning disabilities are appropriately skilled, trained and qualified, and to promote a better understanding of the needs of people with learning disabilities amongst the wider workforce.

Objective 11: Partnership Working
To promote holistic services for people with learning disabilities through effective partnership working between all relevant local agencies in the commissioning and delivery of services.

Source: Department of Health (2001a) p. 26.

with learning disabilities' (p. 5). Finally, the commissioning of services needs to be based on robust evidence about the needs and wishes of people with learning disabilities and of what works and what does not. It is as yet unclear whether such radical changes in organisation and culture, across a range of local authority and health services, can be achieved within the funding available.

Local government changes

In many local authorities the Seebohm model of a social services department has given way to alternative models in which social services are combined with other functions (Hill, 2000a). A recent survey of local authorities indicated that more than two-fifths had combined social services with other services such as housing and health, and a growing number had divided their social services into departments for adult services and for childcare services (Revans, 2002a). Developments in the reform of health care services are likely to further this trend (see Chapter 5).

Alongside this, there have also been changes in local authorities as a consequence of the New Labour programme for modernising local government through the reform of decision-making structures to increase efficiency and accountability. Proposals to replace the committee system with streamlined arrangements such as executive cabinets and executive mayors, which draw a clear distinction between executive responsibilities and the other roles of elected members, had appeared in the local government White Paper (Deputy Prime Minister, 1998). What does this mean for the future governance of the social services? *Modernising Social Services* provides some guidance (pp. 120–3). Councils must continue to appoint a Director of Social Services but will no longer be required to have a social services committee. Instead a named councillor or councillors will have executive responsibilities for social services and be responsible for monitoring the performance of the Director of Social Services and his or her staff. Non-executive or 'backbench' councillors are to be responsible for holding both the executive and senior officers to account through arrangements such as social services scrutiny committees. Early reports suggest that the new structures have contributed to more efficient decision-making whilst presenting new challenges (Brodie, 2001). In particular, Brodie argues, it is important to ensure that 'backbench' councillors feel involved in service issues and that there is a constructive relationship between the executive councillor and the scrutiny committee.

A further local government White Paper, *Strong Local Leadership – Quality Public Services* (Department of Transport, Local Government and the Regions, 2001a), confirmed the government's determination to improve the quality of services through the use of performance assessment. Performance indicator data and data from service-based inspections and reviews will be used to classify local authorities into one of four categories: high-performing, striving, coasting and poor-performing. High-performing councils will be rewarded with extra freedoms, such as reduced revenue ring-fencing and a lighter inspection regime, whilst poor performers will face intervention measures and the possibility that other bodies may be brought in to run their services. In addition the Department of Health has introduced a system of star ratings for social services as a further incentive to councils to improve their services and as a way of identifying and tackling poor performance. These annual league tables, the first of which was published in May 2002, are also intended to provide easily accessible information for local people to compare the performance of their services with those of other authorities. The rating system is based on all the available performance data, including information from inspections and joint reviews (Platt, 2002).

Modernisation – an initial assessment

Initial reactions to the White Paper *Modernising Social Services* from the local authorities and other interested groups were generally muted. There are several possible explanations for this. Its analysis of the weaknesses in social care provision was uncontroversial and it contained little that was unexpected as its main points had already been announced in *The New NHS*, the health service White Paper that preceded it, in the Labour manifesto or elsewhere. Also, as the overall legal framework for service organisation and provision was to remain intact, it was unclear to what extent the array of measures and initiatives it contained heralded fundamental change. In contrast to the reforms of the early 1990s the changes were to come into force gradually and in some cases not for several years (Department of Health, 1999d).

Many of the changes were welcomed, in particular the establishment of the General Social Care Council, the extension of direct payment schemes and the Fair Access to Care initiative. The proposals for a new system for inspection and regulation received a more mixed response, with doubts expressed by local authorities and by the independent care sector (see above). There was disappointment about the extended timetable for implementation and concerns that not enough attention had been paid to the funding arrangements for community care (Hunter, 1998). In advance of the White Paper and as a result of the government's first comprehensive spending review, an additional three billion pounds funding for social services had been announced. However, the White Paper made clear that this money would be used, through the creation of a Social Services Modernisation Fund, for change and modernisation, with much of the additional funding to be delivered in the form of specific grants for development purposes, such as the partnership and prevention grants (p. 11).

Soon after the 1997 election, the introduction of the comprehensive spending review and the production of national figures for each sector of public expenditure over a three-year period had made it easier for local authorities to plan their expenditure. However, despite the increased funding and the further announcement of an extra £2.8 billion over three years for the personal social services under the comprehensive spending review of July 2000, reports of severe financial problems in community care persisted. Thus, at the Local Government Association annual meeting in July 2001, only a month after the Labour government was returned to office in the 2001 general election, the local authorities called for an urgent increase in funding for social services to avert 'inevitable disaster'. It was claimed that the authorities were already spending £1 billion over and above the amount allocated by government to social services through its standard spending assessments (Revans, 2001c).

The government's assessment of local needs, as represented in the standard spending assessments, is central to the local authorities' case. The level at which the assessments are set fails to take account, they argue, of the increasing pressures on social services. Demographic growth, market pressures, higher public expectations, increased pressure to respond to need and the implementation of the government's modernising agenda, in particular the development of partnerships with the health service and other agencies and of new preventative services, have all contributed to a widening gap between expenditure and resources (Service Working Group for Personal Social Services, 2002). A significant increase in funding for the social services, 6 per cent a year guaranteed for the next three years, was announced in the budget of April 2002 (Downey, 2002). The details provided in the comprehensive spending review of July 2002 revealed that the bulk of this expenditure, £1 billion a year of which two-thirds is to be ring-fenced, is to go to older people's services (Hayes, 2002). Whilst it is too early to assess the likely impact of these changes, initial reactions suggest that it may not go far enough to address the long-term difficulties created by underfunding and, in particular, the problems of workforce recruitment and retention (Martin, 2002).

The growth in inspection and review has placed further demands on local authority resources. Whilst there is general agreement on the importance of information about strengths and weaknesses in service provision, uncertainty remains about the extent to which these resource-intensive activities actually lead to improvements in services and in outcomes for service users.

A survey of local authorities about their experiences of inspection found widespread support for the principle of external inspection, as a catalyst for improvement, that would be beneficial to both service users and staff, and as a way of increasing accountability (Local Government Association, 2001). However, less than half the respondents felt that inspection had actually resulted in improved services for users, or that the process had identified and shared best practice; even fewer (27 per cent) felt that inspection had led to innovation. The burgeoning number of inspectorates also presented problems, with only 10 per cent of respondents feeling there was effective co-ordination between inspection regimes and only 7 per cent that there was consistency between them. More encouragingly, there was some evidence of an improvement in the relationship between the local authorities and the inspectorates. In the case of the Social Services Inspectorate, 51 per cent of councils reported an improvement and only 7 per cent a deterioration in the relationship. The growth in joint inspections may help to overcome some of the problems reported. However, another study, from the inspector's angle, suggests that there are challenges here too. Whilst joint inspection regimes were seen as enabling the cross-fertilisation of ideas and leading to fresh approaches to inspection, there was also potential for conflict where different inspectorates were operating with different models of the service under inspection (Mordaunt, 2000).

Perhaps the most detailed account of the challenges of inspection and review, for both inspectors and the services they inspect, has emerged from the national evaluation of the Best Value pilot projects. The problems identified include how to develop a common and clear set of standards for assessing local service performance and how to secure a consistent interpretation of these standards by inspection teams (Boyne, 2000). From the local authority perspective there are questions such as how to consult a sufficiently wide range of stakeholders, how to obtain sufficiently rigorous data for analysing and comparing services and how to ensure that the results of Best Value reviews inform political decision-making within local authorities, when the two processes operate with very different timescales and pressures (Martin and Davis, 2001). It is by no means clear that the resources required to conduct Best Value reviews and to implement the changes required will be balanced by service improvements, whilst determining what constitutes improvement, and from whose point of view, is also likely to pose difficulties (Boyne, 2000). These initial findings were echoed in a later study of the experiences of Best Value in 41 local authorities (Copus and Raine, 2002). Concerns were reported about the reliability of the data available for making cost and quality comparisons between authorities and there was a widely held belief that the Best Value regime was far too demanding for organisations of the limited scale and resource base of local councils. The researchers found a consensus view emerging which welcomed the goals and philosophy of Best Value but sought a more flexible, less prescriptive, regime in relation to timescales, review requirements, procedural expectations and data gathering that would be more in keeping with the individual circumstances and resource limitations of local councils.

The surprise announcement in April 2002 that the newly established National Care Standards Commission would be merged with the Social Services Inspectorate to form the Commission for Social Care Inspection went some way to meeting the demands of local authorities for a rationalisation of the inspection regime (Brown, 2002a). The new body will have responsibility for: the inspection of all social care organisations to ensure they meet national standards; the registration of services; the inspection of local authority social services; the validation of all performance assessment statistics on social care; the publication of star ratings for social services and for recommending when special measures are necessary; and for publishing an annual report to Parliament on the progress of social care with an analysis of the use of resources. The announcement also contained an important clue to government thinking on the future relationship between social and health care. The Department of Health would keep under review the possibility of a merger between the new Commission for Social Care Inspection and the proposed Commission for Healthcare Audit and Inspection, to create a single commission covering both health and social services.

A rather different issue is whether the use of performance indicators and targets provides an appropriate basis for assessing the performance of social services and an effective strategy for improvement. Critics point to the risk that performance indicators, which inevitably focus on single aspects of a complex reality, may present a misleading picture and bear little relation to outcomes for service users (Plank, 2000). They may also distort service priorities, as in the case of the NHS where, in an effort to reduce waiting times, people with non-urgent problems may be seen more quickly whilst urgent cases may be delayed. In social services the use of performance indicators may introduce a further barrier to preventive work, which is more difficult to measure. Concerns have also been raised about whether the methodologies that underpin the assessment of performance are sufficiently robust to take account of the substantial differences between authorities in respect of their social and economic characteristics (Wellard, 2000).

The associated strategy of 'naming and shaming' poor performers through the publication of performance league tables has also been criticised, especially for its potential impact on staff morale and on the continuing recruitment crisis in social care (Revans, 2002b). Denise Platt, Chief Social Services Inspector at the Department of Health, writing shortly after publication of the first star ratings for social services, strongly defended this approach to monitoring performance and the methodology used. In particular, she suggests, it is important to identify councils that need intensive support to improve their services, as such support and monitoring do enable significant changes to take place (Platt, 2002).

The extended timetable for the programme of modernising social services and the continuing announcement of new initiatives make any overall assessment of progress difficult. However, at the time of writing a number of important issues can be identified.

First, one of the key objectives in the White Paper *Modernising Social Services* was to raise the status of social care, in particular through measures to improve the workforce. Much has been done, for example with the creation of the General Social Care Council, the Social Care Institute for Excellence and the changes in social work training. It is as yet unclear whether such initiatives will be sufficient to resolve the crisis in recruitment and retention of staff and to raise the overall standard of practice, particularly in traditionally low-status services such as those for older people.

Second, a more prescriptive approach from central government about all aspects of service delivery necessarily involves a reduction in both local and professional autonomy. It is likely therefore to also reduce the possibility for user empowerment where users' wishes conflict with the rules laid down. A recent example of this has been the closure or transfer of care homes, against the wishes of the residents, after the introduction of national standards for such establishments.

Third, the reform programme contains ample evidence of positive efforts to challenge discrimination, to empower service users and to raise standards, for example in the White Paper on learning disabilities, the National Service Frameworks and the introduction of care standards. It has yet to be seen whether these initiatives will be adequately resourced and whether consistency will or should be maintained across such a wide range of initiatives.

Conclusion

At the beginning of the 1990s the continuing importance of local authority social services seemed undisputed. They had become the lead agency for community care with the task of implementing a complex series of reforms in a challenging climate. By the end of the decade the process of reform was set to continue, after the election of a New Labour government with a programme for modernising both national and local government and the National Health Service. As this chapter has shown, the modernising agenda has had a considerable impact on social services, even though the exact nature of that impact is still in many respects unclear. However it is changes elsewhere that are likely to have the most radical effect on the future shape of social care. The next chapter therefore focuses on the reforms in the National Health Service and their implications for the health and social care interface, and for the future of local authority social services.

5 Health and Social Care: From Collaboration to Incorporation?

Introduction

Labour governments since 1997 have announced on numerous occasions that they are determined to break down the supposed 'Berlin Wall' between health and social care agencies. This chapter focuses on the shifting boundaries between health and social care, and explores whether or not there has been a fundamental policy shift from an emphasis on collaboration between equal partners to one where social services are to be largely incorporated into health.

Shifting boundaries, 1948–93

An immediate answer can be given to the question of whether a Berlin Wall exists between health and social care services. The answer is 'no'. Walls demarcate fixed boundaries – on one side of the Berlin Wall was East Germany and on the other was West Germany. It stayed as a fixed locational point until torn down as part of the reunification of Germany.

The situation with regard to health and social care is far more complex. The issue about 'what is health?' and 'what is social care?' has been regularly disputed and redefined since the Second World War (Means and Smith, 1998b; Glendinning and Means, 2002). It is argued here that there has been a tendency for social services to be expected to take on more and more responsibilities from health without any significant transfer of resources.

Within the confines of this chapter, it is possible to give only a glimpse of these debates. Prior to the late 1970s, the central role of health care professionals with regard to people with learning disabilities and mental health problems was rarely questioned. However, the debate over lead agency roles for elderly and physically disabled people goes back much further. Certainly, by the mid-1960s, Titmuss (1968) was able to say:

> In all this discussion at the present time of who is responsible for what, the family doctor is being cast for the role of co-ordinator, mobiliser,

director, stage manager and leader of community care ... Others, however, are seeing the medical officer of health performing this role partly
on the grounds that the family doctor is too busy and is trained as a clini-
cian and medical diagnostician. Still others propose that the chief welfare
officer should assume some or most of these responsibilities. (p. 100)

In other words, should such services be led by health care professionals or
social care professionals? Medical officers of health were responsible for
local authority health departments, and hence were left with the residue of
local authority health functions after the removal of hospitals from local
government responsibility under the National Health Service Act 1946.
Consequently, they had the prestige of being medically qualified but the
problem of overseeing a declining empire (Means and Smith, 1998b).
Several medical officers of health attempted to counterbalance this by arguing that residential care and domiciliary services under the National
Assistance Act 1948 should be under their control rather than that of either
a chief welfare officer who was not medically qualified or overstretched
family doctors.

The eventual restructuring of services in the early 1970s was based on
assumptions about the distinction between health care services (for example, GP, health visitor, district nurse) and social care services (for example,
social worker, home help). The National Health Service Act 1973 was an
attempt to tackle some of the perceived ineffectiveness associated with the
NHS structure created by the 1946 Act. Brown (1979, p. 6) claimed the
local authority health services were seen as 'a rag-bag of functions' that
needed to be integrated into the hospital and general practitioner services.
The 1973 Act was a mechanism by which 'local authority health services
were nationalised and brought under the same management as hospital services' (p. 22). District nurses and health visitors were no longer to work in a
local authority department but were rather to be responsible to a district
nursing officer who would be a member of the district management team of
the newly formed district health authority.

With regard to local authority services, the leadership role fell to the
Director of Social Services and social services departments from 1 April
1971 (Means *et al.*, 2002). As seen in Chapter 2, the early 1970s saw a
major extension of the powers of local authorities to provide services and
support for elderly people and disabled people. Local authority welfare
departments had become increasingly interested in employing those with
social work skills to help in deciding how to prioritise elderly people wishing to enter residential care, and they had begun to argue that such skills
could help in preventing elderly people even entering such care, especially

if backed up by appropriate domiciliary support such as home care and day care (Means and Smith, 1998b).

On institutional care, a key debate has always been over the meaning of the term 'in need of care and attention' in the National Assistance Act 1948. Godlove and Mann (1980) argued that the authors of the 1948 Act did not envisage residential homes 'as being adequate for people suffering from incontinence, serious loss of mobility, or abnormal senile dementia'. These were health problems requiring placement in a hospital or nursing home. Yet an important aspect of the history of welfare services since 1948 has been the shift of definition of 'care and attention' to include those suffering from these illnesses and medical conditions (Means, 2001).

The early debate on this issue was sparked off by two factors. First, the 1950s saw shortages of residential accommodation, caused by capital restrictions on the building of new homes. Second, the same period saw concerns about the high cost of hospital provision within the newly created National Health Service. A number of questions began to be asked. Were expensive hospital beds being blocked by the lack of residential accommodation, or were local authorities being swamped by residents in need of constant nursing care? Was there a group not catered for in the existing legislation so that they were 'stranded in the no-man's land between the Regional Hospital Board and the local welfare department – not ill enough for one, not well enough for the other' (Huws Jones, 1952, p. 22)? Was there a need for a national system of rest homes or halfway homes that catered for this special group?

As early as 1953, the Minister of Health (Iain Macleod) described this whole area 'as perhaps the most baffling problem in the whole of the National Health Service' (quoted in Means, 1986, p. 94). The government decided that the best approach was to expand local authority residential care in a form which would enable such homes to cope with the needs of those labelled as 'infirm' rather than 'sick'. This approach was supported by the government, which attempted to specify the responsibilities of local authorities and hospital boards in respect of frail and sick elderly people. Ministry of Health Circular 14/57 stated that local welfare authorities were responsible not only for 'active elderly people' in need of residential care but also for:

- Care of the otherwise active resident in a welfare home during minor illness which may well involve a short period in bed
- Care of the infirm (including the senile) who may need help in dressing, toilet and so on, and may need to live on the ground floor because they cannot manage stairs, and may spend part of the day in bed (or longer periods in bad weather)

• Care of those elderly persons in a welfare home who have to take to bed and are not expected to live more than a few weeks (or, exceptionally, months).

Hospital authorities were given their own list of responsibilities by this circular. These included the chronic bedfast, the convalescent sick and the senile confused. 'The partly sick and partly well' seemed to be no longer in no man's land. They would increasingly be directed to local authority residential accommodation even though this was meant to be a form of social rather than health care provision (Means, 2001). Although this situation was further reinforced by a subsequent circular in the mid-1960s (Ministry of Health, 1965), the reality remained one of endless disputes about how to interpret such circulars in terms of the health and social care needs of specific individuals.

The major reforms in both the National Health Service and the personal social services in the early 1970s did little to ease these tensions despite the assertion that they were based upon a clear separation between health and social care functions (see above). Increasingly, disputes focused on the correct placement of adults with health and social care needs and this was often linked to the closure of long-stay hospital beds (Means *et al.*, 2002). Such arguments were often not over the correctness of the policy towards deinstitutionalisation, but the failure either to transfer adequate resources to social services or to ensure adequate health care was available for those now deemed primarily their responsibility.

The research by Means *et al.* (2002) of community care developments in four different local authorities during this period found many respondents taking the cynical view that cutting continuing care beds in the 1980s was a simple way to reduce costs in a health service dominated by acute care and the resource demands of teaching hospitals. For example, a former chief officer for a Community Health Council asserted that 'if you've a teaching hospital in your midst, it's like having a bloody great monster sucking the blood from every other part' of the local health service (p. 82). He felt such a situation often led to a significant under-investment in community health services (quoted in Means *et al.*, 2002, Chapter 5).

The main mechanism created by central government for overcoming these boundary disputes was joint care planning and joint finance. The NHS Reorganisation Act 1973 established joint planning machinery between health and local authorities through member-based Joint Consultative Committees. A key purpose was to help plan for the rundown of long-stay hospitals and the encouragement of community-based services for people with mental health problems, people with learning difficulties and frail elderly people (see Chapter 2). Lack of perceived progress in joint planning led to the subsequent introduction of joint finance. The arrangement was that social services could receive health authority funds for agreed projects over time-limited periods. These projects needed to be community-based and targeted at people leaving long-stay hospitals or to support people so that they would not require hospital-based care (Department of Health and Social Security, 1977, 1978b).

However, joint finance proved to be another source of conflict between health and social services. All four social services authorities studied by Means *et al.* (2002) expressed concern and sometimes anger at the assumption that they would be in a position to pick up revenue costs once the period of joint finance had come to an end. Thus, a county council passed a resolution 'that the health authority be informed that the council regretfully can accept no responsibility for any part of the cost of this programme at present or for the foreseeable future' (p. 89), whilst a London borough complained that 'it would be wrong to commit finance immediately to any long term projects... which would pre-empt decisions in later years on priorities' (p. 89).

As already seen in Chapter 2, *Making a Reality of Community Care* (Audit Commission, 1986) confirmed the failure of joint planning and joint finance to achieve effective collaboration between health and social services with the blame being placed upon organisational fragmentation and the failure to switch funds. Both Chapter 2 and Chapter 3 outlined how the NHS and Community Care Act 1990 attempted to establish a new demarcation line between health and social services. Social services was to be the lead agency for all the main community care groups with health authorities responsible for health, narrowly defined. The emphasis remained on the need for social services and health to work effectively together with the White Paper on community care devoting a short chapter to collaboration (Department of Health, 1989a, pp. 49–52). It was argued that the community care changes would clarify the respective roles of health and social care agencies so that tension and conflict would be greatly reduced. It was accepted that in some areas and over some individuals the distinction remained blurred, but health and local authorities would 'need to decide locally about how they share objectives, responsibilities and the funding of different services' (p. 50).

Joint working between health and social services after the community care reforms: four key issues

The view of Labour Governments since 1997 has clearly been that the reforms of the early 1990s were no more effective than those of the early

1970s in establishing a clear demarcation between health and social services combined with a willingness to work together. It is certainly true that problems continued to occur in some areas while progress was very slow in others. This is briefly illustrated by reference to four important issues: continuing care NHS beds, hospital discharge, the lead role in mental health services and joint commissioning.

Continuing care

Earlier chapters have looked at the spectacular growth of private nursing home care from the mid-1980s (Player and Pollock, 2001) and this, of course, served to speed up the decline in continuing care NHS beds (Wistow, 1995). The community care reforms gave social services the responsibility for assessing and funding people in independent sector nursing home care and this served to encourage health authorities to run down their remaining nursing home and continuing care provision (Lewis, 2001). Once again, local authorities began to complain that some people referred to them from acute hospitals had health care rather than social care needs, and hence remained the responsibility of the health service.

The Conservative government responded to this situation by setting out *NHS Responsibilities for Meeting Continuing Health Care Needs* (Department of Health, 1995a) through Circular HSG(95)8 in a similar way to which Circular 14/57 (Ministry of Health, 1957) had attempted almost forty years previously. The circulars outlined key services which health authorities and GP fundholders had to continue to arrange and fund (see Box 5.1). In terms of which patients should receive such services, the circulars stressed that after a multidisciplinary assessment and consideration of local eligibility criteria, the consultant (or GP in some community hospitals) in consultation with the multidisciplinary team would decide whether:

- The patient needs continuing in-patient care arranged and funded by the NHS because:
  - either he or she needs ongoing and regular specialist clinical supervision (in the majority of cases this might be weekly or more frequent) on account of:
    - the complexity, nature and intensity of his or her medical, nursing or other clinical needs;
    - the need for frequent not easily predictable interventions;
  - or because after acute treatment or in-patient palliative care in hospital or hospice his or her prognosis is such that he or she is likely to die in the very near future and discharge from NHS care would be inappropriate

> **BOX 5.1　Services to be arranged and funded by health authorities and GP fundholders**
>
> - Specialist medical and nursing assessment
> - Rehabilitation and recovery
> - Palliative health care
> - Continuing in-patient care under specialist supervision in hospital or nursing home
> - Respite health care
> - Specialist health care support to people in nursing homes or residential care homes or in the community
> - Community health services to people at home or in residential care homes
> - Primary health care
> - Specialist transport services.

- The patient needs a period of rehabilitation or recovery arranged and funded by the NHS to prepare for discharge arrangements breaking down
- The patient can be appropriately discharged from NHS in-patient care with:
  - either a place in a nursing home or residential home or residential care home arranged and funded by social services or by the patient and his or her family;
  - or a package of social and health care support to allow the patient to return to his or her own home or to alternatively arranged accommodation. (Department of Health, 1995a, p. 9)

Individual health authorities and NHS trusts were given a timetable for translating the above into local policies, with health authorities needing to have arrangements to review decisions on eligibility for NHS continuing care available from 1 April 1996. Conservative governments had encouraged a massively reduced role for the NHS but had become concerned that this trend had gone too far. The circulars were designed to ensure agreed local policies would establish 'a line in the sand' beyond which this withdrawal would not go. The 'Berlin Wall' between health and social services was continuing to shift to a point where it was hard for some not to conclude that such a distinction was becoming impossible to maintain. The second half of this chapter discusses whether this conclusion has now been reached by the Labour government in power at the time of writing.

Hospital discharge

The second issue concerns hospital discharge arrangements for those entering care and for those returning home. This was seen from the outset as a major issue in the implementation of the community care reforms. The Deputy Chief Executive of the National Health Service Management Executive and the Chief Inspector of the Social Services Inspectorate set local authority and health care agencies eight key tasks for 1992/3 in terms of the initial implementation of the community care changes. These included ensuring the robustness and mutual acceptability of discharge arrangements. Subsequently, the handover of social security transfer monies to individual social services authorities became dependent on signing hospital discharge agreements with their health authorities. At one level, this emphasis on improving hospital discharge arrangements deserved to be welcomed since research had pointed to major inadequacies in discharge arrangements for people with support needs returning to their own homes:

> One in three of the people in the sample said they had not been asked how they would manage at home after their discharge. Two-fifths were told about the discharge either the day before or on the day it was due to happen. (Neill and Williams, 1992, p. 74)

However, it was likely that the priority given to hospital discharge issues was driven more by the necessity to avoid bed blockages in the acute hospital sector, rather than from a concern to ensure the capacity of the care manager to offer appropriate care options after hospital treatment.

In fairness, considerable efforts were made to improve the way health and social care professionals worked together over hospital discharge issues, including the production of a hospital discharge workbook (Henwood, 1994). However, research continued to identify major deficiencies in the co-ordination of health and social care agencies over hospital discharge (Audit Commission, 1997; Department of Health, 2000c) and this was soon to become a major concern to post-May 1997 Labour governments. For example, the major review of the National Health Service produced in 2000 stressed how:

> on one day in September last year, 5,500 patients aged 75 and over were ready to be discharged but were still in an acute hospital bed: 23% awaiting assessment; 17% waiting for social services funding to go to a care home; 25% trying to find the right care home; and 6% waiting for the right care home package to be organised ... The 1948 fault line between health and social care has inhibited the development of services shaped around the needs of patients. (Department of Health, 2000d, p. 29)

The clear suggestion of the above quotation is that the fault in such delayed discharge lay with social services, a point confirmed when the government announced financial penalties for local authorities deemed responsible for such delays (Glendinning, 2002). Others disagreed. Social services and community health respondents in research by Help the Aged (2002) complained of a rigid attitude on the part of health professionals to early discharge from acute hospitals leading to 'inappropriate placement in residential settings, to patients returning home with no support in place and to rapid re-admission' (p. 27).

Mental health issues

The third issue relates to mental health services and from the outset there was no shortage of people sceptical of the competence of social services to play a lead role in the way proposed by the White Paper on community care. Thus, the British Medical Association (1992) indicated that 'there is concern ... that most local authorities lack the skills and expertise to take on the responsibility for supporting mentally ill people in the community' (p. 30).

In addition the capacity of social services to take on this lead role was made problematic because of the development of the care programme approach (CPA) as a parallel system to care management for developing user-centred care plans. CPA was introduced in order to provide a clear framework for the care of people with mental health problems outside hospital. Health authorities in collaboration with social services authorities were expected to agree their local CPA approach, which must have four main elements:

- Systematic arrangements for assessing the health and social needs of people accepted by specialist psychiatric services
- The formulation of a care plan which addresses the identified health and social care needs
- The appointment of a key worker to keep in close touch with the patient and monitor care
- Regular reviews and, if need be, agreed changes to the care plan. (Department of Health, 1995b)

However, since the vast bulk of care programme staff were employees of health care agencies, the relation of CPA to the new system of care management began to be identified as a major source of confusion and tension between health and social services (Mental Health Foundation, 1994; Department of Health/Social Services Inspectorate, 1995). In addition, the Audit Commission (1994) pointed out that too many resources remained locked into hospital provision, the development of community services was patchy and service management and co-ordination had to be improved.

Such concerns achieved a very high profile in the mid-1990s for two linked reasons. First, the number of single homeless people was growing and it was clear that a high percentage of these had mental health problems (Bines, 1994). This was bound to lead to concern that people were leaving psychiatric hospitals (or failing to get into them) and drifting into homelessness because of a failure to offer appropriate community services and support. Other research showed that mentally disordered offenders were another group at risk of homelessness because of the poor co-ordination of services on discharge (Lart, 1997).

Second, these concerns were dramatically heightened by a number of mass media portrayals of people with severe mental problems who had killed either care workers or members of the public. For example, on 9 October 1993 John Rous, diagnosed as suffering severe schizophrenia, killed Jonathan Newby, a 22-year-old graduate, working as a volunteer for the Oxford Cyrenians. Ten months previously, Jonathan Zito had been stabbed on the London Underground by Christopher Clunis, also diagnosed as schizophrenic. Reports into both these incidents pointed to a lack of specialist expertise, poor co-ordination of services, a failure to respond to warning signs and a lack of long-term accommodation specifically targeted at those with the most severe mental health problems (Ritchie *et al.*, 1994; Davies Report, 1995).

The initial response of government was to provide good practice guidance on joint working in this area (Department of Health, 1995b) and further changes to the law. In terms of the latter, the Mental Health (Patients in the Community) Act 1995 established a new system of supervised discharge for many of those leaving hospital with the most severe mental health problems. In February 1996 this was followed up with the announcement of a 'new "asylum" plan for severely mentally ill' which would provide 24-hour nursing care for at least 5,000 of the most disturbed mentally ill patients in some 400 new residential homes (*The Independent*, 21 February 1996, p. 1). This trend has continued and at the time of writing the Mental Health Bill 2002 proposes a new legal framework for the compulsory treatment of people with mental disorders which led an editorial in *Community Care* to refer to the bill as owing 'more to the Criminal Lunatics Act of 1800 than to enlightened thinking' (4–10 July 2002, p. 5).

In terms of good practice, the Department of Health (1995b) issued *Building Bridges: A Guide to Arrangements for Inter-Agency Working for the Care and Protection of Severely Mentally Ill People*, whose starting point was:

There has been continuing anxiety, particularly over the last two or three years, concerning the care and treatment of severely mentally ill people in the community. A number of suicides, homicides and other serious incidents have understandably led to great public and professional concern. (pp. 8–9)

The guide stressed that the care programme approach and care management were based on the same principles and so 'the two systems should be capable of being fully integrated' (p. 56) as long as each client has an agreed single care plan and single key worker.

The 'culprit' was being defined as a failure in joint working caused by lack of agreement on roles and responsibilities and poor awareness of each other's networks. Until these deficiencies were resolved, the message of *Building Bridges* was that some people with severe mental health problems would continue to slip through the 'net' of available support into homelessness and possibly worse. However, reviews of CPA continued to identify a failure of co-ordination or integration with care management (Department of Health/Social Services Inspectorate, 1999).

Joint commissioning

One of the themes running through the mental health debate was the lack of community services to support the objective of providing care in the community rather than in long-stay hospitals. This led to a major emphasis on the need for health and social services to work together on joint purchasing strategies, the final issue to be considered in this section. What progress was made on this across the main client groups? Not all the evidence was bleak, since the results of research suggested that, in many areas, an excellent dialogue between health and social services had emerged as a result of the community care reforms (Hoyes *et al.*, 1996), especially where health and social services boundaries were coterminous or nearly so (Hudson, 1992). If nothing else, social services managers and health service managers had developed a greater appreciation of each other's priorities and preoccupations than existed before (Means *et al.*, 2002).

However, the mid-1990s saw a growing belief that joint working at the strategic level needed to become much more formalised and integrated. Thus Knapp *et al.* (1992) argued:

from a procedural standpoint, joint commissioning improves the prospects of moving to clearer and more consistent eligibility criteria. It should raise mutual awareness, foster co-operation rather than competition, and weaken previous tendencies to pass the buck – to shunt people and costs on to other agencies. For example, joint commissioning of residential and nursing home care would provide the opportunity to achieve a much more appropriate balance between congregate and community care across the health and social care system as a whole. (p. 29)

For both those in residential or nursing home care and those still in the community, joint commissioning was felt to be a positive-sum game since it involved 'the pooling of sovereignty to achieve ends which individual agencies are less likely to secure alone' (p. 30).

By the mid-1990s the Conservative government had become convinced of the great value of joint commissioning and was keen to offer advice on how obstacles could be overcome. Guidance distinguished between joint commissioning (two or more commissioning agencies act together to co-ordinate commissioning), joint purchasing (two or more agencies co-ordinate the actual buying of services) and joint provision (agencies jointly provide a service) with a clear view that effective joint commissioning was likely to lead on to the second two activities (Department of Health, 1995c, 1995d). The overall message was that the Department of Health (1995c) remained committed 'to helping authorities achieve the potential benefits for service users and their carers that effective joint commissioning can bring' (p. 9).

Initially, many of the most high-profile joint developments have been in the areas of learning difficulties and mental health. Peck *et al.* (2002) explain the origins of one of these in the following way:

In 1996, Somerset Health Authority and Somerset County Council undertook a review of mental health services in Somerset. The ensuing report catalogued a series of problems that would have been familiar to most localities around England. Amongst the recommendations for dealing with these problems were the proposals to introduce joint commissioning and the creation of the first combined mental health and social care provider in the UK, Somerset Partnership NHS and Social Care Trust, which was formally established in April 1999. (p. 4)

The incoming Labour government in 1997 soon made its enthusiasm for such arrangements clear. The Health Act 1999 not only created a duty of partnership but also significantly extended the ability of local authorities and the NHS to pool budgets for specific groups of services, delegate commissioning to a 'local' organisation and create single provider organisations (Clarke and Glendinning, 2002). Some commentators (Rummery, 2002) have noted how single provider arrangements require a board which changes the fundamental governance of community care. Such governance ceases to be via the simple direct accountability of councillors on a social services committee to the local electorate as argued for in the Griffiths Report (1988). Initially, it seemed that this would only affect services for those with mental health problems and learning difficulties. However, it soon became clear that such developments would quickly affect community care provision for older people.

A key reason for this was the frustration of the Labour government with past failures to encourage collaboration. However, before their approach is outlined further, it is necessary to remind ourselves why the importance of collaboration is very easy to assert yet so difficult to achieve.

Collaborative working: the theory

Over a decade ago, Webb (1991) brutally explained that 'exhortations to organisations, professionals and other producer interests to work together more closely and effectively litter the policy landscape' yet the reality is 'all too often a jumble of services fractionalised by professional, cultural and organisational boundaries and by tiers of governance' (p. 229).

One key difficulty is that governments have often been happy to extol the virtues of collaborative working without ever bothering to address the very real obstacles which exist from the point of view of the proposed collaborating partners (Sullivan and Skelcher, 2002). As Hudson (1987) explains:

> From an agency's viewpoint, collaborative activity raises two main difficulties. First, it loses some of its freedom to act independently when it would prefer to maintain control over its domain and affairs. Second, it must invest scarce resources and energy in developing and maintaining relationships with other organisations when the potential returns on this investment are often unclear and intangible. (p. 175)

Thus in order to commit themselves to joint working, agencies need to be persuaded that it is only by this route that organisational objectives can be achieved. They have to be convinced of the possibility of what Huxham (1996) calls 'collaborative advantage'.

Hudson (1987) suggests there are three main strategies available to foster collaborative working despite these problems. These are co-operative strategies (based on mutual agreements), incentive strategies (based on 'bribes' to encourage joint working) and authoritative strategies (agencies or individuals are instructed to work together). Initially, the tendency of government was to request organisations such as social services authorities and district health authorities to collaborate on various initiatives. Increasingly, governments turned to the use of financial incentives (for example, earmarked monies such as joint finance) to try and persuade health and social care agencies to move in the direction that they wanted. An interesting feature of the present government is its willingness not only to use financial penalties as well as incentives (for example, for delaying hospital discharges) but also to use authoritative strategies (for example, the duty of partnership).

Collaboration and partnership are rapidly becoming 'not optional but mandatory' (Clarke and Glendinning, 2002, p. 37) not just in health and social care, but as central features of policy throughout the public services (Sullivan and Skelcher, 2002). However, this is very problematic because research evidence suggests that joint working is most likely to flourish when there are high levels of trust between the partners (Webb, 1991; Rummery, 2002). It is difficult to see how trust can be enforced and outcomes may well turn out to be disappointing when based on mandated collaboration.

Hudson's framework is focused in the main on co-ordination and collaboration between agencies, and yet Hudson (2002) recognises there is equal concern about how to promote better co-operation on a day-to-day basis between health and welfare professionals involved in providing services for community care clients (see also Owens *et al.*, 1995). These relationships can be equally problematic and some of the reasons for this were pulled together by Means *et al.* (1997):

- *Stereotypes* – different professional groups often hold negative stereotypes about each other. The more entrenched the stereotypes, the harder it will be to develop joint working
- *Cultural differences* – in addition to stereotypes, there are real and very important cultural differences between professional groups in terms of how they understand and respond to need. These cultural differences include the use of jargon particular to each profession
- *Disagreement about roles and responsibilities* – if professionals disagree over their respective roles, responsibilities and competencies, then this is likely to be an obstacle to effective joint working at the local level. This is sometimes referred to as a lack of domain consensus (Hudson, 1987)
- *Misunderstandings* – professionals often have only limited knowledge about other professional groups or other organisations with which they wish to liaise and work. They simply misunderstand the priorities, organisational structures, cultures and working practices of fellow professionals. There is a lack of network awareness.

The policy studies literature indicates that some professionals are adept at overcoming these obstacles and so encourage joint working. Such individuals are sometimes referred to as 'reticulists' (Friend *et al.*, 1974), whilst the Audit Commission (1986) called them 'champions of change'. They are skilled at mapping policy networks and identifying the key resource holders and fellow enthusiasts, both from their own and from other agencies. They tend to feel comfortable working above their hierarchical position, and they are willing to operate in a way not bounded by narrow organisational self-interest. However, a recent study by Hudson (2002) of working relationships between general practitioners, community nurses and social workers found that 'harmonious relationships ... [were] only patchy and partial' (p. 15).

It has long been recognised that staff equally have the capacity to undermine joint working through what is sometimes called 'street level bureaucrat' behaviour (Lipsky, 1980). Hoggett (2001) draws upon the work of Sennett (1998) to illustrate how this is likely to be magnified in times of rapid policy change:

> As the demand for change-embracing and flexible workers intensifies, those who by temperament, age or aptitude cannot maintain the pace or the adaptability required become increasingly vulnerable. (p. 54)

Public sector workers may recognise the imperative need to change but many also feel greater anger and frustration at what is expected of them. Hoggett (2001) has called for a psychosocial perspective on this phenomenon from a belief that 'our capacity to be a reflexive agent is often constrained by the difficulties we have in facing our own fears and anxieties' (p. 42).

Such perspectives underline how difficult it can be to foster collaborative working across agencies especially during periods of rapid change. However, there is a growing body of literature on how to achieve effective inter-professional team working (Ovretreit, 1993) and on how inter-professional education can have a positive impact (Miller *et al.*, 2001). Malin *et al.* (1999) have usefully argued that what is needed is an acceptance of differing views on community care from health and social care professionals, but with shared principles about how to manage disagreements. This is because:

> disagreements ... allow for a diversity of views and therefore for adaptation and creativity. They enhance autonomy. In particular, a diversity of perspectives among professionals, where properly managed, enhances the autonomy of the user. Users who are faced with a monolithic unity of perspective from all the professionals involved run the risk of being disempowered and alienated. (p. 170)

By way of contrast, the rest of this chapter illustrates how an acceptance of diversity amongst health and social care professionals has been seen as something to be discouraged by Labour governments since 1997. A series of policy initiatives have been designed to abolish the health and social care divide.

The Royal Commission on Long Term Care

Ironically, the first example is of a decision by the government *not* to take a major policy initiative, even though its proponents argued that it would dramatically reduce this divide. An early focus of the incoming government was on the specific manifesto commitment to set up a Royal Commission on Long Term Care. Sir Stewart Sutherland was asked to chair the commission with a remit:

> to examine the short and long term options for a sustainable system of funding of long term care for elderly people, both in their own homes and in other settings, and within 12 months, to recommend how and in what circumstances the cost of such care should be apportioned between public funds and individuals. (Sutherland Report, 1999a, p. ix)

There was growing criticism of how the capital resources (and especially the home equity) of older people was being used to fund their nursing home care in later life, because it was felt such care should be free under the National Health Service (Rummery and Glendinning, 1999). However, Commission members were unable to agree on the best way forward for funding and so they were forced to publish both a main report (Sutherland Report, 1999a, pp. 1–111) and a note of dissent (Joffe and Lipsey, 1999, pp. 113–43).

The main report argued for free personal care on the grounds that no logical distinction could be made either between health care and social care or between those services which should be free and those which should be means-tested:

> Older people need long term care not simply just because they are old, but because their health has been undermined by a disabling disease such as Alzheimer's disease, other forms of dementia or a stroke. As yet these diseases cannot effectively be cured by medical care, but people suffering from them will require ongoing therapeutic or personal care of different kinds in order to enable them to live with the disease. In this regard, the

only difference between cancer and Alzheimer's disease is the limitation of medical science. (Sutherland Report, 199a, p. 67).

The main report, therefore, felt justified in calling for a common system of funding for what it defined as personal care (see Box 5.2). This common system was to be based on general taxation so that all personal care would be free at the point of consumption rather than being means-tested or based upon some system of insurance. It was argued that although the resultant public expenditure costs would be considerable (see Table 5.1), they were perfectly affordable.

The authors of the note of dissent were unconvinced by the affordability argument. They were concerned that 'this huge addition to the burden on public expenditure would not, however, increase spending on services for elderly people by a single penny' (p. 113). The Labour government proved to be much more supportive of the note of dissent than the main report. It decided that the nursing care component of personal care in nursing homes should be free, but that social care in nursing homes, residential care and the community would continue to be means-tested and chargeable. This rejection of the central recommendation of the main report was justified on the grounds that actioning the proposal would have absorbed large sums of

---

BOX 5.2   Definitions of personal care

Personal care would cover all direct care related to:

- personal toilet (washing, bathing, skin care, personal presentation, dressing and undressing and skin care);
- eating and drinking (as opposed to obtaining and preparing food and drink);
- managing urinary and bowel functions (including maintaining continence and managing incontinence);
- managing problems associated with immobility;
- management of prescribed treatment (e.g. administration and monitoring medication);
- behaviour management and ensuring personal safety (e.g., for those with cognitive impairment – minimising stress and risk).

Personal care also includes the associated teaching, enabling, psychological support from a knowledgeable and skilled professional, and assistance with cognitive functions (e.g. reminding, for those with dementia) that are needed either to enable a person to do these things for himself/herself or to enable a relative to do them for him/her.

Source: Sutherland Report (1999a) p. 68.

TABLE 5.1   Estimates of health and social services expenditure where personal
care is provided without charge in residential and domiciliary
settings (normal living costs in residential care of £120 per week,
personal care costs of £122 in residential care and £217 in nursing
home care), UK, at 1995 prices

	1995 prices	2010	2021	2031	2051
Cost £billion	8.2	10.9	14.7	20.8	33.4
Tax base on earnings + pensions + investments (%)	2.5	2.1	2.1	2.4	2.6
% GDP	1.2	1.1	1.2	1.3	1.4

Source: Taken from Sutherland Report (1999a) p. 70.

money without increasing the range and quality of care available to older
people (Department of Health, 2000d). The government had decided to
reassert that a real distinction continued to exist between health and social
care even if this was done because of pragmatic concerns about public
expenditure rather than through ideological beliefs. The extent of this practical concern was confirmed subsequently by the way in which free nursing
care was defined in government guidance – as care provided by registered
nurses only and not by nursing assistants (Pearce, 2001).

The authors of this book welcomed the recommendation on free personal
care by the Royal Commission and were disappointed although not sur-
prised by the response of government. However, it is important to stress two
features of the main report which are rarely commented upon by its enthusiasts. The main report does *not* recommend that all services should be
'free' at the point of consumption. The chosen definition of personal care
was based upon 'touching a person's body' (p. 67) and hence excluded
cleaning and housework, laundry, shopping services, specialist transport
services and sitting services where the focus was only companionship
(p. 68). Second, the Royal Commission made no recommendations about
the need to change the main organisational boundaries between health and
social care. Arguments about whose budget should pay for 'free' services
were therefore likely to remain as acrimonious as ever.

The debate about free personal care has continued apace rather than
abated. This has been driven by the decision of the Scottish Assembly to
support the Majority Report of the Royal Commission and fund free
personal care for older people (Jerrom, 2002). Against this, England and
Wales have seen considerable acrimony develop over the complex procedures for defining the now 'free' nursing component of nursing home care.

The government also seems to be reviewing its approach with the Secretary of State for Health announcing in July 2002 that all intermediate care (see below) will be 'free', irrespective of whether it is provided by health or social services (*Community Care*, 25–31 July 2002, p. 6).

The NHS Plan and care trusts

Reforming the National Health Service has been a central concern of recent Labour governments from 1997 onwards, and its ideas were set out in Green and White Papers on the NHS in general (Department of Health, 1997b) and public health in particular (Department of Health, 1998c, 1999f).

The proposed public health changes stressed the need to balance a recognition of the wider determinants of health with the fact that decisions by individuals (for example, to smoke or not) were equally crucial to health outcomes. A key development related to a requirement for each health authority to publish a health improvement programme (HiMP) in consultation with a range of other agencies including social services. HiMPs were expected to reflect both local needs and concerns but also national health targets in priority areas such as accidents, cancer, coronary heart disease and mental health. However, HiMPS were clearly to be driven by health. How this new system was intended to mesh together with community care planning was not articulated but it was hard to avoid the conclusion that the new Labour government was looking more to health than to social services to be the lead agency in planning across health and social services. Further confirmation of this came with the announcement from the Department of Health, in April 2002, that local authorities would no longer be required to produce community care plans. It was suggested that amalgamating community care plans into HiMPS could help to ensure that the latter were more jointly owned and developed (Department of Health, 2002d).

The NHS White Paper was entitled *The New NHS: Modern, Dependable* (Department of Health, 1997b) and emphasised the need for a major switch of focus and resources away from hospitals and towards primary care. However, this was not to be achieved through an extension of the GP budget-holding approach preferred by the previous Conservative administration (Department of Health, 1989b). Budget-holding was to be replaced by a completely new system of primary care groups/primary care trusts (PCGs/PCTs) each to serve populations of around 100,000. Box 5.3 outlines the four-stage development process that was proposed and it soon became clear that the government expected all areas to aspire to Stage Four PCT status.

BOX 5.3   From primary care groups to primary care trusts

Stage One	The primary care group (PCG) acts as an advisory body to its local health authority which retains the health care budget
Stage Two	The PCG takes devolved responsibility for the budget but remains part of the health authority
Stage Three	The PCG becomes a primary care trust (PCT) with its own budget and is then a free-standing body accountable to the authority for how it commissions care
Stage Four	The PCT has added responsibility for providing community services and this is likely to include pooled budgets with social services for much of its community care provision.

It was immediately obvious that this primary care revolution in the NHS would have massive implications for social services and that one of the key agendas of the government was to improve joint working between health and social care (Poxton, 1999; Bradley and Manthorpe, 2000; Rummery and Glendinning, 2000). Social services were given formal representation on PCG boards and a number of studies looked at how this impacted upon joint working (Starkey *et al.*, 2001; Glendinning *et al.*, 2002a). Although this was seen to have fostered a spirit of collaboration in some areas, major problems were found to remain. GPs were often found to take a narrow practice and patient focus rather than the broader strategic perspective required of a PCG/PCT, often leading to a marginalisation of the role of the social services representative. Second, PCG board members were concerned whether progress in working relationships could be maintained within the more formal structures of PCTs.

The determination of the government to achieve radical change in the health service was emphasised by its decision to pull together all the strands of policy change and all the proposals for reinvestment into *The NHS Plan: A Plan for Investment, A Plan for Reform* (Department of Health, 2000d). The main publicity for the plan focused on the major expansion in training numbers for doctors, nurses and the professions allied to medicine, but the plan also announced a significant further expansion in the development programme for primary care trusts:

We now propose to establish a new level of primary care trusts, which will provide for even closer integration. Health and social services are already working together extremely closely and wish to establish new single multi-purpose legal bodies to commission and be responsible for all local health and social care. The new body will be known as a 'care trust' to reflect its new broader role. (p. 73)

Localities were being encouraged to bid for care trust status. The NHS Plan, however, also contained the warning that 'where local health and social care organisations have failed to establish effective joint partnerships – or where inspection or joint reviews have shown that services are failing – the Government will take powers to establish integrated arrangements through the new care trust' (p. 73).

Care trusts were a major new proposal since it was clearly intended that they should be part of the NHS and that their focus should be on the delivery of services across the health and social care interface for the main community care groups. This was confirmed twelve months later by the first wave of pilot care trusts announced by the government (see Box 5.4). Such developments only served to confirm the relevance of the question of whether or not social services were losing their lead agency role in community care by stealth (Glendinning and Means, 2002). Such suspicions were further aroused by the publication of *Shifting the Balance of Power within the NHS* (Department of Health, 2001h). This set out an implementation strategy for the NHS Plan but in a way which stressed the dominant role of health rather than local authorities in long-term care and through a discourse which referred to social care rather than community care (see Chapter 9 for a further discussion of this issue).

BOX 5.4   Care trust pilots

- Bexley: older people
- Birmingham: one care trust for mental health and one for learning difficulties
- Brighton and Hove: range of vulnerable client groups
- Bradford: mental health
- Camden and Islington: mental health
- Essex: housing and older people
- Manchester: mental health
- New Forest: older people and physical disabilities
- North Somerset: all services except mental health
- Northumberland: working age adults (except mental health)
- Sandwell: mental health
- South East Hertfordshire: to be confirmed
- Wiltshire: three trusts covering services for older people, physical disabilities, learning difficulties, children's health.

Source: Revans (2001d) p. 35.

Commentators have also focused on the tension between the response of the government to the Royal Commission on Long Term Care and its approach to care trusts (Means *et al.*, 2002). The first stressed the importance of distinguishing between health and social care and the second seemed to deny its relevance. How would staff in the new care trusts explain that support from a nurse is free but that from a home care worker is means-tested?

National Service Framework for mental health

As emphasised in the previous chapter, a strong feature of recent Labour governments is a belief in frameworks and targets that could be used to steer health and social care agencies in a direction that would meet national priorities. An important component of this strategy has been the introduction of National Service Frameworks in such areas as mental health (Department of Health, 1999b) and for older people (Department of Health, 2001i).

The National Service Framework (NSF) for mental health built upon the earlier report *Modernising Mental Health Services* (Department of Health, 1998d) and focused on the needs of working age adults up to 65, and hence excluded the mental health problems of both children and older people. The framework established ten guiding principles (see Box 5.5) and set out seven standards in five areas, namely mental health promotion; primary care and access to services; effective services for people with severe mental illness; caring about carers; preventing suicide. For example, the two standards in the area of primary care and access to services were:

- Any service user who contacts their primary care team with a common mental health problem should:
  - have their mental health needs identified and assessed
  - be offered effective treatments, including referral to specialist services for further assessment, treatment and care if they require it
- Any individual with a common mental health problem should:
  - be able to make contact round the clock with the local services necessary to meet their needs and receive adequate care
  - be able to use NHS Direct, as it develops, for first-level advice and referral on to specialist helplines or to local services. (Department of Health, 1996 p. 28)

The two standards with regard to effective services for people with severe mental illness included the following on the care programme approach (CPA).

BOX 5.5   Guiding values and principles

- Involve service users and their carers in planning and delivery of care
- Deliver high quality treatment and care which is known to be effective and acceptable
- Be accessible so that help can be obtained when and where it is needed
- Promote their safety and that of their carers, staff and the wider public
- Offer choices which promote independence
- Be well co-ordinated between all staff and agencies
- Deliver continuity of care for so long as this is needed
- Empower and support their staff
- Be properly accountable to the public, service users and carers.

Source: Department of Health (1999b) p. 4.

All mental health service users on CPA should:

- Receive care which optimises engagement, anticipates or prevents a crisis, and reduces risk
- Have a copy of a written care plan which:
    - includes the action to be taken in a crisis by the service user, their carer and their care co-ordinator
    - advises their GP how they should respond if the service user needs additional help
    - is regularly reviewed by their care co-ordinator
- be able to access services 24 hours a day, 365 days a year. (p. 41)

All seven standards were backed up by detailed milestones which related to the gradual full achievement of all the standards in all localities.

So what specifically did this NSF have to say about the lead agency role of social services and joint working across the health and social care divide? The NSF starts by stressing that implementation 'will require new patterns of local partnership, with mental health a cross-cutting priority for all NHS and social care organisations and their partners' (p. 6). It also stressed that the range of mental health services could never be unified into a single provider so that 'interfaces and boundaries must be managed effectively to provide and commission integrated services' (p. 9). However, the clear flavour of the NSF is that the central interface is between NHS trusts (increasingly specialist mental health trusts) and the new primary care arrangements. In reading the NSF for mental health, it is hard to avoid the conclusion that the concept of social services as the lead agency for people with mental health problems has been quietly shelved.

National Service Framework for older people

The NSF for mental health referred to the forthcoming NSF for older people in spring 2000 and yet it was not published until March 2001. Major delays were caused by the production of the NHS Plan, the slowness of the government to announce its full response to the Royal Commission on Long Term Care and probably the sheer complexity of an NSF for this client group. The NHS Plan devoted a whole chapter on 'dignity, security and independence in old age' (Department of Health, 2000d, pp. 123–9). This not only confirmed the response to the Royal Commission (see above) but also outlined the establishment of 'a single assessment process for health and social care' backed up by 'a personal care plan' (p. 125) to be held by the service user. The significance of the single assessment process is that it represented a commitment that key agencies at the local level would share assessment tools and approaches rather than each being allowed 'to do their own thing'.

However, the chapter on 'changes between health and social services' (pp. 70–3) had equally far-reaching implications for services for older people. In addition to the description of care trusts, the NHS Plan announced a £900 million investment by 2003/4 on new intermediate care and related services to promote independence. Such schemes were seen as including rapid response teams, intensive rehabilitation services, integrated home care teams, and social work attachments to primary care. Their main focus was seen as (i) reducing the need for older people to enter hospital and (ii) speeding up their ability to leave hospital after their acute care needs were met. The ambitious claim was made that such investment in intermediate care would mean that 'by 2004 we will end widespread bed blocking' (p. 102).

The NSF itself set out eight standards (and related milestones) relating to age discrimination, person-centred care, intermediate care, general hospital care, stroke, falls, mental health in old age and health promotion (see Box 5.6). As with the NSF for mental health, the question needs to be asked about the implications of the NSF for the future lead agency role of social services in community care for older people. The most striking gesture of the NSF in this regard is the complete absence of comment on this issue. Instead, the new flexibilities under the Health Act 1999 and the new possibilities through primary care trusts/care trusts are stressed with the emphasis on partnership, joint commissioning, integrated service and a single assessment process. And the tendency is to refer to 'HiMPS and other relevant plans' (p. 40) rather than to 'community care plans and HiMPS' and to 'the NHS and councils' (p. 49) rather than the other way round. Under these circumstances, the subsequent discontinuation of community care plans is not surprising (see also Chapter 9).

BOX 5.6   The eight standards of the National Service Framework

Standard 1: Rooting out age discrimination

NHS services will be provided, regardless of age, on the basis of clinical need alone. Social care services will not use age in their eligibility criteria or policies, to restrict access to available services.

Standard 2: Person-centred care

NHS and social care services treat older people as individuals and enable them to make choices about their own care. This is achieved through the single assessment process, integrated commissioning arrangements and integrated provision of services, including community equipment and continence services.

Standard 3: Intermediate care

Older people will have access to a new range of intermediate care services at home or in designated care settings, to promote their independence by providing enhanced services from the NHS and councils to prevent unnecessary hospital admission and effective rehabilitation services to enable early discharge from hospital and to prevent premature or unnecessary admission to long term residential care.

Standard 4: General hospital care

Older people's care in hospital is delivered through appropriate specialist care and by hospital staff who have the right set of skills to meet their needs.

$\longrightarrow$

Earlier in the chapter, the NHS Plan (Department of Health, 2000d) was quoted in terms of the 5,500 patients over 75 who were blocking acute beds in September 1999 and how this was linked to the major investment in intermediate care. The NSF for older people has set formidable milestones in this regard so that by March 2004, the government expected there to be:

- At least 5,000 additional intermediate care beds and 1,700 non-residential intermediate care places compared with the 1999/2000 baseline
- At least 150,000 additional people receiving intermediate care services which promote rehabilitation and supported discharge compared with the 1999/2000 baseline
- At least 70,000 additional people receiving intermediate care which prevents unnecessary hospital admission compared with the 1999/2000 baseline. (Department of Health, 2001i, p. 50)

$\longrightarrow$

Standard 5: Stroke

The NHS will take action to prevent strokes, working in partnership with other agencies where appropriate. People who are thought to have had a stroke have access to diagnostic services, are treated appropriately by a specialist stroke service, and subsequently, with their carers, participate in a multidisciplinary programme of secondary prevention and rehabilitation.

Standard 6: Falls

The NHS working in partnership with councils, takes action to prevent falls and reduce resultant fractures or other injuries in their populations of older people. Older people who have fallen receive effective treatment and rehabilitation and, with their carers, receive advice on prevention, through a specialised falls service.

Standard 7: Mental health in older people

Older people who have mental health problems have access to integrated mental health services, provided by the NHS and councils to ensure effective diagnosis, treatment and support, for them and for their carers.

Standard 8: The promotion of health and active life in older age

The health and well being of older people is promoted through a co-ordinated programme of action led by the NHS with support from councils.

Source: Department of Health (2001i) pp. 12–14.

Such milestones raise numerous questions. What is the evidence that inter- mediate care is cost-effective? What types of intermediate care work best with what types of client? Are the milestones realistic? Above all, will this new investment in intermediate care produce the dramatic effects so strongly desired or, as Martin (2001) put it, 'can it do what its backers prom- ised when it becomes mainstream, the gloss has faded and the charismatic leaders have been promoted away' (p. 18)?

A fundamental difficulty is the existence of continuing disagreements in the way in which intermediate care is conceptualised. Steiner (2001) has identified some significant points at issue. First, there is a lack of consensus about whether intermediate care should be concerned primarily with patient-focused goals, such as 'recovery' and 'maintaining people in their own homes', or whether it should focus on organisational objectives such as 'shortened lengths of stay' and 'lower cost'. The intensity of care is also at issue with alternatives ranging from low-tech nurturing to the delivery of intensive technologies in hospital or community settings. There is a lack of consensus about who should receive intermediate care so that frail or demented patients are included or excluded according to the way in which intermediate care is defined. Finally, there is a question about the similarities and differences between intermediate care and rehabilitation, given the resistance of many rehabilitation professionals to the seemingly passive notion of 'care'. Steiner (2001) herself is clear that intermediate care should not be seen as 'the health sector's synonym for community-based (or residential) continuing care', but should be both short-term and therapeutic (p. 34).

A review of rehabilitation research in the late 1990s found few studies that had tracked clients over time and even fewer that had focused on community- rather than hospital-based forms of rehabilitation (Nocon and Baldwin, 1998). Although the findings from research studies continue to be published in such areas as hospital at home schemes (Department of Health, 2001i, p. 45) and community rehabilitation teams (Means *et al.*, 2001), the overall evidence base remains very limited and presents a 'mixture of benefit, deficit and considerable uncertainty' (Steiner, 2001, p. 37). Intermediate care represents a massive leap of faith with a danger that a myriad of overlapping schemes will emerge in each locality but with no overall rehabilitation strategy. If this does occur, GPs and consultants will refer older people to their 'pet' intermediate care scheme rather than the one most likely to help them.

There is also a real danger that the stress on the required number of new beds and places will encourage this pursuit of quick fixes. We have seen in Chapter 3 how the nursing home industry is in financial crisis in many parts of the country (Laing and Saper, 1999) and may be very attracted to redefining many of its beds as reserved for intermediate care. After all, if rehabilitation 'fails', the older person can always transfer to a long-term bed. Banks (2002) has pointed out how the stress on meeting acute care targets places enormous pressures on emergent health and social services partnerships. This may make it difficult for such agencies to recognise that the establishment of multidisciplinary rehabilitation services which draw upon the skills of social workers, nurses, physiotherapists, occupational therapists and home aides can be a long and painful process. Such teams require joint commitment from health and social services and it will take considerable time for members from very different backgrounds to establish clear working relationships (Thomas and Means, 2000). However, this is a government impatient for quick progress.

From collaboration to incorporation?

It would appear that the government has lost patience with the Berlin Wall between health and social services and it seems intent on the slow incorporation of social care into what will be health-dominated care trusts. The final chapter will return to this issue, so at this stage it is necessary to make just a few initial points.

If we return to the analogy of unification and nation states, the evidence is extremely equivocal. It may be feasible to create a country such as Yugoslavia to embrace potentially warring factions, but it is much harder to keep it together. Even if such countries do survive, different factions may continue to be in conflict with each other. Reunified Germany is not without its problems. Eastern Germany remains culturally distinct and economically weak. Reunification led to a massive disruption of the West German economy.

New configurations of health and social care face many of the same challenges. The social care element of a care trust may well end up being not only culturally distinct, but also lacking in power and influence relative to health care interests. A crucial factor may be whether social care feels it has chosen reunification rather than experiencing forced incorporation. The Yugoslav example underlines that differences are not overcome through the removal of (organisational) boundaries. Difference still has to be coped with and collaboration between different groups has to be fostered within the single organisation. In other words, the challenge of collaboration and joint working as outlined by Hudson (1987), Webb (1991) and others cannot be met just through a simple organisational fix, but rather through the sustained pursuit of a cultural change.

6 Housing and Community Care

It has long been accepted that the 1989 White Paper on community care was right to stress that 'suitable good quality housing' was essential to social care packages (Department of Health, 1989a, p. 9) and that as a result 'social services authorities ... need to work closely with housing authorities, housing associations and other providers of housing of all types in developing plans for a full and flexible range of housing' (p. 25). This message has been subsequently reinforced through the Audit Commission (1998), independent research (Quilgars, 1998; Cameron *et al.*, 2001; Foord and Simic, 2001) and a range of government reports and policy documents (Sutherland Report, 1999a; Department of the Environment, Transport and the Regions, 2001).

This chapter focuses on housing issues from the perspective that housing is an essential element of community care. However, the emphasis of the chapter is not solely on the politics of what is usually called 'special needs' or supported housing, but will also include a consideration of much broader issues such as the meaning of home and the impact of general housing policies on frail elderly and disabled people. It will conclude with reflections on whether the housing dimension of community care is likely to be reinforced or undermined by the key 'modernisation' changes in health and welfare which were outlined in the two previous chapters.

The meaning of home

Community care policy in the United Kingdom is based on the belief that nearly everyone prefers to live in ordinary housing rather than in institutions, because institutions lack the capacity to be a home. Higgins (1989) went so far as to argue that the very concept of community care should be abandoned because 'the real distinction is actually between the institution and home which differ markedly in terms of their core characteristics' (see Table 6.1). Ordinary houses (homes) are preferable to institutions because it is claimed that they offer more privacy, informality, freedom and familiarity. The rest of this section explores theoretical thinking about the home and goes on to consider the implications of this for the users of community care services.

TABLE 6.1   The key characteristics of institutions and home

Institutions	Home
1. Public space, limitations on privacy	1. Private space, but may be some limitations on privacy
2. Living with strangers, rarely alone	2. May live alone or with relatives or friends, rarely with strangers
3. Staffed by professionals or volunteers	3. Normally no staff living there but they may visit to provide services
4. Formal and lacking in intimacy	4. Informal and intimate
5. Sexual relationships discouraged	5. Sexual relationships (between certain family members) accepted
6. Owned/rented by other agencies	6. Owned/rented by inhabitants
7. Variations in size but may be large (in terms of physical space and numbers living there)	7. Variations in size but usually small
8. Limitations on choice and on personal freedom	8. Ability to exercise choice and considerable degree of freedom
9. Strangeness (of people, place, etc.)	9. Familiarity (of people, place, etc.)
10. 'Batch' or communal living	10. Individual arrangements for eating, sleeping, leisure activities which can vary according to time and place

Source: Higgins (1989) p.15.

In doing this, one is immediately struck by the complexity of the term 'home' and the extent to which it does or does not relate to living in specific buildings. Even 'what does home mean to you?' can generate the following wide set of responses:

- A set of relationships with others
- A relationship with the wider social group and community
- A statement about self-image and identity
- A place of privacy and refuge
- A continuous and stable relationship with other sources of meaning about the home
- A personalised place
- A base of activity
- A relationship with one's parents and place of upbringing
- A relationship with a physical structure, setting or shelter. (Rapaport, 1995)

The extensive literature on the home emphasises how responses will vary according to gender, class, ethnicity, country and age of the respondent, and that ideas about 'home' are constantly changing and evolving within any given society (Heywood *et al.*, 2002).

The meaning of home became a source for fierce debate in urban sociology during the late 1980s and early 1990s, although such arguments paid little attention to elderly and disabled people. The background to the debate was a belief in the emergence of a new 'middle mass' in British society with shared goals and aspirations, one of which was the desire to be owner-occupiers. Britain had become, as Saunders (1990) put it, *A Nation of Home Owners*. In terms of concepts of home in the UK, Saunders argued that owner-occupiers identified their house as a home and 'a place where they feel relaxed and where they can surround themselves with familiar and personal possessions' (p. 272). Council tenants, on the other hand, associated 'home' much more with their relationships with family and neighbours. He concluded from this that the great advantage of owner occupation over other tenures was its capacity to enable people to express themselves and their identity in a private realm which was free from surveillance. However, his work was highly contentious because of its apparent celebration of owner occupation over renting, a point made by his critics, especially after the collapse of the housing market in Britain in the early 1990s (Forrest *et al.*, 1994). Owner occupation could be the cause of misery through negative equity and mortgage foreclosure, rather than always a place of security.

In terms of elderly and disabled people, a number of authors have criticised the heavy emphasis placed by Saunders on tenure difference as the core of the meaning of home and have called for a greater stress on what Gurney (1990) called 'the emotions of home' (see also Heywood *et al.*, 2002). These emotions can be both negative and positive. For the majority, home is a positive experience since it is where supportive and loving relationships most often take place. This is certainly true for many older people as the research by Phillipson *et al.* (2001) on social networks and social support in late twentieth-century Britain clearly demonstrated. Their updating of the three seminal studies by Young and Willmott (1957) in East London, Sheldon (1948) in Wolverhampton and Willmott and Young (1960) in a London suburb supported a growing role for friends but also 'that kinship ties have stood up well to the developments affecting urban societies over the past fifty years' (p. 251). Marriage remained a crucial support for many, while close kin tended to act 'as the first port of call if help is needed in the home' (ibid.).

It has long been argued that older people are especially likely to value the home as a place of privacy and retreat:

Mr: It's a place of retreat really.
Mrs: ... and home's always been a place where you want to go back to, however humble it is. Even when we go to town we're still glad,

well I am, to get back ... It's a place of our own. (Quoted in Langan
et al., 1996, p. 6)

Another respondent in the same study saw home as a place where you had
'freedom to do what you want, when you want' (p. 6).

It has often been shown that many older people see home in terms of a
strong emotional attachment to a specific house lived in for much of the life
course:

Home was the old armchair by the hearth, the creaky bedstead, the
polished lino with its faded pattern, the sideboard with its picture gallery
and the lavatory with its broken latch reached through the rain. It embodied
a thousand memories and held promise of a thousand contentments. It
was an extension of personality. (Townsend, 1957, p. 27)

Such views may appear dated and hence irrelevant to present-day debates.
However, research by Askham *et al.* (1999) suggests that many older people
continue to retain a strong bond with the homes which they own.

This emphasis on the positive aspects of home must not be allowed to
obscure the fact that it can also be a negative experience for some. For many
elderly owner-occupiers house repair can become a major worry, while this
can also be true of more general maintenance, including gardens (Heywood
et al., 1999; Heywood *et al.*, 2002). More sadly, the home can be the site of
elder abuse or the abuse of other vulnerable adults free from surveillance,
especially when carried out by a spouse or another close relative (Biggs
et al., 1993). Those in private rented accommodation may experience
harassment from landlords, especially if the landlord wishes them to leave
prior to selling off into owner occupation (Carlton *et al.*, 2003).

Despite the earlier emphasis on the strong link between 'feeling at home'
and attachment to specific houses for many older people, great care must be
taken not to overgeneralise. There is evidence that owner-occupiers who
move to a different part of the country on retirement establish a sense of
home in their new accommodation and environment. Langan *et al.* (1996)
looked at a small number of households which had moved from the
Midlands to Lake District villages. One stressed that 'I love my little cottage, you know' while a second stressed the friendliness of her village
which also had excellent facilities, including a shop and easy access to a
GP. It seems likely that many middle-class older people are used to moving
periodically for career and other reasons, and perhaps have always seen
their house as an asset through which wealth can be released as a result of
trading down in later life (Means, 1997a). Such individuals are likely to

have learned the skill of how to transport a sense of emotional security from one building (home) to another.

There is also extensive evidence that many older people do manage to re-establish a sense of home when they move into good-quality sheltered housing (Heywood *et al.*, 2002, Chapter 7) and that this includes very sheltered housing schemes which aim to promote a high level of care (Oldman, 2000). Such findings have led Oldman to argue that 'it cannot be always assumed that older people do not want to move' (p. 18). Brenton (2001) has taken this argument further by researching the popularity of co-housing schemes in the Netherlands and their relevance for the UK. Although the details of such schemes vary, their essence tends to be self-contained units with some communal support facilities in which each scheme member knew others prior to moving in. Thus, such schemes build on existing friendships and networks rather than artificially creating a community of strangers.

The conventional wisdom is that a willingness to move does not extend to the more institutional environments of residential care and nursing homes. Willcocks *et al.* (1987) suggested that strong emotions and attachments to houses are expressed by many elderly people when they feel threatened by a possible move into residential care, since 'to leave homes which may be inconvenient and difficult ... would be to relinquish a hold on a base from which personal power can be generated and reinforced' (p. 8). Or as Steinfield (1981) explains, housing moves in later life are often linked to negative rather than positive status passages and hence the desire of many to 'stay put'. However, the research by Willcocks *et al.* (1987) also indicated that once in such a home, older people often appreciate the care support from staff, but continue to dislike the lack of privacy and private space. These authors used their findings to argue the need to develop flatlets in which residents would have a key to their own rooms (see also Peace *et al.*, 1997; Brenton *et al.*, 2002, p. 28). This is close to what very sheltered housing actually provides (Means, 1999) and suggests that such types of specialist and age-segregated accommodation can become a home if the privacy issue is properly tackled. This underlines just how stressful it is likely to be when older residents have to leave their residential or nursing *home* because of refurbishment or closure (Wild *et al.*, 2002). Against this, it also needs to be remembered that staying put in one's own home when one has very high dependency needs may be the best option for many, but the reality of near 24-hour health and welfare support can be a loss of control and privacy as one's own home almost begins to take on the features of an institution (Hoyes *et al.*, 1994). The growth of assistive technology will open up the 'staying put' option for many more elderly and disabled people, but this could involve high degrees of surveillance which are in stark contrast to Saunders's view of the private domain of the owner-occupied home (Holland and Peace, 2001; McClatchey *et al.*, 2001).

Finally, there is the need to address the tenure difference question since relatively little is known about the meaning of home to older people in rented accommodation (Heywood *et al.*, 2002). Is it easier to settle in a residential home if one had previously rented rather than owned? Are attachments to particular rented houses less strong? Certainly, older tenants of both local authorities and housing associations are often under pressure to move from the house where they brought up their children in order to release family housing to those on the waiting list. Many such tenants have been willing to consider a move to modern prestigious sheltered housing schemes (Means, 1997b) yet seem increasingly willing to reject offers from older schemes, many of which are becoming hard to let (Tinker *et al.*, 1995). However, there is a shortage of research about the emotional feelings experienced by older people on leaving rented accommodation. One key factor is almost certainly the quality of rented accommodation lived in in the past and the extent to which there has been a single 'family' home rather than a series of moves into different rented accommodation during the life course. For some elderly people their present rented accommodation may hold little emotional attachment and for some the memories may be largely negative. A move in later life may represent an opportunity to establish a sense of home (Carlton *et al.*, 2003).

Towards independent living?

So far the focus of this chapter has been on the meaning of home for older people and how this has been used to justify the emphasis of community care policy on remaining in one's own home rather than moving into residential or nursing home care. However, the same assumptions have also been applied to the other main community care groups, namely people with learning difficulties, people with mental health problems and physically disabled people. Independent living is usually seen as requiring one to live in an ordinary a home as possible. Morris (2002) has stressed how moving into your own home can be a key element to moving into adulthood for many young disabled people.

In terms of people with learning difficulties, the key policy thrust of the 1990s was resettlement from institutions where they had lived for many years to new homes and hostels in the community. The justification for this was the nature of the institutions, as summarised by Higgins (1989) and described in Chapter 2. This policy change was often supported by individuals with learning difficulties:

> It's a lot better to live on your own. It's important that people with learning disabilities have the right to their own home and their own key and live by themselves. (Quoted in Mental Health Foundation, 1996, p. 50)

However, Saunders (1990) did underline that home for some can be as much a matter of networks and relationships (for council tenants) as of privacy (for owner-occupiers). One danger of the resettlement process was that the hospital-based networks and relationships would be shattered but not replaced by equivalent networks in new surroundings. The privacy of the new home or hostel might end up being experienced by some as a prison of loneliness and despair.

Research evidence was to dispel such pessimism. Cambridge *et al.* (1994) tracked 200 people with learning difficulties from twelve localities over a five-year period from when they left long-stay hospital care. They were thus able to evaluate the quality of life achieved and how this related to the community care services provided. Their overall conclusion was unambiguous:

> From our involvement with the twelve services included in the evalua-tion, we know of no reasonable basis on which to challenge the policy of care in the community for people with learning disabilities who would otherwise be long-term hospital residents. In fact, most people are demonstrably better off living in the community than in hospital, over both the short and long term. (p. 105)

Positive outcomes included more choice for most over living environments and improved support networks. This was despite the fact that they did find 'some community accommodation which was some distance short of ideal in terms of quality, scale or institutional regime' (ibid.).

Emerson and Hatton (1996) reviewed 71 resettlement studies of people with learning difficulties going right back to 1970. The overall message was of improvements in standards of living and quality of life with a wide degree of acceptance by neighbours and local businesses. In nearly all the studies, people with learning difficulties felt that life in the community was superior to life in a hospital, with a key factor in 'success' or 'failure' being the quality of staff in community-based accommodation.

The Labour Government of the early 21st century remained committed to the link between independent living and access to mainstream housing options. *Valuing People: A New Strategy for Learning Disability for the 21st Century* (Department of Health, 2001a) listed one of its key objectives as enabling 'people with learning disabilities and their families to have greater choice and control over where and how they live' (p. 70). The White Paper argued that people with learning disabilities can live successfully in a variety of settings from self-contained properties to village communities but stressed the advantages of ordinary housing:

> David inherited the tenancy of a housing association bungalow following his mother's death. He has a support package from a care provider and had some intensive support from the Community Team for Learning Disabilities to improve his cooking and domestic skills. His brother and sister-in-law live nearby and provide emotional and practical support. He is now coping well. (Quoted in Department of Health, 2001a, p. 270)

The range of schemes and initiatives designed to foster independent living continues to increase (Simons, 1997) while independent advice schemes for people with learning disabilities have also begun to develop (Simons, 2000). However, the White Paper notes a continued shortage of appropriate housing, care and support options especially for those wishing to leave the parental home. This has been backed up by research by Mencap (2002) which showed the lack of planning by local authorities for the estimated 29,000 people with learning difficulties who live with parents aged 70 or over. The tendency was 'to act in a crisis situation, only arranging alternative accommodation when parents die' (p. 2). This does raise a major issue about housing and community care policies. Although it is argued that institutions undermine independence, is there not a danger that this is just as likely to happen to young adults in the family home if they are not supported to 'move on'? Under these circumstances, greater independence may be achieved through some kind of housing with support accommodation rather than through over-reliance on parents. This is also an important issue for those physically disabled people who have been brought up in the family home but now wish to branch out as adults who are largely independent from their parents (Hendey and Pascall, 2002). However, Morris (2002) cautions that housing with support options are accepted rather than chosen by young disabled people because of the lack of mainstream housing opportunities.

The issue for large numbers of people with mental health problems may also be the limits of a family home, although for many others it is the lack of any home at all. The National Service Framework for mental health estimated that 'between a quarter and a half of people using night shelters or sleeping rough may have a serious mental disorder, and up to a half may be alcohol dependent' (Department of Health, 1999b, p.14). Research suggests that only about one-third of these will receive any kind of treatment (Social Exclusion Unit, 1998).

Despite such figures, the seven standards of the NSF (see Chapter 5) make only minimal reference to the potential role of housing and housing organisations in achieving these standards, apart from the passing recognition of the need for an expansion of specialist housing with support schemes. This is despite the growing research evidence of the scope for supporting people with mental health problems in both mainstream housing (Audit Commission, 1998) and in specialist housing with support schemes (Quilgars, 1998).

The Audit Commission (1998) used focus group research of people with mental health problems to confirm that most preferred to live in mainstream housing rather than being what they perceived as ghettoised in special units. However, this was only if the housing was of reasonable quality including being quiet and secure, next to sympathetic neighbours and close to informal care networks. Quilgars (1998) evaluated Home-Link, an inter-agency project in Yorkshire, which was designed to help ensure some of these needs were met since it provided permanent housing and low-level, practical support for people with mental health problems. It was found that most users of the scheme felt that Home-Link made an appreciable difference to their lives, especially in terms of access to good-quality housing but also because of the support that was available for issues such as household finances.

Interestingly, one aspect of the scheme that met with only limited success was the attempt to encourage mutual support amongst users of the scheme. Earlier in this section it was stated that the main criticism of resettlement and care in the community initiatives had been that independent living would lead to community isolation (Cox and Pearson, 1993). One feature of the modernisation agenda of the Labour government is the emphasis on tackling social exclusion (Powell, 1999) especially in deprived neighbourhoods, and yet evidence suggests that both older people (Riseborough, 2000) and small community groups representing vulnerable people (Winchester, 2002) are the least likely to be involved in such initiatives. Social networks in neighbourhoods can be crucial to vulnerable people and yet very little priority is given to how they can be fostered and developed.

Supported housing or supporting people

The Higgins typology of home and institution which was outlined at the start of this chapter left open the question of exactly what an institution is and how neatly it can be distinguished from a home and ordinary housing. This has become an important issue given the increasing range of specialist housing and housing with support options available to all the main community care groups.

'Supported housing' is increasingly the term used to describe this varied provision. It is seen as encompassing all forms of sheltered housing, including very sheltered housing for older people (Means, 1999). It also includes a wide variety of staffed and unstaffed shared housing and self-contained accommodation with support attached. The main distinguishing feature is that services are provided that would not be provided to occupiers of general needs housing. However, this still covers a very wide range of provision:

> At one end of the spectrum the distinction between hostels that are part of supported housing and institutions that are not classed as housing provision is sometimes rather fine. At the other end, services can be provided to residents in dwellings that in themselves are part of the mainstream stock, according to need, sometimes through services referred to as 'floating support'. (Hoyes *et al.*, 1996, p. 67)

In 1998, the Audit Commission (1998) estimated in *Home Alone: The Role of Housing in Community Care* that in England and Wales there were 450,000 units of sheltered housing with on-site wardens and a further 82,000 units of supported housing for people with mental health problems, physical disabilities, learning difficulties and other needs. The same report not only illustrated the complexity of both capital and revenue funding for supported housing but also noted that 'the development of specialised housing was not the result of a planned, multi-agency approach but the ragged inheritance of uncoordinated historic decisions' (p. 23).

Supported housing, including sheltered accommodation, has come under increasing criticism, partly because of the complex funding and lack of rational planning identified by the Audit Commission (1998). Schemes are seen as developing in response to the availability of subsidy and local political popularity rather than through the targeting of resources to meet identified need. In addition, the financial viability of many supported housing schemes required the increasing use of housing benefit (HB) to allow low-income people to pay for the support element of their housing with support. Even if this was a justified use of 'housing' benefit, the Audit Commission (1998) pointed out 'the service charge element of HB can be paid only to tenants of specific housing schemes and is not generally available to those in mainstream housing, even though their need for help may be similar' (p. 73). Finally, this 'bricks and mortar' approach to funding had encouraged the building of specialist accommodation long after it was still required with the growing problem of 'hard to let' sheltered housing schemes being the most obvious example (Tinker *et al.*, 1995). Letting problems have arisen in some sheltered housing schemes because basic features of the design of many older schemes (for example, bed-sits, communal facilities) made them unpopular with many older people.

The main response of government has been the development of the *Supporting People* initiative (Interdepartmental Review of Funding for Supported Accommodation, 1998; Department of Transport, Local Government and the Regions (DTLR), 2001b). *Supporting People* is an immensely complex programme (Griffiths, 2000). It 'combines two of the main funding streams which provide support to those who need help to live in their own home – Housing Benefit and Supported Housing Management Grant – into an integrated programme at the local level' (p. 42). Local authorities will be expected to 'run' the new system in collaboration with health and to do this on the basis of a detailed analysis of the need for supported housing within their locality (Foord and Simic, 2001). Resultant 'subsidies' can be used to underpin specialist supported housing schemes but equally to bring support services to people who live in mainstream housing. The new system will be fully operational in April 2003.

Supporting People raises massive implementation issues (Griffiths, 2000; DTLR, 2001b). What are the implications for existing supported housing schemes? More specifically, how will the viability of sheltered housing be maintained within the ring-fenced monies allocated to local authorities? Will the system become driven by the community care concerns of social services to the detriment of those who fall outside the main community care groups, such as those leaving prison and women escaping domestic violence (Rickford, 2001)? How is local need to be estimated and how will the likely mismatch between need and resources be responded to at both the local and national level (Foord and Simic, 2001)? And how clear are the boundaries between personal care fundable by social services as part of their community care responsibilities and support needs which can be met through the *Supporting People* programme (Griffiths, 2000)?

Mainstream housing and community care

It can be argued that an emphasis on 'special needs' housing and supported housing deflects attention away from inadequacies within mainstream housing provision which, in turn, can lead people to drift into residential care or end up homeless. This section therefore looks at mainstream housing provision in terms of availability, affordability, repair and access, drawing out the implications of the findings for the users of community care services.

Any review of mainstream housing needs to be understood in the context of the emphasis by recent Conservative and Labour governments on the superiority of owner occupation over renting. A key element of this growth was the sale of around 2.2 million council houses into owner occupation from 1980 to 1996 as a result of the 'right to buy' (Office for National Statistics, 1997). The majority of elderly people are now owner-occupiers (Peace and Holland, 2001; Heywood *et al.*, 2002) while significant numbers of physically disabled people and people with mental health problems are also owners. The present number of owner-occupiers with learning difficulties may be very small but more and more are likely to inherit the family home and the recent White Paper stressed that 'they can cope with the full range of tenures, including home ownership' (Department of Health, 2001a, p. 70).

Availability

Whether or not there is a shortage of housing in England and Wales is a more difficult question than it first appears since it requires much more than just checking the overall number of units against the overall number of households. To be used by existing or potential households, houses must be affordable, in the right part of the country and of an appropriate design and size, as well as being in good condition. Studies which try to take all these factors into account suggest major housing shortages exist.

The Joseph Rowntree Foundation (2002) reviewed the available research and came to the following conclusions:

- Between 1996 and 2021, England will need to accommodate an extra 4.3 million households
- The above figure excludes the backlog of housing shortage in 1996, estimated to be 650,000 households (that is, homeless people, those in temporary accommodation and so on)
- The newly arising need for new dwellings per annum is around 210,000 units per year
- Existing house completion rates could leave a shortfall of new homes of 1.1 million in England by 2022
- By far the greatest house pressure will be experienced in southern England with the South East alone needing one million extra homes by 2021.

In terms of the focus of this book, it is interesting to speculate how many people with support needs could manage in mainstream housing if it was available, affordable and in reasonable repair, and if the necessary support services could be brought to such housing. It is certainly the intention of the

Supporting People programme (DTLR, 2001b) to help more vulnerable people to remain in mainstream housing by enabling them to access support services. However, it is also the case that supported housing is often used to 'rescue' homeless people who have suffered from the shortage of affordable mainstream housing (Pannell *et al.*, 2002) and the above figures on house shortages suggest that this will continue to be the case.

Affordability

In terms of affordability, our main focus is on rented housing. This is not to deny that issues of affordability in owner occupation do not arise, as the growth of repossessions in the 1990s served to illustrate. However, elderly owner-occupiers tend to have paid off their mortgage by the time of retirement (Peace and Holland, 2001) and hence the major issue for them is often house disrepair (see below). In contrast, younger owners of properties do experience mental health problems; younger physically disabled adults who are owner-occupiers get made redundant; and the house-owning parents of people with learning difficulties die. All three of these situations can raise affordability issues.

However, issues of affordability are most visible in terms of rented property. A raft of housing legislation had the effect of driving up rents in the council house, housing association and private sectors (Heywood *et al.*, 2002). At the same time the growth of owner occupation has inevitably meant that renting, apart from the 'de luxe' end of the private sector, has seen an ever more intense concentration of vulnerable households comprising the unemployed, disabled people, low-income elderly people and people with multiple problems (Carlton *et al.*, 2003). In terms of social renting, this trend has been reinforced by the fact that homelessness has become the main route into new tenancies.

The vast majority of 'vulnerable' tenants in the public and private sectors have been able to afford their accommodation only because of the housing benefit system. This can be seen in a very positive light:

Housing benefit is uniquely adaptable to the accommodation-related needs of people who require support to live in the community. It is cost-effective – payments can be tailored to the type of supported accommodation required as the individual's capacity for community living increases or diminishes over time. (Griffiths, 1997b, p. 23)

However, the response of government has been one of horror at the rapidly increasing level of housing benefit, the annual costs of which rose from £4.5 billion in 1986 to £14.7 billion in 1996 (Wilcox, 1997). One of the key reasons for this growth has been the increased use of housing benefit to pay for support needs, especially for those older tenants in sheltered housing. Another reason has been rising rents because of lower capital grants.

The government strategy for reducing costs has included the development of the *Supporting People* programme (see previous section) as a ring-fenced alternative to the continued use of housing benefit to meet support costs. The second approach has seen the introduction of a series of restrictions on housing benefit through the Housing Act 1996 over such issues as the amount of space for which benefit will be paid on new tenancies and the 'setting [of] "local reference" rents for an area, leaving tenants to find the difference out of money intended for their minimal sustenance needs' (Heywood *et al.*, 2002, p. 46).

The end result has been that the concern for the public purse has far outweighed concern for low-income vulnerable people who rent. This leads Heywood *et al.* (2002) to conclude that:

> All these attempts to reduce the cost of housing subsidies fail to accept the economic realities of housing poorer people in a society with such an uneven distribution of incomes. The lesson the Victorians took so long to learn, that the market unassisted by redistributive taxation could not meet the housing needs of those who had never been paid enough, is in danger of being forgotten again. (p. 47)

Finally, the link between tenure options and affordability needs to be recognised. Morris (2002) points out how high social housing rents deny young disabled people the opportunity to save up the resources to become owner-occupiers in a situation where 'their family is less likely than the families of non-disabled young people to be able to assist them with buying their first home'. (p. 9)

Housing conditions

In all tenures, some appalling housing conditions can be found (Leather, 2000) and Table 6.2 profiles the backlog of disrepair in private sector housing while Table 6.3 profiles the household characteristics associated with poor condition housing across all tenures. The implications of such poor housing conditions for people with support needs are immense. In terms of estates with a large amount of socially rented housing, a concentration of people with social and health difficulties in poor housing has helped to generate almost total environmental and social collapse requiring broad

TABLE 6.2   The backlog of disrepair in private sector housing, England, 1996

Type of repair cost	Cost per dwelling (£)			Aggregate cost (£ million)
	Owner-occupied	Private rented	All private	
All comprehensive (longer-term)	3,620	5,030	3,790	60,500
All current observable	1,850	3,250	2,020	32,200
Urgent current observable	1,250	2,370	1,380	22,100
Number of dwellings in sector (000s)	14,066	1,894	15,960	

Source: Leather (2000), based on Department of the Environment, Transport and the Regions (DETR) (1998a).

strategies of regeneration to tackle the resultant problems rather than just the repair of the housing stock. More specifically, there is growing research evidence about the impact of poor housing on health (Marsh *et al*., 2000) in areas such as excess winter deaths related to inadequate home heating (Wilkinson *et al*., 2001).

For those in owner occupation, and especially for low-income elderly people, there is a constant pressure about how best to maintain property to a reasonable standard. Limited repair help to some groups on a discretionary basis has been available through renovation grants and home repair assistance grants under the Housing Grants, Construction and Regeneration Act 1996 (Heywood *et al*., 2002). However, the government has been reviewing this system and has decided as of July 2003 to bring an end to the current legal framework for the provision of grants and instead give local housing authorities a new broad discretionary power to provide assistance in any way that they choose but linked to an agreed local private sector renewal strategy. It is difficult at this stage to be clear about the implications of this for elderly people and vulnerable people living in mainstream private sector accommodation. However, concern is already being expressed about the adequacy of the level of resources available to local authorities to use this new discretionary power (Care and Repair News and Policy Update, Summer 2002, pp. 1–2).

One option increasingly used by elderly and disabled people with repair problems is to turn to a specialist home improvement agency (HIA) for advice. These are non-profit-making bodies which offer independent advice and support on how to repair, improve and adapt homes (Heywood *et al*., 2002, Chapter 6). Such agencies are often called Care and Repair or Staying Put projects, although some agencies use other names. There were over 250 such agencies in England by 2002 and a further 30 in Wales. Their work in England is supported by a national co-ordinating body called Foundations

TABLE 6.3 Household characteristics associated with poor condition housing,* England, 1996, all tenures

Household characteristics	Percentage living in poor housing
All households	14
Household type	
Lone person aged 60 or more	19
Lone parent with dependants	18
Lone person aged under 60	18
Large adult household	16
Age of oldest person	
16–24	29
75 or more	20
Ethnic group	
Pakistani/Bangladeshi	35
Black	23
Indian	19
Length of residence	
30 years or more	27
Less than one year	16
Other groups	
Ethnic minority under 60	26
In full-time education	25
Unemployed under 60	25
Employed part-time under 60	19
Long-term sick	16

* Poor housing was either unfit, had urgent repair costs of over £48 per square metre, or required essential modernisation to kitchen, electrical fixtures and wiring, or space heating.

Source: Leather (2000), based on DETR (1998a).

and in Wales by one called Care and Repair (Cymru). HIAs are extensively used by people with support needs. For example, monitoring data reviewed by McClatchey *et al.* (2001) showed that over 60 per cent of clients in England during 1998/9 had mobility problems. This included just under 10 per cent who needed to make full or partial use of a wheelchair and just over 17 per cent who needed other kinds of help with walking. McClatchey *et al.* (2001) also showed how HIAs are also beginning to develop a significant role in supporting older people with dementia to remain in the community. This overall client profile has meant not only an expanding role in home adaptation (see next section) as well as home improvement, but also the development of a range of new services such as handyperson, home security and home safety schemes (Care and Repair, 2001).

Owner occupation in later life will be a boon to many. With the mortgage paid off, housing costs will drop at a time when weekly income is reduced, thus avoiding a major decline in living standards. For many, there is the prospect of a move from a family home to a smaller property, thus releasing equity to be used in a variety of ways, including meeting future care needs. But others will be trapped in poorly repaired property of limited value with few assets with which to develop a maintenance and repair strategy. The housing dimension of community care needs to include a strategy for offering support to elderly and disabled people facing these kinds of repair problems.

Access (new build and adaptation)

Despite a general trend towards deregulation in housing construction, recent years have seen the emergence of concerns about the importance of access standards (Milner and Madigan, 2001). In looking at the issue of access, it is crucial to distinguish between the concept of visitability and that of Lifetime Homes.

Box 6.1 sets out the minimum criteria for meeting visitability standards. The concept of visitability derived from the idea of mobility housing and reflected an awareness that most ordinary housing denied minimal access to disabled people. Lifetime Homes, on the other hand, rest on the much more challenging philosophy of 'sustainability, flexibility and adaptability of design which caters for the changing needs of the population throughout their life-course, and enables older and disabled people to "stay put" as and when their mobility needs change' (Milner and Madigan, 2001).

BOX 6.1   Definition of visitability

- Level entry to the principal or suitable alternative entrance
- An entrance door wide enough to allow wheelchair access
- WC provision on the entrance or first habitable storey
- Adequate circulation and wider doors within the entrance storey
- Switches and socket outlets at appropriate heights from floor level
- Level or gently sloping approach from car parking space to the dwelling or, where this is not possible, easy going steps, but not a stepped ramp
- Where a lift is provided in flats, a minimum lift capacity and dimensions will be recommended
- Where a lift is not provided, the common stair to be designed to suit the needs of ambulant disabled people.

Source: Langton-Lockton (1998) p. 5.

BOX 6.2   Definition of a Lifetime Home

Access

1. Where car parking is adjacent to the home, it should be capable of enlargement to attain 3.3 metres width.
2. The distance from the car parking space to the home should be kept to a minimum and should be level or gently sloping.
3. The approach to all entrances should be level or gently sloping. (Gradients for paths should be the same as for public buildings in the Building Regulations.)
4. All entrances should be illuminated and have level access over the threshold, and the main entrance should be covered.
5. Where homes are reached by a lift, it should be wheelchair accessible.

Inside the home

6. The width of the doorways and hallways should accord with the Access Committee for England's standards.
7. There should be space for the turning of wheelchairs in kitchens, dining areas and sitting rooms and adequate circulation space for wheelchair users elsewhere.
8. The sitting room (or family room) should be at entrance level.
9. In houses of two or more storeys, there should be space on the ground floor that could be used as a convenient bed space.
10. There should be a downstairs toilet, which should be wheelchair accessible, with drainage and service provision enabling a shower to be fitted at any time.
11. Walls in bathrooms and toilets should be capable of taking adaptations such as handrails.

$\longrightarrow$

Box 6.2 sets out the main design criteria for Lifetime Homes and it should be noted that even their full implementation would fail to deliver full access to all living areas within a home for wheelchair users.

The response by government to the growing debate about lifetime homes and access standards was to implement changes in building regulations to meet visitability rather than lifetime standards for all new housing (Brewerton and Darton, 1997). This decision not to implement a 'lifetime approach' reflected concerns about cost as well as the resistance of the building industry (Kelly, 2001; Milner and Madigan, 2001; Sopp and Wood, 2001). Despite the limited nature of the changes, an improvement in the access standards of all new-build housing has been achieved although it needs to be remembered that this will affect only a small percentage of the overall housing stock within the foreseeable future.

12. The design should incorporate provision for a future stairlift and a suitably identified space for potential installation of a house lift (through-the-floor lift) from the ground to the first floor, for example to a bedroom next to the bathroom.
13. The bath/bedroom ceiling should be strong enough, or capable of being made strong enough, to support a hoist at a later date. Within the bath/bedroom wall, provision should be made for a future floor-to-ceiling door, to connect the two rooms by a hoist.
14. The bathroom layout should be designed to incorporate ease of access, probably from a side approach, to the bath and WC. The wash basins should also be accessible.

Fixtures and fittings

15. The living room window glazing should begin at 800 mm or lower, and windows should be easy to open/operate.
16. Switches, sockets and service controls should be at a height usable by all (i.e. between 600 mm and 1,200 mm from the floor).

Source: Cobbold (1997) p. 2.

This means that the vast majority of older and disabled people will continue to depend on adaptations to their existing homes if they are to 'stay put'. The main public subsidy for adaptation work is through the disabled facilities grant and Table 6.4 outlines the main features of this complex grant. Although annual expenditure on this grant had risen to over £220 million as early as the mid-1990s, it has completely failed to keep pace with demand (Heywood, 2001). The Audit Commission (1998) pointed out that allocated resources restricted grants to an average of around £5,000 per annum although the government's own research suggested there were 650,000 eligible households in the private sector alone (Department of the Environment, 1996).

From 18 July 2002, housing authorities have had the discretionary power to give grants to help a disabled person to move (and adapt) as an alternative to adapting their current dwelling, where moving would be a more cost-effective solution. Until 19 July 2003, housing authorities may give discretionary disabled facilities grants or home repairs assistance as supplements or alternatives to mandatory disabled facilities grants. After 19 July 2003, these grants will be abolished but housing authorities may give help in whatever ways they have agreed to publicise. Social services authorities have duties under the Chronically Sick and Disabled Persons Act 1970 and

TABLE 6.4 Funding for adaptations

A. Name of grant	B. Purposes	C. Eligibility	D. Terms	E. Conditions
Mandatory disabled	To facilitate use by disabled people of their homes specifically to provide ● Access to building ● Making dwelling safe for disabled persons or others ● Access to and provision of living room, bedroom, lavatory, bathroom (including use of bath and/or shower) and washbasin ● Suitable cooking facilities and suitable power, lighting and heating controls	Anyone over 18 in any tenure who is either disabled themselves or needs the grant to allow them to adapt the house for a disabled person. The definition of disabled person for the purposes of this grant is given in Section 100 of the Housing Grants, Construction and Regeneration Act 1996. It includes a very broad range of older and disabled people, including disabled children. From 19 July 2003 occupants of park homes and houseboats will also be eligible.	Mandatory for the purposes defined in Section 23 of the Housing Grants, Construction and Regeneration Act 1996. Maximum grant £25,000 in 2002. From July 2003, councils may give more if they have an agreed and publicised policy to do so. Test resources as prescribed by the Secretary of State. Housing authorities must be satisfied that works are: (a) 'necessary and appropriate' and (b) 'reasonable and practicable'. In deciding (a) they shall consult the social services authority if it is a different authority.	Disabled person (or parent if the disabled person is a child) must complete a test of resources which takes into account their income and that of their partner or spouse. This means test does not take existing outgoings into account, and there are therefore serious problems for people with mortgages or other debts DoE Circular 4/97 provides for test of resources to be applied to people over 16 and under 19, in receipt of income support and no

TABLE 6.4 Continued

A. Name of grant	B. Purposes	C. Eligibility	D. Terms	E. Conditions
	• suitable heating system • movement around dwelling in order to care for someone • support for other purposes as may be specified by the Secretary of State.		Payment of a grant may in exceptional cases (i.e., where it would not cause hardship to the applicant) be deferred for 12 months from the date of application.	longer at school, in their own right, even if they are living with their parents.

Note: This information is provided only as a guide. Full details need to be checked in the Housing, Grants, Construction and Regeneration Act 1996, Part 1, and in subsequent circulars.

Source: McClatchey *et al.* (2001) p. 13 (based on the work of Heywood in Means *et al.*, 1997, and further updated).

other legislation to ensure that adaptation needs are met. They also have powers to help with the costs.

The disabled facilities grant has been criticised not only for the lack of overall resources allocated to fund adaptations but also because of a number of other deficiencies. These include the complexity of the whole system (Heywood *et al.*, 2002), tensions between housing and social services over how best to proceed (Pieda plc, 1996), delay in obtaining an assessment (Audit Commission, 1998) and the unfairness of the tough means test (Sapey, 1995). In terms of the help available to older and disabled people to assist them through the 'adaptation maze', it is important to note both the potential role of home improvement agencies (see previous section) and the development of specialist disabled persons' accommodation agencies, which are more limited in numbers (Means *et al.*, 1997).

Finally, it needs to be stressed that a well-thought-out home adaptation (see Box 6.3) not only has the capacity to transform the lives of older and disabled people (Heywood, 2001) but has the capacity to do this in a cost-effective way (Smart and Means, 1997). Recent research by Heywood (2001) is crucial in this respect. She co-ordinated teams of professionals working with two disabled researchers to assess the long-term effectiveness of work carried out through the disabled facilities grant. Drawing upon

---

BOX 6.3   Using adaptations to support people in the community: case study

Mr and Mrs Grey

HIA staff explained that last year Mr Grey's parents had returned from Montserrat where their home had been destroyed by the volcano. Both are physically disabled; his father has to use a wheelchair and his mother suffers from dementia, said to have been brought on as a reaction to the shock of the volcano.

Their son has given up his job to care for them but hopes to return to work once a ground floor bathroom, recommended by the OT, has been installed. He would like to move his aunt in, as their carer. Understandably he wants to retain the living room for his exclusive use – he needs to feel that he still has a life of his own.

To give his parents and aunt a living room, the HIA is drawing up plans for a small extension. This will mean that a kitchen/diner can be fitted in as well as the shower room. The disabled facilities grant will pay for the shower and an increase in the mortgage will cover the rest.

The HIA said it saw itself as having a duty to consider the wellbeing of the carer as well as the person suffering from dementia.

Source: McClatchey *et al.* (2001) p. 22.

interviews with 104 recipients of major adaptations and 162 postal questionnaires, Heywood was able to demonstrate how:

• Minor adaptations (grab rails, handrails and so on) produced a range of lasting, positive consequences for nearly all recipients (for example, 62 per cent felt safer from the risk of an accident such as a fall)
• Major alterations such as bathroom conversions and chair lifts were seen by most as having transformed their lives.

Home adaptation meets the core community care objectives of the government and yet it continues to be massively under-resourced (Heywood, 2001; Heywood *et al.*, 2002).

Conclusion: towards an integrated response

This chapter has emphasised the importance of the housing dimension of community care, and hence the need to draw housing agencies and housing professionals into the centre of community care. However, Chapter 5 outlined the obstacles to effective joint working because of conflicts over roles and responsibilities, a lack of knowledge of each other's networks and a tendency for professionals to hold stereotypical images about each other.

Many of these difficulties have existed in respect of housing and social services. On stereotypes, housing professionals have been described as seeing social workers in the following terms:

> There is a stereotyped image of the social worker as young and freshly qualified, straight from school via college without any practical experience, who would be entirely subjective and idealistic about clients and will seek all manner of handouts and special treatments for them without ever expecting them to stand on their own two feet. (Quoted in Means *et al.*, 1997)

Social workers, in their turn, have characterised housing workers as follows:

> I am not saying that they are a lot of heartless villains. I just think they are conditioned and they have little scope to do anything other than reach their targets in terms of rent arrears. (Quoted in Clapham and Franklin, 1994)

In terms of roles and responsibilities there are clear tensions at both the strategic and operational levels in areas such as homelessness and supported housing. At the centre of this tension lies the issue of who should provide the care and fund the care of people whose housing and support difficulties are not so great as to ensure they meet the priority criteria for care management and a care package (see Chapter 3). Thus, housing may define a single homeless person as in priority need on the grounds of old age, mental health problems, learning difficulties or a physical impairment but be concerned that this individual will fail to retain any tenancy offered and drift into homelessness unless provided with care support from social services. However, social services will often feel unable to respond, and hence housing workers and housing agencies feel they are being 'dumped upon' (Means *et al.*, 1997; Heywood *et al.*, 2002).

A number of studies in the mid-1990s pointed to a failure to fully develop the housing dimension of community care. The government's own study of community and housing/homelessness devoted a chapter to joint assessment and found that:

> although housing agencies are beginning to be engaged in community care implementation, housing solutions for people with 'special' needs and homeless people are still being developed in isolation, and links between community care and housing assessment procedures are rare. (Department of Health, 1994)

Arblaster *et al.* (1996) carried out a national postal survey backed up by three case studies on inter-agency working to address the housing, health and social care needs of people in ordinary housing. They found a lack of effective communication between agencies, caused partly by a lack of conceptual understanding about the overall functions of each other and this was combined with a lack of awareness about what each other did in practice on a day-to-day basis. Lund and Foord (1997) studied the housing strategies and community care plans of a range of local authorities and concluded that there was a need for improved integration of assessment procedures, a systematic recording of need and 'robust performance indicators' which are 'relevant to community care' (p. 47).

However, this period also saw considerable efforts by government to move forward the integration of housing into the community care agenda through the encouragement of joint working between the Department of the Health and the then Department of the Environment. *Housing and Community Care: Establishing a Strategic Framework* was a joint circular designed 'to provide a framework to help housing, social services and health authorities to establish joint strategies for housing and community care so that at a strategic level the necessary co-ordination between housing, health and social services is achieved' (Department of Health/Department of the Environment, 1997, p. 1). This was backed up by operational guidance supported by both central departments through the publication of *Making Partnerships Work in Community Care: A Guide for Practitioners in Housing, Health and Social Services* (Means *et al.*, 1997). This argued the need for field-level staff to increase their knowledge and confidence about what each could contribute to community care (see Box 6.4).

BOX 6.4   Housing and social services staff: key knowledge skills

Housing staff need to have the following skills and knowledge:

- Awareness of how social services and health are organised locally, what their priorities are and what they might realistically be likely to provide
- Knowledge of how to make appropriate referrals to health and social services, including information required by social services
- Knowledge of signs of possible dementia and when to seek further advice
- Ability to recognise possible signs of crisis and vulnerability
- Alternative sources of help and advice (advocacy groups, organisations of service users/disabled people, specialist voluntary agencies etc.)
- A commitment to work in partnership with the tenant, housing applicant or their advocate.

Housing staff cannot demand that health and social services provide services, but they can encourage a specialist assessment to be made where they have concerns about a client or tenant.

Social services staff need to have the following skills and knowledge:

- Awareness of how housing is organised locally, what their priorities are and what housing agencies might realistically be likely to provide (NB: housing authorities must provide free copies of a summary of their housing allocation schemes)
- This awareness to include an understanding of options for both homeless people and vulnerable tenants, together with options for those seeking advice on home improvement and/or adaptation
- Knowledge of how to make appropriate referrals to housing agencies
- Knowledge of how to respond appropriately to referrals from housing agencies
- Awareness of alternative sources of help and advice (advocacy groups, organisations of service users/disabled people, specialist voluntary agencies etc.)
- Commitment to work in partnership with service users and their advocates.

Social services staff cannot demand a response from housing agencies but they can encourage a (re)assessment to be made where they have concerns about their client's housing situation.

Source: Means *et al.* (1997).

Both the joint circular and the joint policy guidance recognised the need to include health as well as housing and social services in any consideration of the housing dimension of community care. This has become even more evident since 1997 because of the pivotal role given to primary care by the government as part of its modernisation of health and welfare. It is certainly possible to point to some encouraging developments. Its public health strategy has been very clear in recognising the environmental influences on poor health including that resulting from inadequate housing (Department of Health, 1998c, 1999f). The emphasis by the government on the role of local authorities in developing local strategic partnerships (LSPs) has recognised the pivotal role of housing in social care. These new strategic arrangements are complex:

> PCTs ... will be the lead NHS organisations for partnership working with local authorities and other partners to improve the health of local communities and to deliver wider objectives for social and economic regeneration. PCTs will work as part of Local Strategic Partnerships to ensure co-ordination of planning and community engagement, integration of service delivery and input into the wider government agenda including Modernising Social Services, Sure Start, Community Safety, Quality Protects, Youth Offending Teams and Regeneration Initiatives. (Department of Health, 2001h, p. 13)

The government has supported this new structure for strategic planning by developing an agreement with independent providers about how they can work with commissioners to build capacity and partnerships in care (Department of Health, 2001j). This agreement covered the statutory and independent social care, health care and housing sectors, a clear recognition of the importance placed on housing. At a more practical level, recent guidance on intermediate care has included a section on housing as well as a case study on the potential role of HIAs (Department of Health, 2002f).

It also needs to be appreciated how the new LSPs are very much about neighbourhood renewal. Hence they increase the scope for considering community care in a broad community/neighbourhood as well as a narrow housing context (Riseborough, 2000), the feasibility of which is further considered in Chapter 9.

However, such positive comments need to be tempered by reservations about the willingness and capacity of health to engage with housing/neighbourhood issues and with housing professionals. The creation and development of primary care trusts has created a massive programme of organisational change (see previous chapter) and one in which the emphasis is on the links between primary care and acute care (Glendinning and Means, 2002) rather than the links with housing and neighbourhood. The whole sensitivity and complexity of the care trust debate will do little to ease this situation. There is a real danger that 'housing organisations may struggle to keep housing high on the agenda of primary care and public health in the next few years' (Heywood *et al.*, 2002, p. 68).

7 Community Care: Critical Perspectives

There have been several critiques of community care from user and other perspectives. Many of the changes in policy and practice reported in earlier chapters have occurred in response to such critiques. In this chapter we return to what we see as currently the most significant critical perspectives to report developments and to assess their implications for the future.

A concern with the position of service users and carers in their dealings with the agencies of community care is a common thread linking critics of the reforms. The chapter begins, therefore, with a reminder of how users and carers have continued to occupy a disadvantaged position within a rhetoric of user empowerment. This leads to a discussion of empowerment and of the social model of disability which locates the oppression of disabled people in social organisations and structures. The disability movement has used this model to powerful effect in its demands for independent living and for legally based rights for disabled people. The chapter also considers the perspectives of groups other than younger physically disabled people, who may face different forms of oppression and be unable or unwilling to adopt a 'disabled identity'. Black and feminist perspectives on community care highlight the diversity of service users and carers and of the oppressions they may experience. Practitioners, who may be seen as complicit with the oppression of disabled people, offer a rather different perspective on a system which may frustrate the development and use of their skills whilst failing service users. The chapter ends by viewing community care, and the possibilities for change, within the context of developments in the public and private sectors and within a globalised economy.

An uneasy settlement

A recurrent theme in the discussion so far has been the tension at the heart of the community care reforms between two central, and potentially conflicting, policy objectives: to limit public expenditure and to create 'needs-led' services. How this tension would be managed on the ground, in the negotiations between practitioners and service users, became clear only after the publication of the policy guidance (Department of Health/Social Services Inspectorate, 1991a, 1991b). The needs of service users were to be identified through a process of assessment in which the practitioner would pay particular attention to the views of the user, but would alone be responsible for defining the user's needs. The power to define what counts as 'need' would rest not with the practitioner but with the local authority, whose role is to provide services to individuals with needs which fall within published eligibility criteria (1991a, p. 53).

Ensuring professional and agency control over the definition of need provides a neat solution to the problem of potentially limitless demand for 'needs-led' services, but one that sits uneasily alongside the consumerist rhetoric of the reforms. *Caring for People* had stressed that its proposals were intended to promote 'choice and independence' (Department of Health, 1989a, p. 4). The policy guidance went further, declaring that:

> the rationale for this reorganisation is the *empowerment* of users and carers. Instead of users and carers being subordinate to the wishes of service providers, the roles will be progressively adjusted. (Department of Health/Social Services Inspectorate, 1991a, p. 9, emphasis added)

The guidance recognises that the practitioner's control over resources means that the relationship with service users 'will never be totally equal', and practitioners are advised to correct this imbalance by sharing information and encouraging users and carers to play a full part in decision-making (p. 16). This raises the question of whether access to information and participation in decision-making offer a realistic strategy for the empowerment of service users and carers to counterbalance the practitioner's gatekeeping role. To answer this we need to look briefly at what is meant by user empowerment.

What is empowerment?

There is no simple answer as to what does and what does not represent user empowerment, since it is a contested concept. However, most would argue that it involves users taking or being given more power over decisions affecting their welfare and hence it probably involves taking at least some power away from service providers, although some writers (Oliver, 1996; Servian, 1996) draw upon the work of Foucault to stress that power is a relational concept rather than a zero-sum game.

Any discussion of empowerment has to consider the concept of power. Lukes (1974), in his illuminating analysis of this concept, outlines three main perspectives. The one-dimensional concept of power focuses on observable conflict and seeks to study whose preferences prevail. The two-dimensional view is more subtle in that it takes into account the way in which the powerful mobilise bias so as to ensure that the rules of the game operate in their favour so that they can keep some sources of conflict or potential conflict off the political agenda. However, Lukes argues the need to develop this perspective one stage further into a three-dimensional view of power which:

> allows for consideration of the many ways in which potential issues are kept out of politics ... What one may have here is a latent conflict, which consists in a contradiction between the interests of those exercising power and the real interests of those they exclude. These latter may not express or even be conscious of their interests. (p. 25)

In other words, the victims of non-decision-making may not always be aware that they are victims because they do not always appreciate their real interests. This perspective, if accepted, has major implications for the empowerment debate in community care. It suggests that creating opportunities for greater participation, dialogue and even control over services will not be enough, since many service users and potential service users will not be fully aware of their real interests. It suggests that empowerment requires a general raising of awareness about how society discriminates against and oppresses older people and disabled people.

The social model of disability and the case for disability rights

Understanding of the ways in which society oppresses and discriminates against disabled people has increased substantially with the growth of the disability movement in Britain and elsewhere. Campbell and Oliver (1996) provide an excellent account of the development of the movement in Britain. They chart the growth of traditional voluntary organisations such as the Royal National Institute for the Blind and the formation of single-issue pressure groups such as the Disablement Income Group. Both tended to be ineffective in terms of improving the situation of disabled people, who began to appreciate the need to establish their own organisations. More specifically, 1981 was the International Year of Disabled People and saw the establishment in Britain of the British Council of Organisations of Disabled People (now the British Council of Disabled People), which by 2002 comprised 130 independent organisations representing over 400,000 disabled people (BCODP, 2002, quoted in Barnes, 2002). Equally important was the subsequent formation of Disabled People International. This organisation of disabled people was formed after Rehabilitation International rejected a resolution at its 1980 conference that at least 50 per cent of the members of each national delegation should be disabled people. Morris (1991) sees this as a crucial moment of fighting back which required a struggle for power between organisations of disabled people and organisations for disabled people: 'disabled people had to assert their autonomy and attempt to take power away from the professionals who controlled not only the disability organisations but also the individual lives of disabled people' (p. 175).

The theoretical starting point of the UK disability movement is their commitment to a social model of disability. This model is highly critical of previous definitions of disability because of their tendency to individualise and medicalise, so that disability is seen as ultimately reducible to the functional limitations of disabled individuals (Oliver, 1996). In contrast to this, the social model of disability is based on the following distinction:

- *Impairment*: lacking part or all of a limb, or having a defective limb, organism or mechanism of the body
- *Disability*: the disadvantage and restriction of activity caused by a contemporary social organisation which takes no or little account of people who have physical impairments and thus excludes them from the mainstream of social activities. (Quoted in Oliver, 1990, p. 11)

Such an approach recognises that people have impairments but argues that it is society which disables them. This is through its imposition of, for example, segregated special schools rather than mainstream education; income maintenance benefits rather than access to the labour market; care management rather than direct payment schemes; and inaccessible housing rather than Lifetime Homes. The way forward is for disabled people to take control of their lives by gaining sufficient resources to decide how best to meet their own personal assistance needs rather than, as at present, being expected to live on poverty benefits and to receive care services under the control of welfare professionals or family members. Disability thus becomes a political issue in which disabled people are invited to join a struggle or social movement with a manifesto to win their right to be full citizens of the society in which they live (Campbell and Oliver, 1996).

In adopting a rights-based approach to cash and/or care for disabled people, the disability movement is arguing not just for a right to fair treatment and consideration (often called procedural rights) but for legally based rights. They see this as needing to cover not only the right to appropriate services or the cash to buy those services, but also a right to an income which ensures material comfort and an environment which does not disable those with impairments. Coote (1992) has summarised the case for social rights in the following way:

> People do not start out on the proverbial 'level playing field': many have disadvantages, of which some are constructed and avoidable, while others are inherent or insuperable. Welfare policies should therefore aim to minimise the avoidable disadvantages and compensate for the others, in order to equalise the 'life chances' of all. The idea of 'life chances' is closely linked to the idea of individual empowerment as a requirement of citizenship. Citizenship entails being able to participate in society, to enjoy its fruits and fulfil one's own potential, and it follows that each individual citizen must be equally able (or 'empowered') to do so. (p. 4)

Campaigning for rights

By raising awareness of the social injustices experienced by disabled people the disability movement has made significant progress in recent years in the campaign for legally based rights for disabled people (Barnes, 2002). Despite the opposition of successive Conservative governments to the granting of such rights, sustained campaigning by nationwide organisations such as Rights Now (formerly the Voluntary Organisations for Anti-Discrimination Legislation Committee) resulted in the passing of the Disability Discrimination Act 1995. Although limited in scope and in the protection it provided against discrimination, this Act enshrined in law the notion of disability rights and was followed by the Community Care (Direct Payments) Act 1996 (see Chapter 3). The incoming Labour government was more sympathetic to the movement's demands, promising in its manifesto to 'support comprehensive, enforceable civil rights for disabled people against discrimination in society or at work' (Labour Party, 1997). During its first term it strengthened the existing legislation by extending direct payment schemes to people aged 65 and over, and appointed service users to senior positions in the new social care bodies: the General Social Care Council, the National Care Standards Commission and the Social Care Institute for Excellence. Most significant of all was the creation under the Disability Rights Commission Act 1999 of a body with responsibility for: working to eliminate discrimination against disabled people; promoting equal opportunities for disabled people; encouraging good practice in the treatment of disabled people; and advising the government on the working of disability legislation. The Commission started work in 2000 and, in its first two years of operation, brought 150 legal actions under the Disability Discrimination Act, as well as campaigning for strengthening of the Act to make it harder for employers to justify discrimination and to improve access to business premises and transport (Brown, 2002b).

Despite these advances, disabled activists have continued to argue that far more is needed to secure independent living and full participation in society for disabled people. Part of the problem, in their view, is the government's limited understanding of what is meant by independent living and of the ways in which disabled people are marginalised in society (Campbell and Hasler, 2001). The *Disability Manifesto*, produced in advance of the general election of June 2001, set out the disability movement's view of independent living and of what is necessary to achieve it:

> Independent living means enabling disabled people – regardless of age, impairment or where they live – to achieve the same rights and opportunities as non-disabled people. Independence is not about doing everything for yourself. Nobody does that. It is about having choices about what happens to you.
>
> Independent living encompasses the full range of human and civil rights, including the right to privacy, to personal and sexual relationships and parenthood. It also means having the right of equal access to all aspects of society, including education, health services, training, employment, welfare and support services, housing, transport, public buildings, leisure, information and the media. The cornerstone of independent living for the many disabled people who need support with aspects of daily life is personal assistance. (Disability Daily, 2001, p. 11)

Measures to enable disabled people to access the assistance they need are, therefore, central to the manifesto's recommendations for independent living and community services (pp. 12–13). These include: involving disabled people in the drafting of national eligibility criteria for community care services; making the provision of direct payment schemes a mandatory duty on local authorities; an end to charging for essential non-residential community care services; and full implementation of the recommendations of the Royal Commission on Long Term Care (see Chapter 5). The manifesto notes a link between care charges and the continuing poverty of many disabled people and calls for care services to be provided, like health services, on the basis of need and funded from general taxation (p. 11). Without such changes, disabled activists argue, there will be a continuing contradiction in government policy which seeks to promote independence for disabled people through employment whilst making work uneconomic for many disabled people because of means-tested charging for social care (Campbell and Hasler, 2001).

Viewed in isolation, the recommendations in the *Disability Manifesto* can be seen as gradualist demands, which could be accommodated through adjustments to the existing arrangements. However, implicit in the extended concept of independent living is a radical challenge to community care as currently organised. To assert the fundamental importance of assistance that is under the control of the disabled person, in every area of life, is to question the right of politicians and managers to determine what kinds of need are eligible for help, the right of practitioners to make decisions about individual need and the whole notion of 'care'.

The demand for rights is increasingly articulated amongst different user groups. The National Pensioners Convention, for example, has long campaigned for an increased state retirement pension, but now its demands include the right to non-means-tested social care, as recommended by the Royal Commission on Long Term Care (National Pensioners Convention, 2000). The passing of the Human Rights Act 1998, which incorporated the European Convention on Human Rights into United Kingdom law, provided a further opportunity for the pursuit of rights-based demands, with pressure groups such as Help the Aged urging older people and their advocates to use the Act to ensure social equality and to end discrimination (Hunt, 2001).

One rights issue that has attracted particular attention in the media has arisen from the closure or transfer in ownership of residential care homes. The impact on residents of uncertainty and upheaval has been highlighted through cases such as that of Alice Knight, whose death at the age of 108 was headline news in June 2002. It was reported that she had gone 'on hunger strike' when forced to move to a new home after the closure of Flordon House, her home for six years. A spokesperson for her new home said:

> Everyone involved in planning Alice's move from Flordon House recognised that everything possible needed to be done if someone of her great age was to settle into a new home. (*Community Care*, 2002)

A study by Wyld *et al.* which examined the impact on residents of temporary relocation, whilst their homes were rebuilt or refurbished after transfer to an independent sector provider, gives some indication of what may be needed for a smooth transition. The researchers identified as core issues: the timing involved in preparation for the move; communication methods; the need to preserve residents' autonomy and rights; and an emphasis on providing continuity of care and the preservation of a social life (Wyld *et al.*, 2002).

The potential threat to physical and social well-being presented by care home closures and transfers formed the basis for a number of legal actions taken on behalf of care home residents in authorities across the country. In a well-publicised case, 89-year-old resident Flossie Hands issued a writ under the Act for an injunction against Birmingham City Council's plans to privatise or close their homes for older people (Winchester, 2001a). Mrs Hands, who was supported by the Residents Action Group for the Elderly (RAGE), claimed that the council had failed to take full and proper account of residents' views, and of the potential impact on residents, and that the action was in breach of the protocols governing the right to life, to protection against degrading or inhuman treatment, and respect for family life (Articles 2, 3 and 8).

Mental health service users are another group for whom the issue of rights is salient. Currently, they may be compulsorily detained and treated in hospital, under the Mental Health Act 1983, and policies on mental health have increasingly reflected a conception of service users as a threat from which the public needs to be protected and safeguarded through control and compulsory treatment (Perkins, 2001; Beresford *et al.*, 2002). Publication of the draft Mental Health Bill in June 2002 confirmed the government's intention to extend the powers of compulsory treatment to people living in the community. This added to the fears of mental health campaigners that the primary concern is with public safety, rather than the well-being of patients, and that the numbers of people subject to compulsory treatment will rise (Mind, 2002).

More positively, other recent legislation has provided mental health service users with opportunities to pursue their rights. The first legal case backed by the new Disability Rights Commission was that of Pravin Kapadia, a man with severe depression who had been compulsorily retired by his employers. The appeal court ruling that Kapadia was disabled under the terms of the Disability Discrimination Act enabled him to bring a case under the Act for discrimination and unfair dismissal (Valios, 2000). The Human Rights Act 1998 was used by seven patients detained under the Mental Health Act 1983 to mount a successful appeal against repeated delays in hearings before the mental health review tribunal (Livesey, 2002).

Rights – difficulties and dilemmas

The introduction of the new community care arrangements in April 1993 encouraged lawyers specialising in community care law to test out through the courts exactly what substantive rights were enshrined in the existing 'hotchpotch' of legislation. A pessimistic view was taken by Roberts (1992) who argued that it was rights to assessment rather than to services which had been strengthened under the 1990 Act, since Section 47(1) states that:

> where it appears to a local authority that any person for whom they may provide or arrange for the provision of community care services may be in need of any such services, the authority (a) shall carry out an assessment of his needs for those services; and (b) having regard to the results of that assessment, shall then decide whether his needs call for the provision by them of any such services,

while Section 47(2) goes on to state:

> If at any time during the assessment of the needs of any person under subsection (1) (a) above it appears to a local authority that he is a disabled person, the authority (a) shall proceed to make such a decision as to the services he requires [under section 2(1) of the Chronically Sick and Disabled Persons Act 1970] without his requesting them to do so, and (b) shall inform him they will be doing so and of his rights under the Disabled Persons (Services, Consultation and Representation) Act 1986.

Roberts interprets this to mean that 'the duty of a local authority in relation to assessment will be strengthened, but the nature and content of the services which can, or must, be provided remain unchanged' (p. 16). Carers too now have a right to an assessment under the Carers (Recognition of Services) Act 1995 although not to a subsequent service response.

A series of legal judgments have confirmed Roberts's view. These include the landmark ruling by the House of Lords which upheld the decision by Gloucestershire County Council to withdraw services, provided to the complainants after an assessment of need, on the grounds of budgetary constraints (Thompson, 1997).

Service users and carers thus have only limited rights under existing community care legislation and little scope for challenging the decisions taken by professionals on their behalf. They can challenge the fairness with which they have been treated by their social services authority using the mandatory complaints procedure established under the 1990 Act. But this offers the hope of procedural justice rather than any prospect of substantive rights.

Efforts to secure rights for service users through use of the Human Rights Act have had only limited success to date. The case brought by Flossie Hands against Birmingham City Council (see above) was dismissed as the court was not satisfied that the council had failed to adequately consult with residents or that privatisation would lead to closure (Winchester, 2001b). A similar case, in Plymouth, reached the Court of Appeal but was dismissed on the grounds that the issues could be dealt with by the complaints procedure or through independent mediation. The Lord Chief Justice, Lord Woolf, warned against the use of litigation to resolve such disputes, given the use of public money involved (Cragg, 2002). A further ruling in the Court of Appeal, in a case brought by residents of Le Court, a home owned by the Leonard Cheshire Foundation, established that independent sector providers are not subject to the terms of the European Convention on Human Rights and therefore the Foundation's decision to close the home could not be reviewed by the courts. Unless overturned on appeal to the House of Lords, this ruling places significant limits on the use of the Human Rights Act by service users (Revans, 2002c).

Is the disappointing record of attempts to establish rights for service users through the courts a temporary setback, or evidence of the limitations of a rights-based approach in pursuing the interests of disabled people?

Although sympathetic to the demands of the disability movement, an analysis by Drewett (1999) supports the latter view. Whilst acknowledging the symbolic importance of rights as a campaigning tool, she doubts their effectiveness as a strategy for effective change and identifies a number of weaknesses in the rights-based approach. First, the discussion of rights in the disability literature lacks a systematic theoretical basis, to the extent that even fundamental questions about the source and status of rights claims have been ignored. Second, she is critical of the distinction drawn in this literature between needs-based and rights-based approaches. The concepts of need and of rights are, she argues, often linked as a 'belief in the existence of universal needs often underpins support of rights' (p. 123). Third, it is unclear how rights-based approaches would translate into practice and how they would be administered differently. Finally, Drewett is doubtful about the possibility of establishing legal rights to social goods, such as social care, as historically the law has endorsed only a basic and limited view of needs and rights. The outcome of the cases described above only confirms this to be the case.

In a further contribution to this debate, Handley (2000) pursues Drewett's concerns about needs and rights and the question of how rights-based approaches would translate into practice. His critique focuses on the suggestion by Oliver, a prominent disability theorist, that the allocation of resources should be based on self-defined need, not on ascribed need (that is, need defined by experts) as at present: 'it is rights to appropriate [welfare services to meet] *their own self-defined needs* that disabled people are demanding, not to have their needs defined and met by others' (Oliver, 1996, p. 74, quoted in Handley, 2000, p. 317, emphasis added).

This reliance on self-defined need is, Handley argues, problematic as it is hard to see how self-defined needs could form the basis for rights claims given the difficulty of distinguishing between self-defined needs and wants and preferences:

> If everyone is demanding the satisfaction of their self-defined needs by right, then how are we to sort out the almost inevitable conflicts that this will generate? How are we to prioritise all of these competing claims, and who will arbitrate between them? (p. 318).

Such was the dilemma highlighted by Birmingham's Assistant Director of Social Services, when interviewed about the case brought by care home resident Flossie Hands. If the action was successful, he suggested, the expenditure on the local authority's homes to raise them to the standards required for registration under the Care Standards Act would have a devastating impact on other services (Winchester, 2001a). Such responses serve as a reminder that enacting rights through the courts does not solve the problem of how to allocate scarce resources equitably.

Young and Quibell (2000) introduce another angle to the rights debate with a discussion of the failure of rights-based strategies to ensure justice for people with learning disabilities. They question whether such strategies alone can bridge the gap between the lived experience of the learning disabled and the failure of the 'able-minded' to understand their situation. The problem, they suggest, is that the concept of rights as developed in western societies is essentially mechanical and individualistic and linked to the notion of autonomy. Despite its symbolic power, it provides a questionable basis for determining relations between the powerful and the powerless and for facilitating understanding between them:

> 'rights' are often unsuccessful simply because people still do not know how to treat others who are different; they are not aware of the variety of social institutions or practices necessary for particular 'entitlements', or even that such 'entitlements' are necessary. The irony is that *it is the conception of human nature which the notion of 'rights' promulgates that reinforces this situation*, where individual autonomy and the force of law take precedence over the necessary ability of humans, as social animals, to understand each other. (p. 758, original emphasis)

Young and Quibell do not reject the call for rights, rather they propose a reconceptualisation of the notion to incorporate understanding of the disadvantaged, primarily through access to their stories. Understanding, they suggest, is a necessary condition for any advance in rights:

> *They do not understand us, but once we are understood, we can finally have justice. We have the right to be understood.* (p. 761, original emphasis)

Who is disabled?

The disability movement argues that the way forward is for disabled people to organise together and hence to act as capable agents rather than passive victims. Above all the focus is upon their common experience of discrimination by society which means they have a common interest in fighting for their civil rights to meet their common needs. However, from the outset the movement has been led by younger physically disabled people and thus, as Campbell and Oliver (1996) have acknowledged, cannot claim to be a mass movement when other groups, especially older disabled people, participate hardly at all. Although the increasing demand for rights amongst different user groups points to a strategic convergence of some kind, the shared discourse of rights may conceal quite different perspectives as Young and Quibell's analysis suggests.

To what extent, therefore, does the disability movement articulate the needs and concerns of other user groups? In principle, the social model of disability provides the basis for an inclusive understanding of the ways in which social factors shape experiences of impairment. However, both the rhetoric of the disability movement and the social model itself have been accused of ignoring the diversity of disabled experience. The 'disabled' identity itself is at issue as users with, for example, age-related illnesses or mental health problems differ in the extent to which they perceive themselves as 'disabled'. Similarly the disability movement's rejection of the traditional 'private tragedy' model of disability can be seen as an implicit denial of the pain and suffering many users and carers experience.

The experiences of De Wolfe (2002), a long-term ME sufferer, illustrate these difficulties. The discourse of disability activism seemed irrelevant to her needs until, faced with an access problem, she drew on the social model to argue her case. However, her pain and fluctuating energy levels leave her distanced from a movement that she associates with basically vigorous people with a fixed impairment. De Wolfe locates the problem in the contested divide between disability and illness and the way in which social responsibility for those who are seen as having long-term or intractable illness is understood mainly in terms of individual health care provision and personal support. Worse still:

> The taboos that surround the topic of long-term illness, and inhibit the discussion of the experience it generates, make it hard to formulate suggestions about the social changes that would make it more tolerable. Even those with an interest in promoting such a discussion may find that they are floundering to express needs and concerns for which they are unable to find words. (p. 263)

This reluctance to even acknowledge such experiences, which in the case of disability activists may be heightened by their concern to avoid the association of impairment with personal tragedy, may leave the chronic sick feeling powerless and stigmatised. They are excluded both from a society that is intolerant of illness and from the positive images of impairment presented by the disability movement.

De Wolfe's analysis is also relevant to the largest disabled group, those with age-related impairment and disease, who may have difficulty in identifying with people who have been disabled from childhood or early adulthood and are further disadvantaged by negative attitudes towards ageing and older people. Paralleling the development of the social model of disability, there is now a considerable literature examining ways in which dependence in old age is socially constructed (Phillipson and Walker, 1986; Jamieson *et al.*, 1997). In particular work has been done on the links between poverty and retirement and pension policies and on the impact of the dominant medical model of ageing (Estes and Binney, 1989). Here the emphasis on technologically advanced treatments is compared with the relative neglect of rehabilitation services and the lack of social support for those with chronic disease in old age.

Whilst disabled people themselves have been largely responsible for the theoretical advances in the understanding of disability, older people have played no such role in the study of ageing and thus have been distanced not only from the insights of the disability movement but from equivalent developments relating to old age. This is likely to change, however, as older people become unwilling to simply accept their disadvantaged status as an inevitable consequence of growing older, thus increasing the possibility of links with disability activists. A study by Priestley and Rabiee (2001) of local voluntary organisations serving older people in one large metropolitan area begins to unravel some of the complex and often contradictory understandings that may promote or impede such an alliance. Their informants' responses revealed a 'medico-functional model of disability with apparently little awareness of the social model', but there was evidence of 'social model thinking in the definition of barriers facing older people with impairments' (p. 10). The interviews also uncovered divergent understandings of old age, of disability and of the relationship between the two. The respondents were divided between those who considered as disabled anyone with a significant impairment, regardless of age or of the cause of impairment, and those who saw age-related impairment differently. The latter were likely to describe older people as disabled only if they were functioning in a way that deviated from their perception of what was normal for old age. Older people were also seen as either having fewer needs than their younger counterparts, with the implication that a restricted lifestyle is more acceptable in old age, or as having more needs, for example, because they have not 'learned to live with it' (p. 11).

Survivors of the mental health system are another group who do not fit easily into the disability movement. They have developed their own organisations but these have tended to engage with the mental health system in an effort to achieve reform from within, in contrast to the separatist approach of the disabled movement (Beresford *et al.*, 2002). There are uncertainties too about whether a disabled identity is appropriate in the absence of any physical impairment and a perception that 'the unintentional colonisation of survivors by the disabled people's movement' may threaten their distinct identity (Plumb, 1994, in Beresford *et al.*, 2002). Nevertheless there is growing evidence of collaboration between both groups around shared experiences of discrimination and oppression.

Theoretical attempts to develop the social model in ways that more fully take account of the diversity of impairment, and of individual experiences, are likely to contribute to such collaboration. The extent of these developments is chronicled by Tregaskis (2002) who speaks of separate and competing strands each of which adds to an understanding of disabled people's oppression (p. 458). Marks (1999) provides an example of how such strands may be woven together to create a more holistic understanding of disability which starts from the social model but draws on psychoanalytic insights, narrative accounts of disability and physiological and sociological accounts of the body. Acknowledging the reality of the impaired body, she speaks of disability as something that is lived and experienced physically and psychologically. Disability is, she concludes, 'socially constructed, materially embodied, and invested with fears and fantasies' (p. 177).

Disablism and other oppressions

An announcement in May 2002 that the government was considering a merger between the Disability Rights Commission, the Equal Opportunities

Commission and the Commission for Racial Equality, the equality organisations for gender and race, was greeted with dismay by disability campaigners (Brown, 2002b). The intention of the merger, it was reported,
would be to ensure a more unified approach to equality by creating a single
contact point for advice and support in these common areas of discrimination. Disability campaigners, however, were worried that the plan would
lead to a dilution of the disability rights agenda.

The reaction to the announcement highlights a continuing difficulty for
the disability movement, the charge that it does not take adequate account
of the ways in which the experiences of impairment are shaped by the interaction between disablism and other forms of oppression, such as racism and
sexism. Black disabled people in particular may feel that their perspective is
ignored:

> I got fed up to the back teeth of being told by white disabled people that
> as black disabled people we shouldn't be concerned with issues of race
> and disability; that we should be concerned only with issues of disability
> because that was the fight; that was the most important element in our
> character. I am of the belief that black disabled people share a lot in com-
> mon with white disabled people. We have lots of issues in common, but
> we cannot ignore the fact that to a very large extent there still is that
> added element of racism that we have to encounter as black people.
> I didn't think that the white disability movement was taking that on
> board. (Hill, quoted in Campbell and Oliver, 1996, p. 132)

One implication of such an analysis is that community care services and
relations between welfare professionals and black service users need to be
understood in terms of racism as well as disablism. This requires 'white cultural assumptions underpinning current community care policies being
recognised, their limitations understood and their relevance to services for
people ... from black and ethnic communities challenged' (Baxter *et al.*,
1990). Changes are needed in services at every level, as identified in a report
by the Social Services Inspectorate on services for black and minority ethnic older people. The inspectors found there was little choice in the services
available to these groups and the ethnocentric nature of service provision
often meant they had difficulty in getting their needs met (Department of
Health/Social Services Inspectorate, 1998). A growing number of studies
illustrate how the colour-blind nature of provision means that many potential recipients of services fail to come forward to express their needs. This
in turn helps to perpetuate complacency about previous services and to
encourage sweeping assumptions about the capacity and desire of black

families to care for all their members without support from publicly funded services (Askham *et al.*, 1995; Ahmad and Atkin, 1996).

There is, for example, consistent evidence of unmet need amongst black and ethnic minority elders that challenges such assumptions and points to the varieties of experience within different communities. Ahmad and Walker (1997), in a study of Asian older people in Bradford, uncovered a complex web of disadvantage. Poverty and poor housing were widespread, especially amongst women and the Bangladeshi community. There were high levels of chronic health problems and of difficulties in self-care. For example 54 per cent of the men interviewed, and 48 per cent of the women, had difficulty cooking meals, whilst 19 per cent of both men and women had difficulty dressing. Awareness of domiciliary services such as home care was very limited. Seeking help or accessing information was rendered more difficult by the low levels of fluency in English and of literacy in any language. A particularly worrying feature of this study was that the respondents were relatively young, with only 12.5 per cent aged 70 or above. The assumption that older people are looked after by their families is perhaps particularly strong in the case of Chinese communities. Drawing on two studies of the family care of older people in Chinese communities in London, Chiu and Yu (2001) found that Chinese families were indeed highly motivated to care for older family members but were, nevertheless, unable to meet all their needs. There were significant gaps in the care provided, especially in the area of personal care and in social contact. The authors argue for a model of shared care that supports the existing pattern of care, by enabling different ethnic minority groups to define their needs according to their cultural values.

People from ethnic minorities are particularly disadvantaged in their contact, or lack of contact, with mental health services (Watters, 1996; Bhui, 2002). There are reports of high rates of depression amongst Asian women and of a suicide rate that is about twice that of the population as a whole (Mental Health Foundation, 1995). Numerous studies have confirmed that Afro-Caribbean people are more likely to be compulsorily admitted to hospital and to be diagnosed as psychotic, particularly if they are male (Bebbington *et al.*, 1994; Davies *et al.*, 1996). The complexity of the difficulties facing users, carers and service providers is addressed in a recent review of the relationship between African and Caribbean communities and mental health services by the Sainsbury Centre for Mental Health (2002). The report speaks of services in which prejudice, cultural ignorance and a fear of violence influence assessment and lead to treatment that relies heavily on medication and restriction. This increases the reluctance of service users to ask for help, and to comply with treatment, which in turn reinforces the fear and prejudice of staff. These ' "circles of fear" in which staff see service users as potentially dangerous and service users perceive services as harmful' (p. 8) prevent black people from engaging with services. Once they do engage they may find a system which:

> reproduces the individual and institutionalised racism of society, often exacerbating and compounding our distress as, for example, we get defined in terms of Eurocentric norms and our cultural differences (in particular our culturally determined expressions of emotional distress) get pathologised. This may then drive us into a vicious circle of racism, distress, more racism, more distress, which is only likely to be broken if the true issues are acknowledged and addressed. (Trivedi, 2002, p. 78)

Trivedi, a black user of mental health services, calls for service providers to work with users in empowering ways, which enable them to see how racism (both internal and external) contributes to mental distress.

The Sainsbury Centre report concludes that change is needed in the experience of service users at each point in the care pathway. It proposes a programme of action to cover every aspect of service development and delivery, the main aims of which would be to:

- Ensure that Black service users are treated with respect and that their voices are heard
- Deliver early intervention and early access to services to prevent escalation of crises
- Ensure that services are accessible, welcoming, relevant and well integrated with the community
- Increase understanding and effective communication on both sides including creating a culture which allows people to discuss race and mental health issues
- Deliver greater support and funding from the statutory sector to services led by the Black community. (Sainsbury Centre for Mental Health, 2002, p. 76)

The lack of appropriate community-based services for black users is a particular concern, so an important element in the proposed strategy for reform would be the development of 'gateway agencies', to build bridges with statutory agencies, whilst advocating for black service users (p. 76).

Exploration by disability theorists of the links between disablism and other forms of oppression such as racism, sexism and heterosexism (Morris, 1991; Thomas, 1999) confirm the need for explicit recognition of the racial and cultural diversity of disabled people and of the benefits of subgroupings within the movement based, for example, on ethnic grouping or sexual orientation (Vernon, 1996 1999). Tregaskis (2002) acknowledges that such accounts may undermine the primacy of the disabled identity, but also provide a potential bridgehead between the ideology of the disabled movement and of other oppressed groups striving for social change (p. 466).

The investigation of the links between disability and other forms of oppression, and of the potential for strategic alliances, has perhaps developed most clearly in the work of disabled feminists and in the feminist literature on care. Early feminist critiques of community care focused on the caring relationship, from the perspective of the carer, and on community care policies as a source of exploitation of women in their role as unpaid or low-paid carers (Finch and Groves, 1983; Ungerson, 1987). By highlighting the demands of the caring role, and the way in which caring may exclude women from active participation in the labour market, this work contributed to the campaigning of carers' organisations and thus helped to raise the profile of carers on the policy agenda. However, critics identified significant limitations in this literature. It tended to concentrate on certain types of care situation to the exclusion of others and, in particular, too little attention was given to the co-resident carer (usually a spouse or long-term partner) where the sense of exploitation and lost labour market opportunities may be far less pertinent (Arber and Ginn, 1991). Evidence cited by Fisher (1994) indicated that the extent of the female imbalance in the caring role had been exaggerated, since the 1992 General Household Survey suggested that 2.9 million of the 6.8 million carers were men. More generally, such critiques were seen as failing to recognise the satisfactions of caring as well as the costs (Nolan *et al.*, 1996), and as creating a misleading dichotomy between carer and cared for, as many disabled people are involved in active caring roles (Morris, 1993). By largely ignoring the experiences of those receiving care, many of whom were women, and the reciprocity of the caring relationship, it also contributed to 'polarised constructions of the disabled person as a burden and the informal carer as an oppressed woman' which do an injustice to the experiences of women (Lloyd, 2001, p. 721).

Such criticism has been central to the development of an account of informal care which more accurately represents the diversity of experience amongst disabled and non-disabled women. Through their struggle to access and fulfil traditional female roles, Lloyd argues, disabled women have contributed to a reconceptualisation of 'care' and 'care-giving', in three distinct ways:

● By legitimising the perspective that *caring is something that women might want to do*, or at the very least would not want someone else to do when it is their own intimate relationships which are involved

- By demonstrating, through their own situation, that the *caring role is not synonymous with the caring function*
- By re-establishing, through their position as both givers and receivers of care, that *informal caring takes place within a relationship*, and is thus likely to be mutual and reciprocal. (Based on Lloyd, 2001, pp. 721–5)

In questioning the assumptions in the early literature on caring, disabled feminists and other users also present a challenge to the 'conflict between attention to the needs of carers, and specifically women as informal carers, and the rights and needs of users which is at the core of much of community care policy and practice' (Orme, 2001b, p. 31).

Parker and Clarke (2002) see this as a conflict which cannot be resolved without a fundamental shift in community care policies. This is because those policies contain at their core a commitment to deinstitutionalisation and to the family as the proper provider of welfare, together with a concern to reduce costs which leads inevitably to reliance on unpaid informal care and to limited options for both users and carers. The National Strategy for Carers (Department of Health, 1999g), despite welcome initiatives such as ring-fenced funding for regular breaks for carers, provides further evidence for this view through its failure to take account of the complex nature of caring relationships and of the perspectives of those who receive care (L. Lloyd, 2000). A way forward, Parker and Clarke argue, is provided by the social model through its questioning of the assumption that home-based care and the involvement of carers are inextricably linked. This opens the way to the development of a common agenda for action between users and carers, around four main points:

- Policy must be underpinned by an acknowledgement that disability is socially created
- Different people may have their disability created in different ways and will wish to have their needs for personal support met in different ways
- Family members and friends will still be involved in providing care, but both parties must have choice over this with scope for negotiation
- There will be a continuing need for recognition and support of people who provide unpaid care. (Based on Parker and Clarke, 2002, pp. 356–7)

Taken together, Parker and Clarke suggest, this constitutes a radical critique of the central tenets of community care policy through its questioning of the assumption that older and disabled people should have no option but to rely on the unpaid labour of family and friends if they are to continue living in their own homes.

A practitioner critique

Underpinning much of the critique by the disability movement of community care policy and practice is the charge that the community care system is designed to serve the interests of welfare professionals from the statutory and independent sectors rather than those of community care clients (Oliver, 1990). Very similar criticisms have been made by several of those writing within the political economy of ageing tradition with Estes (1979) in particular referring to 'the ageing enterprise' as operating to the advantage of both welfare professionals and commercial interests (drug companies, private residential homes and so on).

Previously in this chapter we referred to Lukes's three dimensions of power. Drawing on the work of Foucault (1979), Servian (1996) describes a fourth dimension of power in which power is no longer a thing to be won or lost but rather a process by which the identities of individuals are socially constructed, often by welfare professionals and welfare institutions. Such 'disciplinary' power has often been forged through the use of institutions such as school, prison and hospital with discipline in these institutions being made possible by the application of surveillance techniques. The movement of people out of closed institutions into broader society has required the development of micro-techniques of power and surveillance for those in the community, such as assessment, diagnosis, screening, codification and categorisation, all of which serve to help define the client, and the nature of his or her problems, in technical, legislative and bureaucratic terms. Such methods may function as explicit means of control, as in the measures proposed for the surveillance of people with mental health problems in the draft Mental Health Bill (see above) where 'mental illness' is linked to 'dangerousness'. The mechanisms of control may also function in more subtle ways, as Kaufman (1994) demonstrates from her study of a community-based multidisciplinary geriatric assessment service in the United States. Referral to the service was likely to result in increased surveillance and interventions designed to minimise risk and, as far as possible, to preserve autonomy in spite of functional limitations. However, the interaction between competing discourses of risk avoidance and autonomy, both of which are central to American culture, has paradoxical results. In order to retain their independence and avoid institutional care, older people may be required to make lifestyle changes that leave them feeling trapped by the solutions proposed for problems that others have defined.

The continuing power of professionals and agencies has been a continuing feature of community care under the new arrangements and Chapter 3 included evidence of how this power has been exercised. Implementation of the reforms saw the development of bureaucratic procedures through which access to assessment, and to services intended to promote independence, has been linked to risk and to the need for assistance with personal care. Chapter 4 then explored the growth of what has been called the audit culture (Power, 1997) with its heavy emphasis on the direction and surveillance of local agencies by central government. Together these developments have led to changes in the practitioner role and unease amongst many practitioners. A particular concern is the impact of these changes on relationships with service users, on the exercise of professional judgement and decision-making and on the overall focus of their work. There is a perception that professional autonomy has been reduced but that power has shifted to senior management and central government agencies rather than to service users and carers (Lymbery, 1998).

The transformation of social workers into care managers, with responsibilities for assessing needs and for designing, purchasing and monitoring care packages, is a symbol of the changing culture within care agencies and of its uncertainties. From the outset, it was unclear whether care management was simply a reframing of the social work task, reflecting the language and the separation of functions of the new managerialism in the public sector, or something entirely different. The policy guidance (Department of Health/Social Services Inspectorate, 1991a, 1991b) did not address this question. However, a case was made for continuity which rested on the argument that the skills required for care management are identical or very similar to those required for social work (Payne, 1995; Sheppard, 1995). An implication of this argument was that in traditionally low-status sectors, such as work with older people where social work skills were underdeveloped, the introduction of care management could lead to improvements in practice. However, this would depend on the way in which care management is utilised and, as Hugman (1994) observed, the development of an administrative rather than a client-centred model would be unlikely to result in an increase in either professional status or skills. As Hugman predicted, the dominant interpretation of the care management role that emerged from the reforms has emphasised the administrative aspects of the process, such as the completion of forms and the application of eligibility criteria, rather than human relations skills (see Chapter 3).

This 'dominance of administrative activities over client-focused work' (Gorman, 2000, p. 151) is central to the practitioner critique of community care. These activities, which are essential to the allocation, purchasing and monitoring of care services, serve not only to categorise and control the client but also to gather data on which to judge the quality of the service. The latter, as we argued in Chapter 4, is a key element in New Labour's plans for modernising public services. However, the consequence of all this has been a 'mechanistic approach to the assessment and planning of care in the community' and a move 'away from quality time with clients to a notion of quality bound up with the monitoring of interventions' (Gorman, 2000, p. 153).

An insight into care management, as experienced by its practitioners, can be gained from a number of observational studies. Postle (2002), who studied care managers working with older people, describes them as working within an overall context of uncertainty and change. Particular aspects of this context were significant: the restricted resources; the need to operate within a market for care; and the increasing emphasis on risk. They gave rise, Postle argues, to five positions of tension and ambiguity in the care management role:

- Restricted resources to meet needs: emphasis on assessment of needs
- Focusing on the minutiae of financial assessments: dealing with the person
- Spending time on paperwork and IT: taking time to develop a relationship
- Increasingly complex work: more reductionist processes such as checklists
- Concern about all aspects of risk: speed of work throughput increasing risk. (From Postle, 2002)

Whereas in the past bureaucratic tasks had appeared secondary to direct work with service users, now such tasks could not be delayed if systems were to work effectively. Elsewhere Postle warns against the easy assumption of a false dichotomy between social work and care management. Unfavourably contrasting care management with social work runs the risk of ignoring the lack of clarity and the inherent ambiguity of the social work role, most notably in the tension between care and control which has characterised social work from the outset (Postle, 2001b). And, in the case of social work with older people, there is a danger that the contrast will be with an idealised practice that was seldom found (Marshall, 1989; Hugman, 1994). Nevertheless, as Postle suggests, the difficulties the care managers faced in reconciling the differing aspects of their role were likely to have contributed to the decrease in job satisfaction reported by most of them and to the high levels of stress-related illness in the department where they worked (Postle, 2002).

Gorman (2000) also found care managers struggling with the ambiguities and tensions of their role. She uses the concept of *emotional labour*, an analysis of emotion and the responsiveness to other human beings in the context of work, to describe the area of their work where the impact of the changes was most apparent. She concludes:

> In the shift from social work to care management the significance of the emotional labour within caring work may have become lost within the administrative and managerial process that dominates it. (pp. 154–5)

An ethnographic study of the process of needs assessment for older people yielded similar findings. This poignant example of what emotional labour can entail and of what may be lost for both user and practitioner comes from an interview with a care manager, who had recently placed a frail older man in a rest home:

> If I had more time, more space in my diary, there are a lot of people like Mr Reynolds that I'd like to spend some time with. Just to make sure that he really does want what's happening to him, that he really has come to terms with the disability ... And he's now losing his home, and we have not the time to address that. One would hope that the rest home will give him space to talk about that, because they have more time, but they're not skilled in counselling. At some point all they need is somebody to listen to them, to say something like 'it's OK, it's alright to be sad about losing your home'. Whether they will actually say that or not I don't know. It would be nice if we had, but we haven't the time to do it. I wish we did because it's really the most interesting bit of the job is that kind of work. (Quoted in Richards, 1996 p. 165)

This perception that there was not even time for modest interventions to explore the emotional needs of older people, even though this was something that would have given the care manager real job satisfaction, was a recurrent theme amongst the practitioners in this study.

The same study also yielded evidence of the potentially harmful effects of bureaucratic procedures on the interactions between care managers and service users. A focus on *agency-centred* agendas could distract attention from the user's perspective and thus increase the risk of inappropriate or unwelcome intervention and neglect of pressing needs. Tailoring the assessment process to engage with the problems as defined by service users and with their ideas about how these might be addressed requires highly developed listening and communication skills. Instead the quantity of routine information required to determine eligibility, and for agency information systems, encouraged a mechanistic approach to the assessment task, which could appear meaningless to service users (Richards, 2000).

So far in this chapter we have looked at community care from various insider perspectives, to identify problem areas and to suggest that change may require a questioning of fundamental assumptions about 'care', who provides it, the way in which resources are allocated and about the role of practitioners. Community care services are, however, delivered within a context of developments in public services and the national and global economy which, in significant respects, may determine the possibilities for change. It is to review developments in this wider context that we turn next.

The new public sector management and globalisation

There is a growing literature which stresses how management/managerialism in the public sector tends to reflect developments in the private sector (Hoggett, 1996; Clarke and Newman, 1997; Powell and Hewitt, 2002). In the 1950s and 1960s, industry was dominated by the large-scale production of standard necessities (sometimes called Fordism). It is interesting to note that the newly created social services departments were often disparagingly called 'Seebohm factories' in the early 1970s. The recommendations of the Seebohm Report (1968) on local authority and allied personal services had led to their establishment through the amalgamation of smaller welfare departments. A common concern was that this would lead to more rigid managerial and bureaucratic control over the discretion of field-level staff to agitate on behalf of their low-income clients (Bailey and Brake, 1975). In other words, social services staff were becoming workers in large social work factories.

However, the technological base of bureaucracy in the private sector was undermined during the 1970s by the emergence of flexible automation and information technologies. The result was that the 1980s saw a shift towards a greater degree of market segmentation based upon highly differentiated products with a much shorter lifespan than that associated with Fordist systems of production. In terms of private sector organisation, this saw the development of what Peters and Waterman (1982) called 'tight/loose' systems of organisation in which the centre loosens its grip over many aspects of production so that it can more effectively control the essentials of values, culture and strategy. More specifically, contracting out, decentralised production units and localised cost centres were made possible by the emergence of computerised management and financial systems.

What did all this mean for the public sector? A number of authors spoke of the growth of a New Public Management which Ferlie *et al.* (1996) defined as based on four broad commitments, namely a drive for efficiency, a stress on downsizing and decentralisation, a search for excellence and a stress on public sector excellence. In the mid-1990s, authors such as

Le Grand and Bartlett (1993) defined the resultant public sector reforms as the creation of quasi-markets in which competition through contracts was to be the pivotal mechanism for adhering to the aspirations of the new public sector management.

The election of Labour governments since 1997 may have led to less emphasis on markets and more on partnerships in the public sector (Glendinning *et al.*, 2002b) but this is seen by many commentators as still strongly influenced by private sector developments. However, there is less agreement on the nature of this influence. Does the government have a coherent public policy agenda for modernisation and the third way or is it much more a matter of what Powell (2000) calls 'PAP – pragmatism and popularism' (p. 53).

What is clear is that both recent Conservative and Labour governments have drawn on the private sector to strengthen the techniques of control and surveillance. Thus, writing in 1996, Hoggett argued:

> whilst operations have been devolved to business units such as schools, and trust agencies, control over the policy and the allocation of resources has been increasingly concentrated within Whitehall ... Increasingly, the centre does not simply prescribe performance targets for operational managers but offers incentives and sanctions for meeting targets. (p. 19)

Six years later, Powell and Hewitt (2002) referred to 'the "double jeopardy" of quantitative (performance indicator) and qualitative (peer inspection) performance review' (p. 136) across huge swathes of the public sector. The audit culture is certainly not restricted to monitoring the policy and practice of community care.

The next chapter explores the extent of similarities and differences between community care in England and in the rest of Europe. In general, the stress on the distinctive nature of Thatcherism has been replaced by debates about the extent of convergence between welfare states (Powell and Hewitt, 2002) as a result of the impact of globalisation on social policy (Yeates, 2001). From such a perspective, the crucial issue is not how the techniques of public sector/community care management reflect those of the private sector but how global capitalism and transnational companies (TNCs) limit the scope for individual nation states in the west to develop distinctive public sector/community care responses. As Yeates (2001) explains, 'strong' globalisation theory stresses how:

> states are structurally dependent on global capital while TNCs have unlimited freedom in choosing the most conducive or profitable terms

and conditions for their investment and production operations. Since TNCs owe no allegiance to any state, they (re)locate wherever advantage exists. (p. 10)

From the perspective of the left, such pressures from global capital have led to 'the emergence of an integrated, or unified world economy which has a separate dynamic to that of national economies and which is not fully under the control of political institutions' (p. 10). Such a world economy is likely to have little concern for those requiring support through community care policies. The future may hold the opposite to that advocated by the disability movement – limited means-tested services from declining welfare states rather than rights-based benefits and services.

However, the true nature of globalisation and its implications for social policy are highly contested (Rodger, 2000). Yeates's conclusion in *Globalisation and Social Policy* (2001) is that 'social movements for globalisation cannot simply steamroll over states and populations, or bulldoze national institutions and remould them in their preferred fashion' (p. 168). This suggests that future directions in community care policy will need to engage with globalisation pressures but that the nature of this direction is not inevitable (see Chapter 9).

Conclusion

In certain respects the community care reforms of the 1990s represented a significant change from the past. Funding for care packages in the community, the introduction of care management and assessment and the transformation of local authorities from their role as service providers to that of purchasers and enablers within a social care market were all important new developments. However, in other respects little seemed to have changed. Despite a commitment to user empowerment, the power of professionals and agencies was maintained over what is often the most crucial stage for the service user or carer – the assessment of his or her needs. Also underpinning the reforms were the continuing assumptions that people with impairments or chronic illness would normally be cared for by family or other unpaid carers and that additional needs could be met through individualised care packages.

Much of this chapter has been devoted to the radical critiques of community care articulated by various user interests and by carers. The social model of disability in particular highlights the need to rethink fundamental assumptions about *disability* and *care* and to design systems that enable people with different kinds of impairments to access the assistance and support they require. The conception of independent living proposed by the disability movement challenges not just welfare professionals but society as a whole to consider the ways in which disabled people are disempowered and socially excluded. The campaign for legally based rights by disabled activists points towards a very different vision of community care (assistance) from that which currently exists, yet as a strategy it has important weaknesses that are currently unresolved. Service users are not a united movement; categorised by age and pathology, there are also differences relating to race and gender which are not easily subsumed within a single identity, yet there is evidence of convergence through a growing awareness of shared interests.

Critiques of the community care reforms from a practitioner perspective have also emerged. These have focused on the shift to a managerial culture in care services and on the growing burden of administration which detracts, in their view, from the quality of work with user and carers. Whatever the aspirations of users, carers and practitioners, the possibilities for change may be determined elsewhere through the workings of a globalised economy. The next chapter examines similarities and differences in the organisation of community care in other European countries.

8 European Perspectives on Community Care

Introduction

The policies of the European Union (EU) have an indirect, and occasionally direct, impact on community care strategies in individual member states, including the UK. This chapter starts by referring to key macro-level developments in recent years in EU policies and highlights the tensions between increasing competences at supranational level and demands for powers and responsibilities to be returned to or to remain at the national or subnational level. This is followed by a short introduction to the main institutions of the EU, the relationships between them and the process of policy-making. The first part of the chapter ends with a scrutiny of the impact of EU policies for older people, for disabled people and for the providers of community care.

The second part of the chapter looks at different welfare regimes and examines community care policies in three countries, Denmark, Germany and Greece, which represent welfare regimes different from that of the UK. The focus is on the welfare mix, the role of the family, the level of costs, particularly for institutional care, and the problems of collaboration. The increased exposure to practices in other countries, plus the brokering role of the EU itself, could enable campaigners and policy-makers in the UK to make use of experiences in other countries.

EU institutions and the policy-making process

The key priorities of the European Union are to achieve a dynamic knowledge-based economy, trading successfully in the global market and underpinned by low levels of unemployment. The remit of EU social policy has therefore traditionally emphasised labour market issues such as equal pay, equal treatment, worker participation, support for migrant workers and their families, mobility of the workforce and health and safety matters (Kleinman, 2002). However, more recent years have seen a broadening to an overall concern about discrimination and social inclusion (Geyer, 2000). For example, the 1997 Treaty of Amsterdam stated in Article 13 that the

Council of Ministers 'may take appropriate action to combat discrimination based on sex, racial or ethnic origin, religion or belief, disability, age or sexual orientation'. However, under the terms of the Maastricht Treaty, this expansion has to be tested against the concept of subsidiarity:

> the Community shall act within the limits of the powers conferred on it by this Treaty and of the objectives assigned to it therein. In areas which do not fall within its exclusive competence, the Community shall take action, in accordance with the principle of subsidiarity, only if and in so far as the objectives of the proposed action cannot be sufficiently achieved by the Member States. (Maastricht Treaty, Article 3b)

The specific concern of this chapter is the extent to which resultant EU social policies have embraced a community care component which has impacted on policy and practices at member state level. However, before addressing this question, a brief description of the architecture of the EU and the process of policy-making sets the institutional scene. The latter is likely to be reformed in the first decade of the twenty-first century as the existing fifteen member states agreed in December 2002 to invite ten further countries to join the EU in 2004.

In one sentence, the EU policy process could traditionally be summarised as 'the Commission proposes; the Council of Ministers disposes'. More specifically, the European Commission, the executive arm of the EU, is the body that has the duty to initiate legislation. It is not a large bureaucracy, having at the end of the twentieth century about 17,000 staff in all (Nugent, 2001, p. 164). Following a reorganisation in 1999, it was divided into 23 Directorates-General (DGs). The DG for Employment and Social Affairs is the one most closely associated with social and community care.

Policy proposals are developed within, and sometimes between, the directorates of the Commission and, usually after much debate, are formally presented to the twenty Commissioners. Once a policy proposal is approved by the Commissioners, it is forwarded to the Council of Ministers, which is made up of ministers from member state governments. The actual composition of the Council depends on the subject under discussion. When a proposal arrives from the Commission, it is passed on to the Committee of the Permanent Representatives of the Member States (COREPER). This comprises civil servants from the governments of the member states and one of their key tasks is to make an initial close scrutiny of the proposal.

As well as forwarding proposals to the Council of Ministers, the Commission sends them to the European Parliament. In 2002, the Parliament comprised 626 members from all fifteen member states, 87 of them from the UK. At the outset, the European Parliament did not propose and pass legislation; rather, it debated the proposals and passed opinions. Since the first direct elections in 1979, the Parliament has enjoyed a substantial increase in its powers as well as continuing to be an important influence on the policy process. For many policy arenas, it has co-decision powers with the Council of Ministers and where there is unresolvable disagreement between the two institutions, it has a strong power of veto. One of the developments in the Parliament since direct elections is the establishment of intergroups. They number about 50 and comprise interested members from different political parties who examine particular issues in great detail, including ageing, disabled people and the family.

The opinions of the European Parliament are considered by both COREPER and the secretariat to the Council of Ministers and a common position is adopted either at official level or, in areas of major difficulty, by the appropriate Council of Ministers. On many proposals, the Parliament has a second opportunity to scrutinise the proposed legislation. Where differences remain between the Council and the Parliament a conciliation process is enacted in an attempt to reach agreement. Usually, a compromise is reached. For every proposed law, the Council of Ministers has to play a part in the final decision to adopt primary legislation. The outcome is published in the *Official Journal of the European Union*.

The legislation can take different forms. A regulation applies directly from the day it comes into force; a directive requires domestic legislation in member states if appropriate legislation does not already exist; decisions usually apply to specific problems rather than to the EU as a whole, and are binding on those to whom they are addressed. Where there is a view that legislation is inappropriate, a recommendation or an opinion may emerge. These have no legislative force, though they are not necessarily without influence (Nugent, 1999, p. 247). A wide range of legislative proposals can be adopted by a majority vote (known as qualified majority voting) with voting weighted according to the population of the member state. Other legislation requires unanimity.

The formal process of policy-making has been described, but the informal processes are just as important. First of all, the Commission officials do not just sit behind their desks in Brussels and think up new legislation. They are lobbied from every quarter, including other institutions of the EU, such as the Council of Ministers who can ask them to focus their minds on a particular issue, or the European Parliament which can issue its own views on subjects as well as influence or, as a last resort, block draft legislation. The Commission follows the progress of legislation through the system very closely and is in frequent contact with COREPER working groups.

Meanwhile, it is lobbied by a wide range of interests. Individual members of the European Parliament may press for meetings to be arranged with delegations from a particular region or a particular sector of industry or commerce. It has been calculated that there are in the order of 700 lobbying interests with offices in Brussels, whose main function is to pick up early intelligence about possible new proposals impinging on their or their clients' interests (Greenwood *et al.*, 1999). A substantial number of bodies representing regional and local interests have opened offices in Brussels to be able to hear about and influence the policy debate at very early stages, even before a directive is initially drafted within the Commission (Marks *et al.*, 2002).

As well as regional authorities and business interests, voluntary organisations have also developed a lobbying base in Brussels, some focusing on environmental or consumer issues and others on the 'social dimension' of the European Union. There is an umbrella body called the Platform of European Social NGOs (non-government organisations), which was set up, with support from the European Commission, in 1995. Members of the Platform include COFACE (Confederation of Family Organisations in the European Community), AGE (European Older People's Platform), the European Women's Lobby, the European Disability Forum and the European Anti-Poverty Network. They have been prominent in pressing for EU recognition of the massive social implications of its mainstream economic and trade policies, and for effective implementation in member states of relevant EU legislation.

Against this backcloth of the main institutions of the EU, the policy process and the way interest groups have organised to influence legislative outcomes, we can now turn to the impact of EU policies, practices and procedures on community care.

The impact of EU policies on community care

As already noted, much of social policy is seen as a domestic issue for individual member states of the European Union, as the legal base for intervention by the EU is very restricted. The Commission tends to limit its role, through a series of social action programmes, to the encouragement of convergence of different member state policies, information exchange, support for innovation, the designation of special years and good practice through networking and co-funding of cross-national projects.

However, the EU does recognise that strategies such as the completion of the internal market, the free movement of goods, services, capital and labour and other measures of economic integration do cause problems for particular regions or particular groups of people. Discriminatory effects are addressed, though perhaps not adequately, by special support for disadvantaged regions and by special measures to help groups such as disabled people, migrant workers and women to secure employment in the open labour market (Swithinbank, 1996).

It is, therefore, not surprising that there was no direct reference to social care services in the 1994 White Paper on European social policy (European Commission, 1994), the subsequent three-year social action programmes and associated initiatives. Nevertheless, the EU has over time had a modest impact in terms of a range of EU policies affecting older people, disabled people and the providers of community care (Geyer, 2000; Hantrais, 2000).

Older people

The 1957 Treaty of Rome, the Single European Act 1986 and the 1992 Maastricht Treaty made no mention of older people or disabled people, though in the 1970s there were concerns about older workers and about the poverty and marginalisation of elderly people. However, by the 1980s the European Parliament was paying some attention to the position of older (and disabled) people and had passed resolutions in 1982 and 1986 on improving the situation of older people and the provision of appropriate services and support for them.

The Social Charter, adopted by all member states except the UK at a summit meeting in Strasbourg in December 1989, referred to the rights of workers rather than citizens. From this perspective, it asserted that elderly people, at the time of retirement, should have sufficient resources to provide a decent standard of living, as well as medical and social assistance suited to their needs. Retirement pensions were thus seen as deferred income, so the quality of life for older people did become a concern of the European Union. Following a Commission proposal published in April 1990 and a Council of Ministers decision in November of the same year, a three-year EU social action programme for older people was launched at a conference in Brussels in September 1991, with the aim of encouraging the transfer between member states of knowledge, ideas and experience on ageing and elderly people. It included the creation in 1992 of an Observatory on Ageing and Older People, which was charged to focus on four areas: living standards and way of life; employment and the labour market; health and social care; and the social integration of older people in both formal and informal settings (Walker, 1993, p. 9).

The work of this Observatory and the results of two 1992 Eurobarometer Surveys have been usefully brought together by Walker and Maltby (1997). The main social care issues highlighted by the Observatory included:

- Consensus that care in the community rather than in institutions was the most appropriate policy for older people
- Overall severe undersupply of community care services
- Need for new incentives for the development of community care. (Walker and Maltby, 1997, p. 91)

Hantrais (2000) commented that most member states had developed community care policies but there were major differences in levels of provision:

Provision of care services in the Nordic countries was still recognized as a responsibility of the state ... the southern Mediterranean countries continued to place a clear legal obligation on relatives to care for older people. (p. 159)

However, these legal obligations themselves varied in scope:

In Italy, even in-laws and half siblings were obliged by law to provide support in proportion to income. The legal requirements in Portugal and Spain were such that family members could be taken to court or could lose their right to inheritance if they failed to comply. In Belgium ... France ... Austria, Germany, Greece and Luxembourg, adult children had a legal duty to maintain both their parents and their children. (Ibid.)

The 1991–3 social action programme culminated in the designation of 1993 as European Year of Older People and Solidarity between the Generations. The emphasis was on the contribution that older people make to the community, and the healthy and active life enjoyed by most older people, rather than focusing on the need of some for care and support.

In the same year, the European Commission (1993) published its Green Paper on future options for European social policy. As well as commenting on the financial challenges to the level of official welfare support that would be provided, it also noted the demographic pressures resulting from an increasing number of older people relying on the support of a shrinking number of economically active people. The ensuing White Paper (European Commission, 1994) further emphasised the importance of economic well-being for underpinning state support of welfare services. 'Levels of spending on social protection and social services will be affected by countries' costs of addressing the unemployment problem' (Munday, 1996, p. 27). The strategy for tackling unemployment has remained high on the European agenda and EU policies for older people have not progressed as much as their advocates hoped. However, the lobbying has continued.

In 1984, the European Parliament formed an Intergroup on Ageing, reconstituted as the Third and Fourth Age Intergroup after the June 1999 elections. From the outset, it was serviced by Eurolink Age, the transnational interest group on behalf of older people. At the beginning of 2001 Eurolink Age joined forces with the International Federation of Associations of Older Persons (Paris) and the European Platform of Seniors' Organisations (Brussels) to create AGE (European Older People's Platform) in order to speak with a single voice on EU policies impinging on older people. The aims of the new Platform were:

- To promote the interests of older people at EU level and raise the profile of older people's issues, taking forward the momentum developed through the UN International Year (1999)
- To improve and strengthen co-operation between older people's organisations, making more efficient use of scarce resources and building on existing links with the EU institutions
- To provide a resource centre for organisations across Europe
- To disseminate information on EU developments affecting older people and raise awareness of the ageing of society and its consequences. (*Eurolink Age Bulletin*, March 2000, p. 3)

The 1989–94 Parliament had pressed the Commission to put forward, through the social action programme that followed the acceptance (except by the UK) of the Social Charter, 'specific solutions at Community level' to challenges posed by an ageing population. Citing the Treaty of Rome provision to improve the living conditions of European Community citizens, the European Parliament called for a directive on the right to home care and better provision of home help and health care.

Some of the main concerns of the intergroup in the 1994–9 Parliament were issues faced by older women, the sustained blockage in the Council of Ministers (see below) of a new social action programme on older people, and the inclusion of age in the anti-discrimination clause in the Treaty of Amsterdam. The priorities of the renamed intergroup for the 1999–2004 Parliament included combating age discrimination through the Commission's non-discrimination proposals, implementation of the social inclusion articles of the Treaty of Amsterdam, social protection and following up the May 1999 Commission communication, *Towards a Europe for All Ages* (see below). Despite pressure from the Parliament and older people's organisations, age discrimination in the workplace was not made illegal providing it was seen to be objectively and reasonably justified under national law.

There was growing awareness in the last decade of the twentieth century that the community care implications of completing the single market could be far-reaching. Chapman (1989) argued that the removal of trade barriers in 1992 would create an internal market for social services as well as in industry and commerce. She pointed out that 'some home care organisations are looking at the potential of expanding their services across national boundaries' and 'sources of funding are expected to change as the market for home care opens up' (p. 19). Munday (1996) describes the creation of a Danish social care export/consultation agency called DANSOC: 'The agency existed to make Danish expertise and excellence in child care and services for disabled and elderly people available to interested organisations in other countries' (p. 35).

There are also possible community care implications of international retirement migration, particularly to the coastal areas of Portugal and Spain (for an overview, see Ackers and Dwyer, 2002, especially Chapter 5). Early commentaries focused on the problems and possible responses to anticipated difficulties. It was suggested that over the years elderly migrants from northern Europe would grow 'increasingly frail and dependent in a situation where there is little established structure for collaboration in the personal social services field' (Bongers, 1990, p. 58). What would be likely to happen?

> When, for example, older people from Northern Europe migrate to the south but then fall ill, will they be flown back to their countries of origin as soon as their personal resources run out, or their demands on personal and health services intensify, in a sort of new law of settlement? Or will Member States develop schemes for charging the country of origin for such care? (Room, 1991, p. 4)

Alternatively, might social services agencies combine to establish care services in these retirement areas, or offer consultancy services to the care authorities in these localities? The Director of Social Services for Kent County Council reported that his authority was examining the potential use of respite service for older people in Spain (Gilroy, 2001). The 1992 Eurobarometer Survey reported that a quarter of older people wanted information about services, benefits and facilities available in EU countries other than their own (Walker and Maltby, 1997, p. 119).

More recent studies have developed a less stereotypical view of international retirement migration. For example, Ackers and Dwyer (2002), whilst acknowledging the lack of reliable statistical data, did point out that the 'triggers and motivations' for migration were such that five distinct categories of migrants could be identified (p. 5):

1. Persons who move to another member state for work and then exercise their right to remain (retired community workers)
2. Those who move to another member state for work and then return home on retirement (returning community workers)
3. Persons who retire in the home state and then move (post-retirement migrants)
4. A subgroup of category 3 who move in order to accompany or join their Community migrant children claiming rights as ascendant, dependent relatives (joiners)
5. A subgroup of category 3 who subsequently return home (returning post-retirement migrants).

The 1993 European Year of Older People and Solidarity between the Generations covered an enormously wide range of activities and was reported as having been very successful, even though only one in ten adults surveyed in the UK in February 1994 said they had been aware of the Year (Department of Health, 1995f). A five-year follow-on programme with a budget of 25 million ecus was proposed by the Commission in March 1995. The scope was broadened to cover not only active elderly people but also those approaching retirement and the very old. However, this programme was never implemented as in 1996 the UK government challenged the legality of European Commission spending on these kinds of activities, building on the German government's successful challenge to the proposed fourth poverty action programme, arguing that these issues should, in accordance with the principle of subsidiarity, be dealt with at the national or subnational level (Wendon, 1999). This argument was formally upheld by the European Court of Justice in May 1998 and the UK government subsequently dropped its case on the 1996 budget line in favour of older people. However, 'the rising tide of gerontophobia' (George, 1996, p. 177), based on beliefs in lessening productivity and an increasing financial burden as a result of greater longevity, has yet to ebb. For some, the demographic timebomb has continued to tick.

In May 1999 the Commission published a document on older people's issues in the medium to long term, as a contribution to the UN International Year of Older Persons in 1999. It focused on combating discrimination (following ratification of the Treaty of Amsterdam), research to respond appropriately to health care needs, measures to reduce the level of early retirement and the promotion of lifelong learning and flexible working arrangements for older workers. It also advocated the creation of a European Older Persons' Platform, which resulted in the establishment of AGE at the beginning of 2001. In an attempt to get round the problems of funding developments at the EU level in favour of older people, the Commission's strategy concentrated on intergenerational equity and solidarity, encapsulated in the title of the document, *Towards a Europe for All Ages* (European Commission, 1999). Geyer (2000) argues that the Commission's interest in 'actions in favour of older people' would be sustained by attempting 'to integrate ... proposals ... into the strategies for combating social exclusion and discrimination' (p. 187) and concludes that 'for the foreseeable future EU elderly policy will continue to be a weak adjunct to more successful policy areas, rather than a coherent policy area on its own' (ibid.). He does, however, acknowledge that policies in favour of older people had become more visible than in the early years of the European Community and EU-level organisations representing the interests of elderly people had become more vocal and influential.

It has been in part due to this persistent pressure, and despite the block on developments following the 1993 year, that funds have been made available for a number of initiatives relating to older people. These include (i) support for the exchange of information and best practice in relation to people suffering from Alzheimer's disease and their carers (Tester, 1999b); (ii) underpinning of the transnational activities of charitable bodies and non-governmental organisations dealing with the interests of elderly people, such as the Older Women's Network and the Eldercare Network, as well as umbrella bodies like Eurolink Age and AGE; (iii) payment for comparative studies, such as the project on social protection arrangements for dependent elderly people above retirement age and in need of long-term care (Pacolet *et al.*, 1999); and (iv) ensuring that the Framework Programmes on Research and Development included projects relevant to the elderly population.

Disabled people

As with elderly people, there was no overarching disability policy in the early years of the European (Economic) Community. There was recognition in the 1960s that disabled people faced particular difficulties in the labour market (Geyer, 2000, p. 188) and the reform of the European Social Fund in the early 1970s included support for the 'rehabilitation' of disabled people.

The 1974 social action programme included reference to the employment and social needs of disabled people, but it was not until the early 1980s that the first action programme to promote the social integration of disabled people was adopted. This was a response to the 1981 International Year of Disabled People and ran from 1984 to 1988. A Bureau for Action in Favour of the Disabled was established in the Social Affairs Directorate-General of the Commission and the Disability Intergroup of the European Parliament was set up in 1980. One of the main features of the action programme was to create a network of local projects across the Community, funded 50 per cent from the European Social Fund. Geyer (2000, p. 189) describes the 1988–9 period as 'a watershed for EC disability policy'. It was included in the Social Charter and in the 1989 social action programme, as well as featuring in the 1988 reform of the structural funds.

A second action programme aimed at both vocational and social integration and independent living, called HELIOS (Handicapped People in the European Community Living Independently in an Open Society), ran from 1988 to 1992. In December 1993 a European Disabled People's Parliament was held to mark the first annual European Day of Disabled Persons. One of the resolutions was a call for a general anti-discrimination clause to be included in any amendment to the Treaty on European Union.

A third programme, called HELIOS II, ran between 1993 and 1996 and comprised four themes, which built on earlier programmes: social integration and independent living; functional rehabilitation and economic integration; vocational training and employment rehabilitation; and education integration. The modest funds were to support transnational conferences, visits and training. It also introduced the idea of a European Disability Forum to act as a pressure group on behalf of a large number of NGOs, and the unit in the European Commission responsible for disabled people changed its name from Measures for the Disabled to Integration of the Disabled (Hantrais, 2000, p. 144). The 1994 Social Policy White Paper reinforced the theme of integration and suggested that measures should be brought in to counter discrimination against disabled people in the labour market.

The European Disability Forum (EDF) first met in Dublin in November 1996 and one of its key priorities was to press for a clause on non-discrimination in the revised EU Treaty. By this time, the Commission was putting forward ideas for a rights-based approach to disability (European Commission, 1996), moving away from the 'traditional notions of social and economic compensation' (Geyer, 2000, p. 192). The strategy was endorsed by a Council resolution in December 1996. As with gender equality, the idea was to 'mainstream' issues of disability into all 'appropriate policy developments' (Hantrais, 2000, p. 145). The rights-based approach became a focus for the disability pressure groups, via the EDF, but their campaign did not result in separate treatment in the Treaty revision process. However, disability was integrated into the general non-discrimination clause (Article 13) of the Treaty of Amsterdam.

The 'Jobs Summit' held in Luxembourg in November 1997 introduced employment guidelines for national employment policies and they included targets to promote increased employment rates for disabled people (European Commission, 1997). On the research front, the 1998–2002 Fifth Framework Programme included a key action on the ageing population and disabilities and an action line 'research relating to people with disabilities'. One of the projects funded focused on the use of information technology to prevent disability through functional decline. The theme of information society technologies is one of the research areas proposed for the Sixth Framework Programme (2002–6), and in 2002 eEurope Action Plan includes a target that disabled people should benefit fully from new technologies and the internet.

The theme of 'mainstreaming' was central to the European Commission's May 2000 communication, *Towards a Barrier-Free Europe for People with Disabilities* (European Commission, 2000). The Social Policy Agenda required the Commission to monitor progress on achieving the targets outlined in its communication. One of the features of the communication was the proposal to declare 2003 the European Year of People with Disabilities. This was formally agreed by the Council of Social Affairs Ministers in December 2001. It has a budget of 12 million euros to support exchanges of information, experience and good practice and to stimulate debate on future initiatives to promote equal opportunities for and the rights of disabled people. More than 10,000 events are planned.

In 1990, building on the 1988 reform of the structural funds, the European Community formally agreed three new cross-national grant aid initiatives to improve education and training facilities and to provide new employment opportunities. One of these initiatives, called HORIZON, was aimed at people with physical or mental disabilities, those who work with them and other disadvantaged individuals. As well as focusing on employment issues, including long-term unemployed people or 'women returners' to the labour market becoming carers of older people in need of support, the programme covered the adaptation of public infrastructure to improve access and mobility. In 1994 the HORIZON programme was subsumed under a broad employment/human resources initiative and funds were allocated for the 1994–9 period to support two main kinds of activities: improving the quality of training and creating jobs through new types of work organisation for both disabled and disadvantaged people. In July 1996 the

European Commission published revised guidelines for Community Initiatives to cover the 1997–9 period. One of the proposals was to separate support for disadvantaged people from support for disabled people. The latter were still covered by the HORIZON initiative and the emphasis on training and job creation remained.

The further review of the structural funds at the end of the twentieth century led to a rationalisation in the number of Community initiatives. Four were eventually adopted for the 2000–6 period, one of which was EQUAL and addressed issues of inequality and discrimination in access to the labour market. It was formally launched in the UK in March 2001 with a budget from the European Social Fund of just under 400 million euros. The focus was on themes such as employability, entrepreneurship and adaptability rather than particular groups such as disabled people (though asylum seekers were specified). Thirteen Networking Groups were to be established to implement the main principles of EQUAL and would include in the UK representatives from the Disability Rights Commission.

Providing care in the community

The focus so far has been on groups in the population likely to be users of community care. EU policies also impinge on the providers of care, as the emphasis on the single market and labour market issues would lead one to expect. The completion of the single market, embodying the principle of freedom of movement of people and services, provides opportunities for businesses, voluntary bodies and self-employed individuals from mainland Europe to establish services in the social care field, including community care. It also offers opportunities for statutory, voluntary and private sector community care providers to export their expertise to continental Europe:

> Organisations which have been established by local authorities at arm's length, such as housing trusts, training agencies or occupational therapy and other bureaux, may wish to expand into the European market. (Swithinbank, 1996, p. 76)

On the labour market side, UK doctors and nurses have since 1977 and 1979, respectively, been able to work in any member state of the EU, provided they have the appropriate language skills and are prepared to undertake some locally based training. This has not led to major cross-boundary migrations, but attempts by the UK government to address the problems of the pressures on the National Health Service by importing surgical teams from mainland Europe or exporting patients to other EU countries if they would otherwise have to wait for a long time for their operations is a clear recognition of the existence of a single professional labour market (Munday, 2002, p. 39).

Legislation on the mutual recognition of professional qualifications came into force in January 1991. Rather than looking at each individual profession, a long and laborious process, the position was adopted that a qualification based on three or more years' study at higher education level (whatever that means) in one member state has to be recognised in all member states. This has not been without its problems, since expectations of relevant language skills and training in local procedures remain. It has been reported that small but significant numbers of social workers have moved from France, Germany and the Netherlands to work in the UK (Hill, 1991).

Major cross-boundary moves are not anticipated in the future, but there is an oversupply of social workers in some member states such as Germany (Hansen, 2002, p. 24), and private, voluntary or statutory sector providers of community care in the UK could decide to mount a recruitment campaign, if they were severely understaffed and had the resources to recruit. Recruiters would need to develop some understanding of the training and professional qualifications in social care, social work and social assistance in other member states of the European Union. Likewise, welfare rights advisers need to recognise that people who move between EU countries carry their entitlements with them based on their contributions to the country of origin's social security system.

Over the years the European Union has been concerned to develop an equal opportunities programme, with the primary aim of countering discrimination in the labour market. This has had significant implications for community care providers. For example, the NOW strand of the 1994–9 EMPLOYMENT Community Initiative (New Opportunities for Women) was intended to encourage women to enter or re-enter the formal labour market in which all projects had to have transnational partners. Swithinbank (1996, p. 84) noted that social services had used the NOW programme to retrain traditional care workers or heads of residential homes to become care managers or managers of new business-style enterprises. EQUAL, the successor to the EMPLOYMENT Community Initiative, provides a general remit to counter all forms of labour market discrimination.

The core of the EQUAL initiative is the establishment of Development Partnerships between key players in a geographical area or sector and a link with at least one other partnership in another member state. One of these partnerships is headed up by Carers UK. The overall objective is to work with relevant agencies to enable carers across all disadvantaged groups to overcome the many barriers to formal employment that they face. The focus in the UK is on 2,000 carers in seven pilot areas. The transnational partner is in Vorarlberg, Austria where the project focuses on women entering or re-entering the labour market.

Many of the proposals in the EU 1995–7 social action programme were uncontroversial, particularly in the field of health and safety at work. However, some of the proposals on working hours or those that affected part-time or temporary workers were resisted by the Conservative government in the UK. The UK Labour government's acceptance of the Social Chapter in 1997 had implications for the delivery of community care:

> As social care work requires people to provide round-the-clock cover, social services agencies will have to ensure adequate rest periods and limited hours. This applies especially to residential care staff, after-hours and emergency staff cover and attendance at evening meetings. Any junior staff or pregnant women will be unable to provide night care or be on call. Social services departments in Britain will need to ensure that contracted private and voluntary residential homes abide by these requirements. (Swithinbank, 1996, p. 74)

One of the features of the Social Chapter was to bring opportunities for non-casual part-time workers into line with those of full-time workers. This agreement on part-time work came into effect in Britain in 1999. At the time there were about half a million people who worked part-time in social services departments and nearly 300,000 in the independent social care sector. Most of those affected were women. However, the part-time workers directive did not apply to the large numbers of agency staff used by local authorities or in the independent sector (Thompson, 1997).

The 1977 acquired rights directive had major implications for the transfer of staff from one employer to another, for instance from a local authority to a company responsible for the provision of community care. This directive overrules any domestic legislation with which it is in conflict. There was some uncertainty whether the directive and Britain's Transfer of Undertakings (Protection of Employment) Regulations 1981 (TUPE) applied, for instance, to compulsory competitive tendering, which, it was argued, tended to cut the terms and conditions of local authority workers. In February 1997, the European Commission issued a revised proposal to amend the 1977 directive in which it was made clear that the proposed directive would apply to both private and public undertakings. The new directive was formally adopted in June 1998 and the intention to amend UK legislation was reaffirmed in the White Paper, *Fairness at Work* (Department of Trade and Industry, 1998). New regulations are expected in 2003.

One of the consequences of focusing on the labour market implications of EU policies for community care is that not a little ambiguity has emerged about the role of caring, which is sometimes remunerated but often is not when provided by friends or volunteers and particularly relatives. At one level, the availability of unpaid carers has reduced because of higher rates of involvement by women in the paid labour market, greater mobility and smaller families. This reduction in carer availability can be juxtaposed with the overall ageing of the EU population and an anticipated increase in the demand for care from people in their eighties and beyond, a demand likely to be addressed in the main by women workers (Hantrais, 2000, pp. 158–9). At another level, beyond the labour market, there is a debate about recognition in the EU of unpaid work, such as caring. 'What is lacking is a concept of citizenship which recognizes the importance of care to society' (Leira, 1992, quoted in Ackers and Dwyer, 2002, p. 27). Where women (and sometimes men) leave the formal labour market to support families (elderly dependants as well as children), it can be argued that earnings are forgone and pension entitlements lost:

> In failing to recognise or acknowledge the genuine and significant economic contributions made by informal carers in terms of savings to welfare systems and also the economic burden to the carers themselves in forgoing paid work, the insistence on the exercise of paid work as the trigger to citizenship entitlement disadvantages carers. (Ackers and Dwyer, 2002, p. 42)

Not engaging in paid work also penalises carers in their own later life as they have not been able to contribute to become eligible for the provision of benefits or services that may be needed in the future.

The European Union's employment strategy has recognised the caring responsibilities of those in the labour force and argues for 'family-friendly policies' in member states' employment policies, such as providing affordable, accessible and good-quality care services for both children and other dependants. However, whilst one of the measures of progress in this respect is the provision of childcare, there is as yet no measure or indicator about care for older dependants.

Community care in member states of the European Union

One of the central characteristics of EU social care policy is the exchange of information on good practice in individual member states. The second part of this chapter examines community care policies in three countries, Denmark, Germany and Greece, representing different kinds of welfare regimes from that of the UK. In recent years, governments throughout the European Union have had to address the consequences for their community care policies of demographic pressures, high levels of unemployment, changes in the labour market, shifting social expectations and family make-up, deep recession and public expenditure pressures (Taylor-Gooby, 1996, pp. 204–5). Whilst the pressures on social care policies have not recognised national boundaries, the responses of individual EU states have varied, reflecting differences in welfare traditions and regimes.

There are several contested typologies of European welfare states (see Abrahamson, 1999b; Arts and Gelissen, 2002 for overviews). The categorisation used in this chapter is that acknowledged by Abrahamson (1999a), which broadly reflects the four models of social care outlined by Anttonen and Sipilä (1996) with the four types of welfare state each reflecting a particular kind of welfare regime. The *rudimentary welfare state* (or Catholic social policy) is associated with Latin Rim countries, such as Spain and Portugal. This tradition emphasises philanthropic solutions to welfare provision by traditional institutions such as the church, family and private charity, with limited public welfare institutions and policies developing alongside. 'Greece is an example *par excellence* of the southern welfare model … and is characterized by fragmentation, dualism and ineffectiveness in income maintenance, near universalism in national health care (but with extended scope for private provision), a particularistic–clientelistic welfare state and a peculiar mix between public and non-public actors and institutions' (Symeonidou, 1997b, p. 68).

The *residual welfare state* (or liberal social policy) has been associated in recent years with the UK. As outlined earlier in this book, this is characterised by rolling back the boundaries of the welfare state and by public services being contracted out to the independent sector. The state is a safety net and a regulator rather than a primary provider. The *institutional welfare state* (or corporatist social policy in the Bismarckian tradition) has been linked in particular to Germany. This tradition puts emphasis on labour market solutions to social issues, such as unemployment, sickness or old age. Those outside the labour market are likely to be dependent on local charity. The *modern welfare state* (or social democratic policy) is associated with Scandinavian countries. This is characterised by wide provision of good-quality publicly provided services, with the private and voluntary sectors becoming increasingly involved in the welfare mix.

These four broad categories may in themselves not be robust enough to withstand the societal and economic pressures impinging on EU countries in the early years of the twenty-first century, but they provide a vehicle for examining the core elements of community care in different European countries. The residual model is not, however, considered below, as it is the focus of most of this book. Instead, Greece, Germany and Denmark provide examples of the other three models, although some material has also been drawn from Italy, Spain and Sweden.

The mixed economy of welfare

In the debate about the mixed economy of welfare, Evers and Olk (1991, p. 77) stress the need to distinguish between 'welfare mix' and 'welfare pluralism'. Welfare mix refers only to the proportion of investment provided by the state and the not-for-profit, private and informal sectors. In this respect, all welfare states have a welfare mix, although the proportions vary between them and over time (Baldock *et al.*, 1999). Fargion (2001), for instance, describes how the plans of left-wing regions in Italy to create a local version of the Scandinavian 'modern welfare state' model were undermined by a combination of increasing demand and limited resources, which forced them to endorse a welfare mix rather than a state monopoly.

Welfare pluralism addresses the issue of the preferred mix in the mixed economy of welfare, although it is now recognised that, in all welfare regimes, the informal sector has played the dominant, albeit often invisible, role (Tester, 1996, p. 8). In the rudimentary welfare states, the case is being made for increased state support in response to the changes in society affecting the capability of family and local community to provide the level of care taken for granted in the past.

This trend can be observed in Greece, where the informal sector, especially the family (see below) has dominated, and other forms of support, such as meals services or residential care, have been provided by volunteer organisations such as the Orthodox Church or the Red Cross as well as by some municipalities (Giarchi, 1996, p. 408; Triantafillou and Mestheneos, 2001, pp. 78–9). In the last decade of the twentieth century, policies for the public provision of domiciliary services such as home help were introduced, but there were still major problems of implementation (Petmesidou, 1996; Symeonidou, 1997a). In 1998, a European Social Fund-supported three-year 'help at home' pilot programme was launched in 97 municipalities, staffed by teams of nurse, social worker and home help, plus 1,200 volunteers. The broad aim of this initiative was to provide home support for older people who needed some measure of care, who lived alone and/or had inadequate resources to sustain or improve their quality of life. By early

2002, the scheme had been extended so that approximately 400 programmes were in operation, serving about 9,000 people in all, with funding
via local authorities. Evaluators recommended that, as a low-cost service,
this programme should be extended for a further five years and expanded to
include all 1,100 municipalities in Greece through integration into local
social services or through community day centres (Amira *et al.*, 2002).
They also identified some key issues, including the need for more staff, better support for staff, the lack of transport, particularly in more remote areas,
clear funding sources, improved training for volunteers and those responsible for recruiting and managing them, and a common administrative system
for recording the level and type of services provided and the characteristics
of service users.

In the modern welfare state, the argument for some time has been for
increasing the role of the non-statutory sector. For Denmark, Abrahamson
(1991) has argued for what he calls new concepts in social policy, which for
disabled and elderly people would mean 'they should have the opportunity –
to a much greater degree than beforehand – to purchase services on the
market (privatization), to be serviced by a neighbourhood activity center
(decentralization); and to be encouraged to obtain help from voluntary and
self-help institutions (de-professionalization)' (p. 49). Responding to financial pressures, public authorities in Denmark have sought ways of increasing efficiency, including the use of voluntary bodies (or rather volunteers) in
service provision and the contracting out of services such as home help to
the private sector. So the question is raised whether the public solution is
under threat as a result of increasing welfare mix (Pedersen, 1998).

In the corporatist social policy context, the notion of the mixed economy
of welfare has been central to the ideology of the institutional welfare state,
embedded as it is in the principle of subsidiarity in which non-state institutions play a constitutionally independent role, even where there is extensive
support from the public sector. However, the traditional role of the voluntary
sector has been challenged, for instance, in Germany, by both new-style, that
is, radical, non-profit-making, and private sector initiatives, including the
development of profit-oriented home nursing and of family-type care for
frail older people who had no families of their own. In 1994, the
Dependency Insurance Act was passed to underpin long-term care for vulnerable older people and, following amendment to the legislation in 1996,
to others requiring care as a result of disability or physical/mental illness
(Schneider, 1999, pp. 43, 48). The new social insurance measure provided
for direct financial support and a range of benefits 'designed mainly to
promote community care by voluntary organisations and private agencies'
(Lawson, 1996, p. 43). Reflecting the idea of 'compulsory voluntarism',

about 15 per cent of the staff working in care institutions and 10 per cent in the home care sector were doing the job as an alternative to compulsory military service (Evers and Sachsse, 2003, p. 59).

The overall trend has been for increasing emphasis on the non-state sector, with the possible exception of rudimentary welfare states. This has in turn increased the visibility of the informal sector, not least family members and their availability to provide care. The role of the family in caring is examined in the next section.

The role of the family in caring

The family has remained the main supporter of those needing care across the European Union. National attitudes, behaviour and policy towards caring for adults were examined in a sixteen-country cross-national study on family obligations undertaken in 1994 covering the then twelve member states of the European Union and the four applicant countries of Austria, Finland, Norway and Sweden. Millar and Warman (1996) distinguished between those countries where there were legal obligations on the family to provide care (for example, Germany and Greece) and those where there were no such obligations (for example, Denmark). They also categorised the sixteen countries into those where service provision was locally organised (such as Germany); those where it was locally organised under national regulation (Denmark); and those where it was nationally organised (Greece). Systems of care payments were divided into those made to care givers (Denmark), those made to care receivers (Germany and Greece) and those made to both (the United Kingdom). The adequacy of payments was, however, another matter. In other words, the picture was one of great variety. The role of the family in caring covered a wide spectrum ranging from systems 'where the family provides virtually all the support to situations where family care is an optional extra to state services' (p. 43) and there was no trend towards a common pattern of provision. Work undertaken towards the end of the 1990s suggested no major changes in family care-giving for older people in nine EU countries and Poland (Philp, 2001).

The family continues to hold a central position in rudimentary welfare states. 'Although the urbanisation and modernisation of Greek society in the 1970s and 1980s has influenced the already changing social structure of the Greek family, the family continues to play a central role' (Marinakou, 1998, p. 244). Triantafillou and Mestheneos (2001) pointed out that discussion on the need for public policy to support carers had started towards the end of the 1980s but 'very little priority has been given to this issue and as yet [referring to 1998] support for family carers has not been incorporated on a systematic basis into public policy' (p. 77). Symeonidou (1997a) made the point that in Greece women are the basic prop of the family and have internalised their role as carers. This role transmutes into 'compulsory altruism' which can have a 'negative impact on the carer's physical and/or mental health, especially in more severe cases (such as mental handicap)' (pp. 355, 356).

The family has also been expected to play a central role in the institutional welfare state, particularly for those outside the labour market, creating a major responsibility for and strain on relatives, where they exist. In Germany until the mid-1990s the provision of income support could be made only after a comprehensive examination of the circumstances of family members, following the principle of subsidiarity. One of the consequences of this was that many adult children in Germany struggled to mobilise the resources necessary to carry out caring tasks. Support for carers was a central focus of the reforms of the mid-1990s (see below), providing they were spending at least fourteen hours a week on home care. 'Giving benefits is meant to strengthen the already existing family care potential ... However, the insurance scheme gives also the option to widen the range of possible "care persons" away from family relatives to neighbours and other informal care persons willing to perform care on a regular basis' (Kondratowitz *et al.*, 2002, p. 7). Evers and Sachsse (2003, p. 73) comment that the new scheme encouraged to some extent 'traditional and female dominated forms of caring'.

The modern welfare state has also been under pressure, but here the thrust is to involve the voluntary and private sectors more, rather than require the family to take on the caring role. The argument in Denmark is that the family is not in a position to provide care. Munday (1996) drew on the 1992 Danish report to the European Commission Observatory on Social Exclusion to point out that the institution of the family had weakened substantially in the last thirty years, so care functions were taken over by the state. Research Volume 1 of the Royal Commission on Long Term Care (Sutherland Report, 1999b) noted that in Denmark the proportion of women in paid employment rose from 49 per cent in 1965 to 78 per cent in 1988–9 (p. 159). However, children do care about their older relatives; this takes the form of advocacy and pressure on the professionals. The main burden of informal care in Denmark falls upon spouses or partners, leading Jamieson (1991) to argue over a decade ago that 'perhaps these are the ones who pay the highest price for a welfare system which is geared towards state provided professional solutions to health and social problems' (p. 120).

Salvage (1995) examined future prospects for the family care of older people in the EU over the twenty-year period to 2015. She concluded that governments needed to make urgent plans based on the recognition of the current overdependence on informal care. Four options were put forward (pp. 68–76):

1. Reducing demand for care by improving older people's health and independence
2. Stimulating supply by making it easier for families to support older relatives
3. Developing new ways of providing support, including surrogate families and intergenerational housing schemes
4. Improving the image and experience of residential care.

The European Commission's study of social protection for dependency in old age (Pacolet *et al.*, 1999) argued that the distinction between formal and informal care might be of less relevance in the future 'since informal carers will receive training and become more professional in their work and to some degree even be paid for their work' (p. 28). Daly (2002) concluded that there was an 'increasing willingness of welfare states to pay for private/ family care – a good which was formerly generated free in the family' (p. 268). This has to be encouraging news for those who are both carers and work in the formal labour market. The first annual report on the social situation in the EU published by Eurostat (2000) stated that 5 per cent of men and 9 per cent of women who held down a job of at least 30 hours a week also put in up to four hours per day in caring for a dependent adult.

Cost pressures and the role of institutional care

In a number of European countries with different welfare state traditions, the policy trend since the mid-1970s has been away from institutional provision, particularly for elderly people. The prime reason for this policy shift has been the cost to the public purse, supported by what were seen as inappropriate admissions of people who could live in (cheaper) non-institutional settings. Another factor has been the preferences of disabled and older people themselves. These preferences were shared by the vast majority of the general public in the European Community who thought that older people should be helped to stay in their own homes. This consensus extended across virtually the whole of the age group and was shared by both sexes (Eurobarometer Survey, 1993, p. 29). By the end of the twentieth century Ackers and Dwyer (2002) were able to report, using the results of a six-country study of Greece, Italy, Portugal, the UK, Ireland and Sweden, that there was 'some evidence of convergence in relation to state-provided institutional care (with a general retrenchment)' (p. 78). This retrenchment has been brought about in part by pressures to reduce social expenditure. Fiscal measures were required to ensure compliance with the convergence criteria in relation to monetary union (p. 105).

Italy, for example, has engaged in a policy debate about the need to run down large institutions for frail elderly people (Fargion, 2001). Towards the end of the 1990s, under 3 per cent of those aged 65 or over were in long-term residential care and, rather than providing residential or community services directly, Italian local and regional authorities began to provide a care allowance to frail elderly people on low income or their carers. This allowance could be used to buy low-cost care in the informal economy (Gori, 1999, quoted in Ackers and Dwyer, 2002, p. 81). More broadly, state funding to support the development of community-based social care by local authorities was cut back in the later years of the twentieth century, leading to a shift to provision by non-statutory suppliers (Fargion, 2001, pp. 197–8).

It is not reasonable to class Italy as a rudimentary welfare state (partly because of the enormous regional variation) but Greece is not untypical of such a regime in having only a small minority of elderly people living in residential homes. Ackers and Dwyer (2002) point out that less than 1 per cent of people aged 65 or over were in institutional care (mainly provided by non-profit organisations) compared with the EU average of 8–11 per cent (p. 79). Stathopoulos (1996) adds that in Greece a further 7 per cent are dependent and 25 per cent are housebound (p. 150). As outlined in the previous section, care for elderly people in Greece is mainly a family affair. There is concern that changes in Greek society may reduce the availability of family carers, because of fewer children in the family, greater participation of women in the formal labour market, greater geographic mobility of younger people and increasing divorce rates. Even so, a family which places an elderly person in a home is seen as having failed in its duty (Symeonidou, 1997a, p. 356) and, just as in Italy, some families cope by employing cheap, often immigrant, labour to provide care in the family home (Triantafillou and Mestheneos, 2001, pp. 93–4). In addition, legislation passed in 1994 to decentralise the administration of personal social services in Greece, whilst excellent in principle, was undermined in terms of implementation because of the need to reduce public expenditure (Stathopoulos, 1996, p. 151). Some private sector for-profit homes have been established, mainly in and near Athens, to respond to demand from more affluent frail elderly people (or their families) and day centres have been developed on the initiative of the state. The aim was 'the prevention of organic, psychological and social problems in older people, so that they remain active, equal and participating members of their communities' (Amira *et al.*, 1986). The first opened in 1979 and by early 2002 there were over 350 such centres (Triantafillou, 2002).

In institutional welfare states such as Germany, the policy trend in the 1980s was fuelled by the need to cut costs (Kondratowitz *et al.*, 2002, p. 6), and involved increased day care and domiciliary services at the expense of residential provision. In 1984 the social assistance law gave community services priority over care in institutions (Tester, 1996, p. 18). Residential care for elderly people had in the main been provided by the non-statutory sector and in 1999 served about 5 per cent of the older population of whom 16 per cent were in public institutions (Evers and Sachsse, 2003, pp. 59, 60). This was because the principle of subsidiarity applied not only to the responsibilities of families for their needy members but also to the relationship between statutory and voluntary bodies. Conditional priority had to be given to a small number of leading voluntary non-profit organisations which wished to provide such social help. They were described as forming a 'virtual cartel' in local welfare markets (Schunk, 1998, p. 30).

The financial responsibility of the family to support an elderly relative often meant that the parent moved in with the children rather than entering residential care. However, as in Greece and elsewhere, there was concern that the capability of the family to provide care was lessening because of changes in society and the increasing numbers of older people (Lawson, 1996, p. 40).

Problems also existed in the health care system. In the 1980s, about 30 per cent of all beds in acute hospitals had been occupied by elderly patients with an average length of stay as high as forty days. The extent of hospital care was related to a shortage of domiciliary and day care services. It was officially estimated that some 20–30 per cent of hospital patients over the age of 65 were long-term patients who could be better supported through day clinics, rehabilitation centres or residential/nursing homes. The problem was made more acute by the then social insurance system in Germany which drew a distinction between sickness (covered by insurance) and general frailty (perceived as a personal risk). Alber (1991) explained that this meant that 'prolongation of the stay in acute hospitals is the only way to prevent older patients from having to foot the bill for delivery into nursing homes which they can rarely afford' (p. 25).

Despite the expenditure cutbacks associated with unification in 1990, a major new element in the German care insurance scheme was introduced in the mid-1990s. Home care benefits were payable from April 1995 and institutional care benefits from July 1996. This policy development has had an impact on the major social welfare organisations. After many years of privilege, the leading not-for-profit providers of residential and domiciliary care found themselves under pressure 'to improve efficiency to survive in competition with commercial providers in the social services market developing under the new Care Insurance' (Leisering, 2001, p. 169). Individuals in need of long-term domiciliary care were entitled to choose between payments for care and services in kind bought on their behalf by the insurance funds. The monetary value of the hours of help was greater than the alternative cash payment in order to discourage misuse of funds (Baldock and Ely, 1996, p. 211). By 1999, about two million people were receiving benefits from the scheme, just under 1.5 million in private households and just over half a million in care institutions. Over half were over 80 (Kondratowitz *et al.*, 2002, p. 4) and two-thirds were women (Evers and Sachsse, 2003, p. 59).

The interim judgement is that a good new scheme was introduced which had a number of deficiencies, including lack of advocacy and counselling for potential users, an excluding assessment system and a lack of co-ordination between service deliverers as well as between different sources of funding (Kondratowitz *et al.*, 2002, pp. 13, 18).

It is of interest to note that Denmark, as a modern welfare state with an emphasis on universality, has traditionally had a comparatively high rate of institutional care for older people (Walker, 1992). The principle of universality covers both health and social care in Denmark and is based on citizenship rather than insurance rights. The services are both financed and provided by the public sector (counties and municipalities), leaving the voluntary sector to provide advocacy and act as pressure groups. The home help service was merged in the mid-1990s with domiciliary health care to overcome the conflicts between health and social care staff (Walker and Maltby, 1997, p. 94). Denmark has continued to provide a high level of free home care provision 'with over 20% of those aged 67+ receiving some service [and] from July 1996, there was a legal requirement on local authorities to offer consultations to all those aged 80+ in their homes'. This was extended in July 1998 to those aged 75 or over (Sutherland Report, 1999b, p. 180).

Earlier, in the 1960s, both domiciliary and residential care services for older people had been expanded, and there was no intention to replace institutional care. Rather, the range of services was to relieve families of the caring role and attempt to improve the quality of life for older people. However, in the 1980s there was a growing critique of institutional care, which resulted in major legislative reform in 1987. Deinstitutionalisation was based on an expectation of economic savings as well as philosophies of enhancing self-realisation, increased choice and autonomy (Pedersen, 1998, p. 83). In brief, the principle underpinning the legislation was that the care available to people should not be linked to the kind of accommodation they were living in. The 1980s legislation stopped the building of nursing homes and provided for the building of special dwellings for older people who would be supported, where necessary, by a 24-hour home care service, which focused more on personal domestic help (see Giarchi, 1996).

The point of the reform was that every older person, whatever kind of care he or she needed, had the right to independent housing and care according to his or her needs. The impact of these legal changes was affected by professional resistance, local politics and the economic disruption caused by the recession (Abrahamson, 1991, p. 56). However, in general, care policies have proved popular and have been well-resourced. Denmark does have a practice of fining local authorities if they are slow in providing appropriate accommodation and services for elderly people ready for discharge from hospital (Pedersen, 1998, p. 96). The level of investment in local services means that this is not seen as an unreasonable burden.

Cost containment and collaboration

Problems of collaboration and co-operation between health services and community social services have been a central theme in accounts of home care almost everywhere (Baldock and Ely, 1996, p. 198). In her review of community care developments for older people in France, Germany, Italy, the Netherlands, the United Kingdom and the United States, Tester (1996) concluded that, whilst the need for better co-ordination was widely recognised, implementation was equally widely inhibited:

> Despite the policy initiatives and processes implemented to promote co-ordination, there is little evidence that co-ordinated community care has been achieved. Reports of poor co-ordination, gaps and overlaps in services and lack of information in the countries studied continued to appear in the early 1990s. (p. 170)

Difficulties were compounded by the ambiguous notion of community care as a broadly based social care concept, but one which can refer to where the care is provided, who is providing it and/or who is paying for it (Hill, 1996; see also Chapter 1). Such ambiguity in both the UK and other European states encourages boundary disputes between health and social care organisations (see Chapter 5).

Collaboration difficulties appeared to be less acute in Denmark, where all home care services were the responsibility of the local authority and where the modern welfare state principle of universality implies comprehensive provision based on citizenship rather than insurance rights. Co-ordination was assisted by the development of multidisciplinary teams, decentralisation of service responsibility to small areas based on a health centre, working across care settings, common training programmes and the conversion of nursing homes into health centres (Pedersen, 1998, pp. 92–3). However there were still problems over co-ordination between hospitals and community-based health and social care, including the familiar concerns about cost shunting and bed blocking, in part caused by the demise of the nursing homes (Pedersen, 1998, p. 95). In addition, the moves towards privatisation of the home help service and the contracting out of nursing were thought to be likely to undermine co-ordination of services and the expectation that the same person would be providing support for an individual changing care settings (Pedersen, 1998, p. 99).

The principle of subsidiarity in the context of corporatist social policy and the institutional welfare state required partnership between the statutory and the non-statutory sectors, but the diversity of local supply, intended to offer choice of services to the individual, does not easily promote collaborative endeavour. In Germany, there have been close links between the state and the non-statutory welfare agencies over matters such as finance and the law but the fragmentation of responsibility for service delivery made effective co-operation to support particular individuals problematic. For example, Tester identified serious obstacles to co-ordinated community care 'in the strong divisions in organisation and funding between hospital and ambulatory services, health and social care' (1996, p. 179). The 1994 social insurance scheme has not successfully tackled inadequate co-ordination. It contained no incentives for health and care professionals to collaborate or plan services together (Schunk, 1998, pp. 40, 45). 'Co-ordination of local care services and counselling of care clients have not taken clear shape yet' (Schneider, 1999, p. 70).

In the rudimentary welfare states one of the key concerns has been the co-ordination of the public and private sectors in providing personal social services. In Spain, the role of the public sector increased after the end of the Franco regime but economic difficulties have since led to demands for reductions in public expenditure plus a more flexible, less bureaucratic management style. The outcome in the late 1980s was a very uneven distribution of supply with traditionally provided services not being linked to more recent developments, particularly for specific groups of people (Rossell and Rimbau, 1989, pp. 118–19). In Italy, financial difficulties led local authorities to turn to non-statutory bodies, including new types of not for-profit organisations, such as co-operatives. The outcome was an intricate web of public–private arrangements (Fargion, 2001, p. 197). In Greece, the traditional fragmentation of services is being patchily addressed in the inevitable context of scarce resources (Triantafillou, 2002).

One of the responses to the lack of collaboration because of the variety of providers and funding arrangements has been the attempt to introduce case (or care) management. The UK experience is addressed elsewhere in this book (see Chapter 3) but it is worth noting that one of the main conclusions of a comparative study of innovations in care in the Netherlands, Sweden and England and Wales in the late 1980s was the need to invest in the management of care:

> This problem of management exists at two levels: the level of the individual client and the level of the care system as a whole ... It is no accident that case management at the level of the individual client is more developed in the United Kingdom. It is a solution ... typical of systems where resources are in chronically short supply. (Baldock and Evers, 1991, pp. 193, 196)

It was this pressure to make effective use of scarce resources in an ideological context of consumer choice that made the idea of case management as developed in the United States attractive to the British government struggling to pursue a coherent policy and practice on community care. However, as a result of increasing pressures on public expenditure from the late 1980s, countries like the Netherlands and France were also beginning to undertake case management experiments or at least to debate the means of integrating social care services. Baldock and Ely (1996) concluded that the provision of social care was in practice inherently complex and called it the 'paradox of complex mundaneity' (pp. 202–3), or, less grandly, the complexity of everyday life. In particular, the unpredictability of need at the individual level distinguished people with mental health problems and frail elderly people on the one hand from people with learning difficulties and physically disabled people on the other.

Concluding comments

The impact of EU policies on community care developments in the UK has been in the main indirect and, where direct, modest. What is unambiguous is the increased investment by the European Union in social policy issues in recent years. There is major concern for the social integration of people seen to be in need of support. The implications of moves towards the completion of the internal market have highlighted the social responses needed to address likely problems of dislocation. The debate on political union has brought into focus the position of residents, not only of workers, in the European Union. External migratory pressures demand a social policy as well as a border control response. The increasing role of women in the formal labour market has added considerably to the force of the argument that the European Union is much more than a common market. The Treaty of Amsterdam included age (though with an escape clause) in its anti-discrimination article. The year 2003 is the European Year of People with Disabilities.

This internationalisation of the policy debate may not lead to a high proportion of social (as opposed to economic) legislation being of EU origin, but it will enable campaigners and policy-makers in the UK to become more aware and make use of illuminating policies, practices and procedures in community care in other countries. The second half of this chapter has shown a high degree of diversity in approach to community care in countries with different welfare traditions. The opportunity to benefit from this rich variety is encouraged by the EU institutions, but the context in which interesting developments are located is as important for full understanding of their potential transferability as the policies and practices themselves.

9 Community Care: New Directions and Old Challenges

Much of this book has been about the modernisation agenda for public policy of Labour governments since 1997 and how this has impacted upon the ongoing implementation of the 1993 community care reforms. This final chapter draws the key threads together to reflect upon achievements and failures so far as well as likely future directions.

Modernisation muddles?

Chapters 4 to 7 all explored the implications of the modernisation of the welfare state for community care policy and practice. In doing this, the sheer complexity and range of policy changes and reforms have become apparent.

The emphasis that the government places upon partnership as part of the modernisation process has also been stressed, especially in Chapter 5 which considered joint working between health and social services (see also Glendinning *et al.*, 2002b). An important reason for this is that partnership is seen as one of the mechanisms for achieving joined-up government, which has been called both 'the new mantra' (Heywood *et al.*, 2002, p. 142) and 'New Labour's big idea' (Clark, 2002, p. 107). In terms of health and social care, the argument for the importance of this has been presented in a clear and decisive way:

> people want and deserve the best public services ... It is the responsibility of government, local government and the NHS to ensure that those justifiable expectations are met. People care about the quality of the services they get – not how they are delivered or who delivers them. We all need to ensure that service quality does not suffer because of artificial rigidities within and between service deliverers. (DoH/DETR, 1999)

It is, therefore, quite clear that the government would expect that its influence upon community care should include a much more coherent and flexible approach in which a range of agencies work together in the interests of service users and carers.

However, Chapter 5 outlined how theories of joint working indicate the difficulty in achieving this in practice. In addition, Clark (2002) has pointed out the tension in New Labour approaches between emphasising community orientation and participation as the key to joined-up working at the local level and a desire to impose joined-up working and hence improve performance through centralised indicators which require very specific forms of partnership to be demonstrated.

Indeed, the clear suggestion in Chapters 4, 5 and 6 is that there has been little by way of incremental progress in joined-up working let alone a modernisation revolution in joined-up government. Instead, the impression is of modernisation muddles, in which managers and field-level staff are struggling to keep pace with the demand for policy change and the ever increasing flood of directives, guidelines and indicators.

Why is this happening despite such good intentions which are being backed up by increased resources going into the welfare state? To understand this it is necessary to draw on the well-established literature on policy implementation which stresses how often there appears to be a major gap between the stated objectives of legislative change and what continues to happen on the ground across all policy areas. The seminal book on implementation deficit was a study of a job creation scheme in Oakland, California by Pressman and Wildavsky (1973). The authors argued that such schemes could only be successful if numerous organisations linked up to create a successful implementation chain. Relatively small failures of co-operation between different organisations can easily multiply to create a major implementation deficit, which is what occurred in the Oakland scheme.

Two main approaches to theorising implementation deficit subsequently emerged, namely the top-down perspective and the bottom-up perspective (Hill and Hupe, 2002). The top-down approach tends to offer advice to policy-makers on how to minimise the discretion of actors further along the implementation chain so as to ensure that implementation is consistent with policy objectives. The bottom-up approach emphasises that implementation is the inevitable product of negotiation and compromise between the formal policy-makers and those with the task of working out how to turn policy into practice. As Barrett and Hill (1984, p. 222) argue:

- Many policies represent compromises between conflicting values
- Many policies involve compromises with key interests *within* the implementation structure
- Many policies involve compromises with key interests upon whom implementation will have an impact

- Many policies are framed without attention being given to the way in which underlying forces (particularly economic ones) will undermine them.

Such tensions mean that some decisions on goals and objectives are left to what is normally seen as the implementation stage. Top-down theorists tend to see this as regrettable and undesirable. Bottom-up theorists see this as inevitable and some would perceive it as desirable on the grounds that field-level implementers are in the best position to assess the local situation and set appropriate objectives.

Modernisation muddles are not difficult to understand from this perspective. Major policy change is especially likely to create a large implementation gap (or deficit) because of the complexity of implementation. A government that embarks upon a wide range of interlinking reforms is especially likely to suffer from this problem. Such reforms would not only provoke resistance from vested interests (see Chapter 5) but would also generate a mass of unintended consequences, as the full implications of change would not have been worked through. Attempts by any government to enforce change through 'a top-down approach' are likely merely to further exacerbate problems of this type (see Chapter 4).

The extent of this problem has been well summarised by Appleby and Coote (2002) in terms of health policy. They talk of 'relentless, almost hyperactive intervention' in which:

a formidable torrent of pledges, policy documents, laws, regulations, advice and guidance has been issued by the Department of Health without let-up since 1997, to knock the system into shape: ironing out disparities, raising standards, improving productivity, increasing responsiveness, extending services, meeting unmet need. (p. 5)

Even where the policies have been sound, Appleby and Coote (2002) argue that 'implementation has been of poor quality or uncomfortably slow' (p. 7).

If this is true of health, this book suggests that it is equally true of community care. Writing in 1996, Hadley and Clough spoke of 'care in chaos' which still feels an unfair assessment given the community care achievements of social services within what has often been very inadequate resourcing (see Chapter 3). However, the extent of policy change across health and social services risks pushing community care towards such a situation.

The key question is whether such modernisation muddles are only a temporary phenomenon that will have little salience by the time of the next general election. Will the implementation gap be much narrower at this critical point? In this respect much will depend upon the success of the government's policies on primary care trusts. Community care can no longer be delivered in a coherent way without the central input of these still fledgling organisations which are struggling to cope with all the expectations that are being heaped upon them (see Chapter 5). This issue is, of course, closely linked to whether or not social services will retain the lead agency role in community care or whether this is to become yet another key role for primary care.

Before turning to this issue, it is necessary to warn against becoming too obsessed with the modernisation issue in assessing contemporary community care and practice. If it remains in something of a muddle, much of the blame for this has deep historical roots (see Chapter 2). How to organise and fund long-term care has a much longer history than the Sutherland Report (1999a). The prioritisation of acute health care over primary care is equally long established as is the low priority accorded to community-based health and welfare services for all the main community care groups. Above all, how to distinguish health care from welfare has a long and tortuous history. Modernisation policies may be part of the present community care muddle but this muddle can be traced right back to the Poor Law.

The end of the road for social services?

The logic underpinning the first two editions of *Community Care: Policy and Practice* was the reluctant acceptance by a Conservative government of the main recommendation of the Griffiths Report (1988) that social services should be the lead agency for all the main community care groups. Both editions had a chapter entitled 'Leaders at Last: The Changing Role of Social Services'.

However, there has to be real doubt as to whether this lead agency role remains intact, not just in mental health (see Chapter 5) but for all the other groups as well. One indication of this has been the gradual downgrading of the importance of social services producing their annual community care plan followed by the decision to completely end this requirement. Yet community care plans had initially been seen as a pivotal component of the 'new' community care through which social services would set out their strategy for developing the mixed economy of social care (Hoyes *et al.*, 1994; Lewis and Glennerster, 1996).

The rationale for abolishing community care plans is the plethora of other plans which have to be produced such as health improvement plans (Department of Health, 1998c) but it should be noted how these tend to be led by health with social services input rather than the other way round.

Chapter 5 explored in detail whether the growth of primary care trusts and care trusts signalled the end of the lead agency role for social services and possibly even the incorporation of their community care functions into health.

One of the strongest indicators that this might indeed happen came through the publication of *Shifting the Balance of Power within the NHS: Securing Delivery* (Department of Health, 2001h) as a follow-up to the NHS Plan (Department of Health, 2000e). Although not its intended implication, the shift of balance seems to be very much away from social services and towards health.

This document confirmed primary care trusts as leading 'the NHS contribution to joint work with local government and other partners' (p. 5) and stressed how:

> PCTs working with local authorities should maximise the potential benefits to patients and clients by the integration of health and social care ... Where local partners agree, care trusts will be important vehicles for modernising both social and health care, helping to ensure that integrated services are focused on the needs of patients and users. (p. 39)

As significant for the lead agency role of social services in community care was the announcement in the same document of 'four new Regional Directors of Health and *Social Care*' (our italics) whose responsibilities were to include:

- Overseeing the agreements on health and social care-related targets
- Ensuring integration of planning for the whole system of health and social care
- Ensuring the outcomes from and the arrangements for performance management of the NHS and the performance assessment of social services are properly integrated
- Ensuring that health and social care joint interests are properly represented and integrated into the work of the government offices
- Securing the implementation of Health Act flexibilities and supporting the development of care trusts. (p. 20)

What is significant is not just the content of change but also the terminology. The tendency is to talk of local authorities rather than social services authorities and of social care (never fully defined) rather than community care. The lead agency role of social services in community care is very much under threat.

An end to ideology debate?

The first two sections of this final chapter have focused on policy changes and yet many would claim that the scope for change has become prescribed within very narrow limits because of the end of ideological debate about welfare. Both Labour and Conservative governments are united in their acceptance of the mixed economy of social care, their belief in the greater efficiency of the private sector and their assumption that the general public is reluctant to accept higher general taxation as the best route to fund service improvements.

The globalisation debate has tended to strengthen such perceptions from the belief that global capital and transnational corporations have placed considerable restrictions upon individual nation states (see Chapter 7). However, there is growing recognition of how misleading this can be both at the level of overall welfare provision (Sykes *et al.*, 2001; Yeates, 2001) and in terms of variations in approaches to community care taken by different European countries (see Chapter 8).

This suggests that the new managerialism discussed in Chapter 7 does not mean an end to politics, despite the fact that most commentators accept that there has been some narrowing of options available especially to left-of-centre governments (Powell and Hewitt, 2002). The options and choices are still considerable, as would soon become apparent if the next general election were to see the return of a Conservative government which had campaigned successfully on the basis of the modernisation muddles of Labour. An emphasis on insurance-based schemes for funding health and long-term care might well be pushed to the forefront. The present emphasis on partnerships and planning between the statutory, voluntary and private sectors (Glendinning *et al.*, 2002b) would be dramatically reduced and replaced by an emphasis on individual choice from free markets. Such a Conservative government would create its own implementation deficits and obstacles to radical change but the end product would be a community care system very different from the one presently in operation. Ideological debate over future directions in community care is not at an end.

New directions? New possibilities?

The last point is crucial since to accept the end of ideological debate is to deny ourselves the opportunity to argue for the feasibility of new directions and new possibilities. But what might these be? One of the challenges is to encourage community care policy and practice to focus on quality of life issues. The emphasis on intermediate care or rehabilitation is admirable (Department of Health, 2002f) but the question still has to be asked: what are we rehabilitating people for?

The answer from older people is unequivocal. They wish to maximise their sense of autonomy and independence whether they live in mainstream housing, sheltered housing or residential care (see Chapter 6). Qureshi and Henwood (2000) reviewed research in this area to argue that this in turn requires services which mesh with other life choices as well as being flexible in terms of delivery, and care staff who treat older people with respect. One of the major arguments for direct payment schemes in community care is, of course, that they enable the client to retain autonomy and independence (Glasby and Littlechild, 2002).

Older people want a wider range of services and support than just those concerned with the management of their illness or impairment (Ellis, 2001). This means that they often wish to prioritise very practical preventative services which will maintain their independence in the home (Heywood *et al.*, 2002) or their social inclusion and participation outside the home (Clark *et al.*, 1998; Raynes *et al.*, 2001).

The failure to address fully such quality of life concerns is an issue for all the main community care groups and not just for older people. Thus, Murray (2002a; 2002b) researched how young disabled teenagers, and especially those with learning difficulties, tended to be excluded from 'normal' everyday leisure facilities. Leisure was usually organised through the family when the teenagers wanted to be with other young people, doing things that young people do – discos, karaoke evenings and eating out being hot favourites (2002a, p. 42).

There is also enormous potential to empower a wide range of people with support needs through participation in the arts. Drawing upon a wide range of arts projects, Matarasso (1997) has felt able to argue that:

> participation in the arts does bring benefits to individuals and communities. On a personal level these touch people's confidence, creative and transferable skills and human growth, as well as their social lives through friendships, involvement in the community and enjoyment. (p. 79)

One group with whom art and music therapies are used increasingly are people with dementia because of their capacity to support communication from people with cognitive impairments (Allan, 2001).

From a similar perspective, others have pointed to the importance of using existing practical skills to make a contribution to the community. Thus, Barnes (1997) has described a neighbourhood-based ecological project which 'promotes the development of small-scale, local activities which can enable people experiencing emotional distress ... to take on work which not only contributes to their own personal empowerment but also to the achievement of ecological objectives' (p. 157). Such projects draw upon the capacity of communities to support local disabled people and people with mental health problems.

Barr *et al.* (2001) have drawn upon a three-year action research project in Scotland to argue for a community development approach to community care in which people with support needs become genuinely part of their caring communities. Such a philosophy fits well with the neighbourhood renewal policies of the government, although Chapter 6 indicates that it is these very groups who tend to get excluded from the renewal process. This will change only if health and social services give much greater priority to the prevention agenda and the role that neighbourhood renewal can play in all of this.

Front-line staff matter

The last section stressed that ideological debate is very much alive and others will see very different possibilities to those outlined so far. One possibility is the likely emergence of not just national but international providers of health and social care (Player and Pollock, 2001; Holden, 2003). The former cottage industry of family-run residential and nursing homes has turned into a sector dominated by a small number of national players, some of which are likely to develop international aspirations.

Holden (2003) predicts 'an increasing concentration of provision in long term care, and a deepening of internationalisation as existing large firms utilise their advantages' (p. 122). However, the reason for raising this possibility is not a desire to return to the globalisation debate but rather to stress the importance of front-line staff. Governments come and go. Service provision may move from the statutory to the voluntary or the private sectors. Assessment responsibilities may move between health and social services. However, the experience of community care services by most people is defined by the quality of their contact with professional and non-professional care staff. For service users this close link between the processes and outcomes of care services exists at every stage of service planning and delivery. Thus an assessment that takes full account of the views of the service user is more likely to result in appropriate and acceptable service provision than one that does not (Richards, 2000). Process issues remain central after services are in place, as demonstrated by users of domiciliary care services whose judgements about service quality reflect the nature of the relationship with care staff and the way in which care is delivered (Henwood *et al.*, 1998).

Positive contact with service users, the belief that they are 'making a difference', has traditionally been an important source of job satisfaction for social care professionals. However, as outlined in Chapter 7, many practitioners are critical of the increase in administrative tasks and fear that the reduction in the time available for service users has had a direct impact on the quality of their interventions. The concerns of practitioners have been echoed in an inquiry by the King's Fund which found evidence of a continuing crisis of morale and a lack of appropriate training and support amongst social care staff (Henwood, 2001).

It is clear that the New Labour governments have made considerable efforts to improve the social care workforce through important initiatives such as the establishment of the General Social Care Council and the introduction of registration and of codes of conduct for social care workers (see Chapter 4). What is less certain is the long-term impact of these measures on the continuing crisis of recruitment and retention, which is widely linked to low pay, to high stress levels in the workplace and to the perception among social care workers that their skills and commitment are not valued. Worryingly, there is a widespread view that morale has deteriorated further with the increase in monitoring and regulation that has occurred throughout the public services since New Labour came to power (Jones, 2001).

Chapter 7 showed how social care practitioners are also under pressure from another quarter, from the disability rights and other user movements. However, here at least there is a potential for fruitful alliances around strategies for user empowerment and the social model. An emphasis on user empowerment would involve a radical reframing of the practitioner role, to move away from the bureaucratic processing of service users and towards the development of skills for facilitating change with service users and their communities. Similarly, incorporating the social model into social 'care', more properly 'support', would focus attention on the way in which service users and both formal and informal care-givers are disadvantaged by negative attitudes towards impairment and illness and by a social organisation which continues to exclude people with illness or impairments from full social participation.

Conclusion

There can now be little doubt about the determination of New Labour to radically reform public services including the organisation and provision of community care. Surveying the community care landscape at this point in time we can be confident that key elements of the reforms of the early 1990s, described in earlier chapters, will continue as prominent features. These include the split between commissioning and purchasing and the provision of care and the existence of care markets that are dominated by private and voluntary sector bodies. However, social services departments in their present form are likely to disappear. The integration of health and social care into Care Trusts spells the end not only of their role as the lead agency for community care but of the generic social services established after the Seebohm reforms of 1971. In October 2002, as the authors were completing this book, a speech to the National Social Services Conference by the Secretary of State for Health confirmed this view. He spoke of breaking up 'the old style, public service monoliths' that 'cannot meet modern challenges' and announced the creation of children's Care Trusts which, like Care Trusts, would ensure greater specialisation and the integration of services through partnerships (Milburn, 2002). The speech also signalled government thinking about a radical transformation of the workforce, with a call for the development of new types of social care professional, 'people who can work in the community, combining the skills of the therapist and the home help to provide rehabilitation alongside home care'. Nevertheless, although the shape of the new services is becoming clearer, considerable uncertainty remains about the implementation and outcome of such massive change. New Labour's programme of modernisation seeks to achieve quality services that put the interests of the service user first. Whether this can be achieved by the top-down implementation of the current plethora of reforms and initiatives is likely to form the subject of any future edition of this book.

Guide to Further Reading

Chapter 1   Introducing Community Care

Readers seeking an introduction to the key debates in community care will find
the recent contributions edited by Bytheway *et al.* (2002) and Hudson (2000) are
excellent starting points. The academic journal *Health and Social Care in the
Community* and the professional journal *Community Care* are also important sources
of information.

Chapter 2   From Institutions to Care in the Community:
The History of Neglect

Some readers may wish to learn more about the general development of the British
welfare state and Glennerster (2002), Lowe (1999) and Gladstone (1999) all provide
clear introductions. More detailed service histories can be found in Means and
Smith (1998b), Scull (1993) and Bartlett and Wright (1999). The two classic texts on
political learning perspectives are those by Phillipson (1982) and Oliver (1990).
Psycho-social issues are well-addressed by Marks (1999) and cultural assumptions
by Gilleard and Higgs (2000). Orme (2001b) provides a clear discussion of gender
and community care issues.

Chapter 3   Implementing the Community Care Reforms

The challenges of implementing the reforms are summarised in *Community Care:
Managing the Cascade of Change* (Audit Commission, 1992) and in the policy guidance *Care Management and Assessment: Managers' Guide* (Department of
Health/Social Services Inspectorate, 1991b). For insightful accounts of how local
authorities approached the task of implementation, see Lewis and Glennerster (1996)
and Wistow *et al.* (1996). Hadley and Clough (1996) draw on interviews with managers and practitioners to provide a view of the reform process as experienced by
insiders. For an assessment of the changes, see Bauld *et al.* (2000), a longitudinal
study of the care arrangements for older people in the wake of the reforms, and the evidence of contributors to *Community Care and Informal Care*, Research Volume 3 of
the report of the Royal Commission on Long Term Care (Sutherland Report, 1999c).

Chapter 4   Community Care and the Modernisation Agenda

The context for New Labour's modernisation programme is the restructuring of
welfare provision under the Conservative governments of 1979–97. Clarke and

Newman (1997) provide an interesting account of the rise of managerialism in an increasingly fragmented public sector, whilst Power (1997) examines the 'audit explosion' that has accompanied the growing demand for accountability. The modernisation agenda for social services is set out in the White Paper *Modernising Social Services* (Department of Health, 1998a) and developed in subsequent publications from the Department of Health. Mitchell (2000) provides an invaluable insider account of the rationale and strategy for change. The weekly journal *Community Care* is an excellent source of information about new policy initiatives and a guide to what is happening on the ground. In the rapidly changing world of social and health care the Department of Health website (www.doh.gov.uk) is an invaluable resource.

Chapter 5   Health and Social Care: From Collaboration to Incorporation?

Key government modernisation policies towards health and social care are clearly laid out in the NHS Plan (Department of Health, 2000d). The nature of the challenge of joint working and collaborative working is well-specified by Hudson (1987) while Sullivan and Skelcher (2002) and Glendinning *et al.* (2002b) provide more recent reviews of the issues. Means and Smith (1998b) and Means *et al.* (2002) provide important histories of the shifting boundary between health and social care which was also a central concern of the Royal Commission on Long Term Care (Sutherland Report, 1999a). Glendinning *et al.* (2002b), among others, have started to explore the implications of primary care trusts and care trusts for the future role of social services in community care.

Chapter 6   Housing and Community Care

A useful overview of housing policy is provided by Balchin and Rhoden (2002) while Leather (2000) supplies a profile of housing conditions. Heywood *et al.* (2002) offer a useful introduction to issues around the meaning of home while Higgins (1989) remains a main source for discussion of home versus institution. Key research and policy documents which stress the importance of the housing dimension of community care include the Audit Commission (1998), Cameron *et al.* (2001) and the Royal Commission on Long Term Care (Sutherland Report, 1999a). Heywood (2001) has more specifically looked at the importance of home adaptation while Means *et al.* (1997) provide useful guidance on how to make housing a more integrated element of community care.

Chapter 7   Community Care: Critical Perspectives

Oliver (1996) and Campbell and Oliver (1996) provide excellent introductions to the development of the disability movement and its demand for adequate income, personal assistance and independent living based upon the rights of disabled people to be full citizens of society. Marks (1999) presents a thoughtful analysis of current debates in disability studies and a case for theoretical elaboration of the social model of disability. Ahmad and Atkin (1996) look at issues of race and community care, whilst *Breaking the Circles of Fear*, by the Sainsbury Centre for Mental Health (2002), explores the problems faced by black mental health service users and the ways in which these may be addressed. Orme (2001b) provides a comprehensive analysis of gender and community care. The question of convergence between welfare states is discussed in Powell and Hewitt (2002) and the impact of globalisation on welfare policy in Yeates (2001).

Chapter 8   European Perspectives on Community Care

Useful publications on European welfare traditions and regimes include Esping-Andersen (1990), Abrahamson (1999a) and Arts and Gelissen (2002). For a more specific focus on social care, see Alber (1995), Anttonen and Sipilä (1996) and Tester (1999a). Recent comparative social policy texts include Clasen (1999), Bonoli *et al.* (2000), Kennett (2001), Alcock and Craig (2001) and Kleinman (2002). Commentaries on family policies and policies for older and disabled people are covered in Geyer (2000) and Hantrais (2000). The institutions of the European Union and the process of policy-making in the EU are described in many publications for students of public administration and government. Among the more readable are Nugent (1999), Wallace and Wallace (2000), Bromley (2001), George and Bache (2001), Nicoll and Salmon (2001), Richardson (2001) and Peterson and Shackleton (2002). A longer paper on the theme of this chapter can be found at http://www.bristol.ac.uk/Depts/SPS/information/working_papers.shtml

Chapter 9   Community Care: New Directions and Old Challenges

For an assessment of the state of social services five years after New Labour came to power see *Tracking the Changes in Social Services in England*, the sixth annual report of the Joint Review Team (Social Services Inspectorate and Audit Commission, 2002). For a vision of the future organisation and direction of social care from the influential Institute for Public Policy Research see Kendall and Harker (2002). The greater involvement of service users in every aspect of social care is an important theme in the current changes. Allan (2001) provides an example of how to involve one of the most disadvantaged groups in the development of services.

References

Abberley, P. (1991) 'The significance of the OPCS disability surveys', pp. 156–76 in M. Oliver (ed.), *Social Work, Disabled People and Disabling Environments* (London: Jessica Kingsley).

Abbott, P. and Sapsford, R. (1987) *Community Care for Mentally Handicapped Children* (Milton Keynes: Open University Press).

Abrahamson, P. (1991) 'Welfare for the elderly in Denmark: from institutionalisation to self-reliance', pp. 35–61 in A. Evers and I. Svetlik (eds), *New Welfare Mixes in Care for the Elderly, Vol. 2, Austria, Denmark, Finland, Israel, Netherlands* (Vienna: European Centre for Social Welfare Policy and Research).

Abrahamson, P. (1999a) 'The welfare modelling business', *Social Policy and Administration*, vol. 33, no. 4, pp. 394–415.

Abrahamson, P. (1999b) 'The Scandinavian model of welfare', pp. 31–60 in D. Bouget and B. Palier (eds), *Comparing Social Welfare Systems in Nordic Europe and France, vol. 4, France–Nordic Europe* (Paris: MIRE).

Abrams, P. (1977) 'Community care: some research problems and priorities', *Policy and Politics*, vol. 6, no. 2, pp. 125–51.

Ackers, L. and Dwyer, P. (2002) *Senior Citizenship? Retirement Migration and Welfare in the European Union* (Bristol: The Policy Press).

Ahmad, W. and Atkin, K. (eds) (1996) *'Race' and Community Care* (Buckingham: Open University Press).

Ahmad, W. and Walker, R. (1997) 'Asian older people: housing, health and access to services', *Ageing and Society*, vol. 17, no. 2, pp. 141–65.

Alber, J. (1991) *The Impact of Public Policies on Older People in the Federal Republic of Germany*, Konstanz, Spring (submission to the EC Observatory on Older People).

Alber, J. (1995) 'A framework for the comparative study of social services', *Journal of European Social Policy*, vol. 5, no. 2, pp. 131–49.

Alcock, P. and Craig, G. (eds) (2001) *International Social Policy* (Basingstoke: Palgrave Macmillan).

Allan, K. (2001) *Communication and Consultation: Exploring Ways for Staff to Involve People with Dementia in Developing Services* (Bristol: The Policy Press).

Amira, A., Georgiadou, E. and Teperoglou, A. (1986) *The Institution of Open Care for Older People in Greece – Research on the KAPI Centres* (Athens: National Centre for Social Research [EKKE]) (in Greek).

Amira, A., Stounara, A. and Manara, C. (2002) *'Help at Home' Pilot Programme: Implementation Report* (Athens: Central Union of Municipalities and Communities [KEDKE]) (report summarised in English by J. Triantafillou).

Andrews, G.J. and Phillips, D.R. (2000) 'Private residential care for older persons: local impacts of care in the community reforms in England and Wales', *Social Policy and Administration*, vol. 34, no. 2, pp. 206–22.

Anttonen, A. and Sipilä, J. (1996) 'European social care services: is it possible to identify models?', *Journal of European Social Policy*, vol. 6, no. 2, pp. 87–100.

Appleby, J. and Coote, A. (2002) *Five-Year Health Check: A Review of Government Health Policy, 1997–2002* (London: King's Fund).

Arber, S. and Ginn, J. (1991) *Gender and Later Life: A Sociological Analysis of Resources and Constraints* (London: Sage).

Arber, S. and Ginn, J. (1995) *Connecting Gender and Ageing: A Sociological Approach* (Buckingham: Open University Press).

Arblaster, L., Conway, J., Foreman, A. and Hawtin, M. (1996) *Asking the Impossible? Inter-Agency Working to Address Housing, Health and Social Care Needs of People in Ordinary Housing* (Bristol: The Policy Press).

Arts, W. and Gelissen, J. (2002) 'Three worlds of welfare capitalism or more? A state-of-the-art report', *Journal of European Social Policy*, vol. 12, no. 2, pp. 137–58.

Askham, J., Henshaw, L. and Tarpey, M. (1995) *Social and Health Services for Elderly People from Black and Minority Ethnic Communities* (London: HMSO).

Askham, J., Nelson, H., Tinker, A. and Hancock, B. (1999) *To Have and to Hold: The Bond between Older People and the Homes They Own* (York: York Publishing Services).

Atkin, K. (1996) 'An opportunity for change: voluntary sector provision in a mixed economy of care', pp. 144–60 in W. Ahmad and K. Atkin (eds), *'Race' and Community Care* (Buckingham: Open University Press).

Atkinson, D. (1988) 'Residential care for children and adults with mental handicap', pp. 125–56 in I. Sinclair (ed.), *Residential Care: The Research Reviewed* (London: HMSO).

Audit Commission (1985) *Managing Social Services for the Elderly More Effectively* (London: HMSO).

Audit Commission (1986) *Making a Reality of Community Care* (London: HMSO).

Audit Commission (1992) *Community Care: Managing the Cascade of Change* (London: HMSO).

Audit Commission (1994) *Finding a Place: A Review of Mental Health Services for Adults* (London: HMSO).

Audit Commission (1996) *Balancing the Care Equation: Progress with Community Care* (London: HMSO).

Audit Commission (1997) *The Coming of Age: Improving Care Services for Older People* (London: HMSO).

Audit Commission (1998) *Home Alone: The Role of Housing in Community Care* (London: Audit Commission).

Audit Commission (2000a) *Briefing: Seeing is Believing: How the Audit Commission Will Carry Out Best Value Inspections in England* (London: Audit Commission).

Audit Commission (2000b) *Forget Me Not: Mental Health Services for Older People* (London: Audit Commission).

Audit Commission (2001) *Changing Gear: Best Value Annual Statement 2001* (London: Audit Commission).

Aves, G. (1964) 'The relationship between home and other forms of care', pp. 11–17 in K. Slack (ed.), *Some Aspects of Residential Care of the Elderly* (London: National Council of Social Service).

Bailey, R. and Brake, M. (1975) *Radical Social Work* (London: Edward Arnold).

Balchin, P. and Rhoden, M. (2002) *Housing Policy: An Introduction* (London: Routledge).

Baldock, J. and Ely, P. (1996) 'Social care for elderly people in Europe: the central problem of home care', pp. 195–225 in B. Munday and P. Ely (eds), *Social Care in Europe* (Hemel Hempstead: Prentice-Hall).

Baldock, J. and Evers, A. (1991) 'Concluding remarks on the significance of the innovations reviewed – their implications for social change', pp. 186–202 in R.J. Kraan, J. Baldock, B. Davies, A. Evers, L. Johansson, M. Knapen, M. Thorslund and C. Tunissen (eds), *Care of the Elderly: Significant Innovations in Three European Countries* (Boulder, Colo.: Westview Press).

Baldock, J., Manning, N., Miller, S. and Vickerstaff, S. (eds) (1999) *Social Policy* (Oxford: Oxford University Press).

Banks, P. (2002) *Partnerships Under Pressure* (London: King's Fund).

Barnes, C. (1996) 'Theories of disability and the origins of the oppression of disabled people in western society', pp. 43–60 in L. Barton (ed.), *Disability and Society: Emerging Issues and Insights* (Harlow: Longman).

Barnes, C. (2002) 'Introduction: disability, policy and politics', *Policy and Politics*, vol. 30, no. 3, pp. 311–18.

Barnes, M. (1997) *Care, Communities and Citizens* (London: Longman).

Baron, S. and Haldane, J. (eds) (1992) *Community, Normality and Difference: Meeting Social Needs* (Aberdeen: Aberdeen University Press).

Barr, A., Stenhouse, C. and Henderson, P. (2001) *Caring Communities: A Challenge for Social Inclusion* (York: York Publishing Services).

Barrett, S. and Hill, M. (1984) 'Policy bargaining and structure in implementation theory: towards an integrated perspective', *Policy and Politics*, vol. 12, no. 3, pp. 219–40.

Bartlett, P. and Wright, D. (eds) (1999) *Outside the Walls of the Asylum: The History of Care in the Community, 1750–2000* (London: The Athlone Press).

Bauld, L., Chesterman, J., Davies, B., Judge, K. and Mangalore, R. (2000) *Caring for Older People: An Assessment of Community Care in the 1990s* (Aldershot: Ashgate).

Baxter, C., Poonia, K., Ward, L. and Nadirshaw, Z. (1990) *Double Discrimination: Issues and Services for People with Learning Difficulties from Black and Ethnic Minority Communities* (London: King's Fund Centre/Commission for Racial Equality).

Bebbington, P., Feeney, S., Flannigan, C., Glover, G., Lewis, S. and Wing, J. (1994) 'Inner London collaborative audit of admissions in two health districts. II: Ethnicity and the use of the Mental Health Act', *British Journal of Psychiatry*, vol. 165, pp. 743–9.

Beresford, P., Harrison, C. and Wilson, A. (2002) 'Mental health service users and disability: implications for future strategies', *Policy and Politics*, vol. 30, no. 3, pp. 387–96.

Beveridge Report (1942) *Social Insurance and Allied Services* (London: HMSO).

Bhui, K. (ed.) (2002) *Racism and Mental Health* (London: Jessica Kingsley).

Biggs, S., Phillipson, C. and Kingston, P. (1993) *Old Age Abuse* (Buckingham: Open University Press).

Bines, W. (1994) *The Health of Single Homeless People*, Discussion Paper No. 9 (York: Centre for Housing Policy, University of York).

Bongers, P. (1990) *Local Government and 1992* (Harlow: Longman).

Bonoli, G., George, V. and Taylor-Gooby, P. (2000) *European Welfare Futures: Towards a Theory of Retrenchment* (Cambridge: Polity Press).

Bosanquet, N. (1978) *A Future for Old Age* (London: Temple Smith).

Bovell, V., Lewis, J. and Wookey, F. (1997) 'The implications for social services departments of the information task in the social care market', *Health and Social Care in the Community*, vol. 5, no. 2, pp. 94–105.

Bowl, R. (1986) 'Social work with old people', pp. 128–45 in C. Phillipson and A. Walker (eds), *Ageing and Social Policy* (Aldershot: Gower).

Boyne, G. (2000) 'External regulation and Best Value in local government', *Public Money and Management*, July–September, pp. 7–12.

Bradley, G. and Manthorpe, J. (eds) (2000) *Working on the Fault Line* (Birmingham: Venture Press).

Brenton, M. (2001) 'Older people's co-housing communities', pp. 169–88 in S. Peace and C. Holland (eds), *Inclusive Housing in an Ageing Society* (Bristol: The Policy Press).

Brenton, M., Heywood, F. and Lloyd, L. (2002) *Housing and Older People: Changing the Viewpoint, Changing the Results* (London: London and Quadrant Housing Trust).

Brewerton, J. and Darton, D. (eds) (1997) *Designing Lifetime Homes* (York: Joseph Rowntree Foundation).

British Medical Association (1992) *Priorities for Community Care* (London: British Medical Association).

Brodie, J. (2001) 'The politician's challenge in health and social care', *Managing Community Care*, vol. 9, no. 5, pp. 3–7.

Bromley, S. (ed.) (2001) *Governing the European Union* (London: Sage).

Brown, D. (2002a) 'New care standards body to be axed in favour of merged inspectorate', *Community Care*, 25 April–1 May, p. 16.

Brown, D. (2002b) 'Campaigners fear one equality body will put disability issues on hold', *Community Care*, 23–29 May, pp. 20–1.

Brown, R. (1979) *Reorganising the National Health Service* (Oxford: Blackwell).

Burgner Report (1996) *The Regulation and Inspection of Social Services* (London: Department of Health).

Bytheway, B., Bacigalupo, V., Burnet, J., Johnson, J. and Spurr, S. (eds) (2002) *Understanding Care, Welfare and Community* (London: Routledge).

Cabinet Office (1999) *Modernising Government* (London: The Stationery Office).

Cambridge, P. (1992) 'Case management in community services: organisational responses', *British Journal of Social Work*, vol. 22, no. 5, pp. 495–517.

Cambridge, P., Hayes, L. and Knapp, M. with Gould, E. and Fenyo, A. (1994) *Care in the Community: Five Years On* (Canterbury: Personal Social Services Research Unit, University of Kent).

Cameron, A., Harrison, L., Burton, P. and Marsh, A. (2001) *Crossing the Housing and Care Divide* (Bristol: The Policy Press).

Campbell, J. and Hasler, F. (2001) 'Real joined-up thinking – a systematic approach to the barriers of disablement', *Critical Social Policy*, vol. 21, no. 4, pp. 531–3.

Campbell, J. and Oliver, M. (1996) *Disability Politics: Understanding our Past, Changing our Future* (London: Routledge).

Care and Repair (2001) *Making the Links – Developing Services Which Address the Housing, Health and Care Needs for Older People* (Nottingham: Care and Repair).

Carlton, N., Heywood, F., Izuhara, M., Pannell, J., Fear, T. and Means, R. (2003) *The Harassment and Abuse of Older People in the Private Rented Sector* (Bristol: The Policy Press).

230   *References*

Challis, D. (1993) 'Care management: observations from a programme of research', *PSSRU Bulletin 9* (Canterbury: University of Kent).

Challis, D. (1999) 'Assessment and care management: developments since the community care reforms', pp. 69–90 in Part One of *Community Care and Informal Care*, Research Volume 3, The Royal Commission on Long Term Care (London: The Stationery Office).

Challis, D., Chessum, R., Chesterman, J., Luckett, R. and Wood, R. (1988) 'Community care for the frail elderly: an urban experiment', *British Journal of Social Work*, vol. 18 (supplement), pp. 13–42.

Challis, L. (1990) *Organising Public Services* (London: Longman).

Chapman, K. (1989) 'Trends of home care provision into the 1990s', *Eurolink Age Bulletin*, September, p. 19.

Chiu, S. and Yu, S. (2001) 'An excess of culture: the myth of shared care in the Chinese community in Britain', *Ageing and Society*, vol. 21, no. 6, pp. 681–99.

Clapham, D. and Franklin, B. (1994) *The Housing Management Contribution to Community Care* (Glasgow: Centre for Housing Research and Urban Studies, University of Glasgow).

Clark, H., Dyer, S. and Horwood, J. (1998) *'That Bit of Help': The High Value of Low Level Preventative Services for Older People* (Bristol: The Policy Press/Joseph Rowntree Foundation).

Clark, T. (2002) 'New Labour's big idea: joined-up government', *Social Policy and Society*, vol. 1, no. 2, pp. 107–17.

Clarke, J. and Glendinning, C. (2002) 'Partnership and the remaking of welfare governance', pp. 33–50 in C. Glendinning, M. Powell and K. Rummery (eds), *Partnerships, New Labour and the Governance of Welfare* (Bristol: The Policy Press).

Clarke, J. and Newman, J. (1997) *The Managerial State* (London: Sage).

Clasen, J. (ed.) (1999) *Comparative Social Policy: Concepts, Theories and Methods* (Oxford: Blackwell).

Clough, R. (1990) *Practice, Politics and Power in Social Services Departments* (Aldershot: Avebury).

Cobbold, C. (1997) *A Cost Benefit Analysis of Lifetime Homes* (York: Joseph Rowntree Foundation).

Community Care (2002) 'Woman of 108 dies after hunger strike protest over care home move', 2 July, www.community-care.co.uk.

Coote, A. (ed.) (1992) *The Welfare of Citizens: Developing New Social Rights* (London: Institute of Public Policy Research/Rivers Oram Press).

Copus, C. and Raine, J. (2002) *Best Value and Local Councils* (London: Office of the Deputy Prime Minister).

Cox, C. and Pearson, M. (1993) *Made to Care* (London: The Rannock Trust).

Cragg, S. (2002) 'Judge warns parties to resolve disputes out of court', *Community Care Legal Updates*, 4 February, www.community-care.co.uk.

Craig, G. and Manthorpe, J. (1996) *Wiped off the Map – Local Government Reorganisation and Community Care*, Papers in Social Research No. 5 (Hull: University of Lincolnshire and Humberside).

Crowther, M. (1981) *The Workhouse System, 1834–1929: The History of an English Social Institution* (London: Methuen).

Daker-White, G., Beattie, A., Gilliard, J. and Means, R. (2002) *Marginalised Groups in Dementia Care* (Bristol: Dementia Voice/University of the West of England).

Dalley, G. (1996) *Ideologies of Caring: Rethinking Community and Collectivism* (Basingstoke: Macmillan).

Daly, M. (2002) 'Care as a good for social policy', *Journal of Social Policy*, vol. 31, part 2, April, pp. 251–70.

Davies Report (1995) *Report of the Inquiry into the Circumstances Leading to the Death of Jonathan Newby (A Volunteer Worker) on 9th October 1993* (Oxford: Oxfordshire Health Authority).

Davies, B. (1992) 'On breeding the best chameleons', *Generations Review*, vol. 2, no. 2, pp. 18–21.

Davies, B. and Challis, D. (1986) *Matching Needs to Resources* (Aldershot: Gower).

Davies, S., Thornicroft, G., Leese, M. *et al.* (1996) 'Ethnic differences in risk of compulsory psychiatric admission among representative cases of psychosis in London', *British Medical Journal*, vol. 312, no. 7030, pp. 533–7.

Deakin, N. (1995) 'The perils of partnership: the voluntary sector and the state, 1945–1992', pp. 40–65 in J. Davis Smith, C. Rochester and R. Hedley (eds), *An Introduction to the Voluntary Sector* (London: Routledge).

Department of Health (1989a) *Caring for People: Community Care in the Next Decade and Beyond* (London: HMSO).

Department of Health (1989b) *Working for Patients* (London: HMSO).

Department of Health (1990) *Community Care in the Next Decade and Beyond: Policy Guidance* (London: HMSO).

Department of Health (1994) *Implementing Caring for People: Housing and Homelessness* (London: Department of Health).

Department of Health (1995a) *NHS Responsibilities for Meeting Continuing Health Care Needs* (London: Department of Health).

Department of Health (1995b) *Building Bridges: A Guide to Arrangements for Inter-Agency Working for the Care and Protection of Severely Disabled People* (London: Department of Health).

Department of Health (1995c) *An Introduction to Joint Commissioning* (London: Department of Health).

Department of Health (1995d) *Practical Guidance on Joint Commissioning* (London: Department of Health).

Department of Health (1995e) *Moving Forward: A Consultation Document on the Regulation and Inspection of Social Services* (London: Department of Health).

Department of Health (1995f) *European Year: A Historical Report and Evaluation* (London: Department of Health).

Department of Health (1997a) *Social Services: Achievement and Challenge* (London: The Stationery Office).

Department of Health (1997b) *The New NHS: Modern, Dependable* (London: The Stationery Office).

Department of Health (1998a) *Modernising Social Services: Promoting Independence, Improving Protection, Raising Standards* (London: The Stationery Office).

Department of Health (1998b) *Modernising Health and Social Services: National Priorities Guidance 1999/00–2001/02* (London: Department of Health).

Department of Health (1998c) *Our Healthier Nation: A Contract for Health* (London: The Stationery Office).

Department of Health (1998d) *Modernising Mental Health Services: Safe, Sound and Supportive* (London: Department of Health).

Department of Health (1999a) *You and Your Services: A Charter to Improve Services for People Needing Ongoing Support or Care* (London: Department of Health).

Department of Health (1999b) *A National Service Framework for Mental Health* (London: The Stationery Office).

Department of Health (1999c) *Fit for the Future? National Required Standards for Residential and Nursing Homes for Older People – Consultation Document* (London: Department of Health).

Department of Health (1999d) *Modernising Social Services Implementation Diary* (London: Department of Health).

Department of Health (1999e) *Better Care, Higher Standards: A Charter for Long Term Care* (London: Department of Health).

Department of Health (1999f) *Saving Lives: Our Healthier Nation* (London: The Stationery Office).

Department of Health (1999g) *Caring about Carers: A National Strategy for Carers* (London: Department of Health).

Department of Health (2000a) *A Quality Strategy for Social Care* (London: Department of Health).

Department of Health (2000b) *A Quality Strategy for Social Care: Executive Summary* (London: Department of Health).

Department of Health (2000c) *Shaping the Future NHS: Long Term Planning for Hospitals and Related Services: Consultation Document on the Findings of the National Beds Inquiry* (London: The Stationery Office).

Department of Health (2000d) *The NHS Plan: A Plan for Investment, A Plan for Reform* (London: The Stationery Office).

Department of Health (2000e) *NHS Plan, A Plan for Investment, A Plan for Action* (London: The Stationery Office).

Department of Health (2001a) *Valuing People: A New Strategy for Learning Disability for the 21st Century* (London: The Stationery Office).

Department of Health (2001b) *Fit for the Future? National Required Standards for Residential and Nursing Homes for Older People – Summary of Responses* (London: Department of Health).

Department of Health (2001c) *Care Homes for Older People: National Minimum Standards* (London: The Stationery Office).

Department of Health (2001d) *Nothing About Us Without Us: The Report from the Service Users Advisory Group* (London: Department of Health).

Department of Health (2001e) *Family Matters: Counting Families In* (London: Department of Health).

Department of Health (2001f) *Learning Difficulties and Ethnicity* (London: Department of Health).

Department of Health (2001g) *Community Care Statistics 2001: Residential Personal Social Services for Adults, England* (London: Department of Health).

Department of Health (2001h) *Shifting the Balance of Power within the NHS: Securing Delivery* (London: Department of Health).

Department of Health (2001i) *National Service Framework for Older People* (London: The Stationery Office).

Department of Health (2001j) *Building Capacity and Partnership in Care* (London: Department of Health).

Department of Health (2002a) *Fair Access to Care Services: Guidance on Eligibility Criteria for Adult Social Care* (London: Department of Health).

Department of Health (2002b) *National Care Standards Commission (NCSC) Implementation Project* (London: Department of Health).

Department of Health (2002c) *National Minimum Standards for Care Homes for Older People/National Minimum Standards for Care Homes for Younger Adults (18–65): Proposed Amended Environmental Standards* (London: Department of Health).

Department of Health (2002d) *Briefing Note on Consultation on Community Care Plans* (London: Department of Health).

Department of Health (2002e) *Community Care Statistics 2001: Home Help/Home Care Services, England* (London: Department of Health).

Department of Health (2002f) *Intermediate Care: Moving Forward* (London: Department of Health).

Department of Health and Social Security (1971) *Better Services for the Mentally Handicapped* (London: HMSO).

Department of Health and Social Security (1975) *Better Services for the Mentally Ill* (London: HMSO).

Department of Health and Social Security (1977) *Priorities in the Health and Social Services: The Way Forward* (London: HMSO).

Department of Health and Social Security (1978a) *A Happier Old Age* (London: HMSO).

Department of Health and Social Security (1978b) *Collaboration in Community Care: A Discussion Document* (London: HMSO).

Department of Health and Social Security (1981) *Growing Older* (London: HMSO).

Department of Health/Department of the Environment (1997) *Housing and Community Care: Establishing a Strategic Framework* (London: Department of Health).

Department of Health/Department of the Environment, Transport and the Regions (DoH/DETR) (1999) *Health Act 1999 – Modern Partnerships for the People*, Letter to health and social care agencies, 8 September (London: DoH/DETR).

Department of Health/Social Services Inspectorate (1991a) *Care Management and Assessment: Practitioners' Guide* (London: HMSO).

Department of Health/Social Services Inspectorate (1991b) *Care Management and Assessment: Managers' Guide* (London: HMSO).

Department of Health/Social Services Inspectorate (1991c) *Care Management and Assessment: Summary of Practice Guidance* (London: HMSO).

Department of Health/Social Services Inspectorate (1995) *Social Services Departments and the Care Programme Approach: An Inspection* (London: Department of Health).

Department of Health/Social Services Inspectorate (1998) *'They Look After Their Own, Don't They?' Inspection of Community Care Services for Black and Ethnic Minority Older People* (London: Department of Health).

Department of Health/Social Services Inspectorate (1999) *Still Building Bridges* (London: The Stationery Office).

Department of Health/Social Services Inspectorate (2000) *A Modern Social Services: 9th Annual Report of the Chief Inspector of Social Services* (London: Department of Health).

Department of the Environment (1996) *Providing Indicators of Elderly and Disabled People at the District Level* (London: Department of the Environment).

Department of the Environment, Transport and the Regions (1998a) *English House Condition Survey: 1996* (London: The Stationery Office).

Department of the Environment, Transport and the Regions (1998b) *Modernising Local Government: Improving Local Services through Best Value* (London: DETR).

Department of the Environment, Transport and the Regions (with Department of Health) (2001) *Quality and Choice for Older People's Housing: A Strategic Framework* (London: DETR).

Department of Trade and Industry (1998) *Fairness at Work* (London: The Stationery Office).

Department of Transport, Local Government and the Regions (2001a) *Strong Local Leadership – Quality Public Services* (London: The Stationery Office).

Department of Transport, Local Government and the Regions (2001b) *Supporting People: Policy into Practice* (London: DTLR).

Deputy Prime Minister (1998) *Modern Local Government: In Touch with the People* (London: The Stationery Office).

De Wolfe, P. (2002) 'Private tragedy in social context? Reflections on disability, illness and suffering', *Disability and Society*, vol. 17, no. 3, pp. 255–67.

Digby, A. (1978) *Pauper Palaces* (London: Routledge & Kegan Paul).

Disability Daily (2001) *The Disability Manifesto for Rights, Equality and Inclusion* (London: SCOPE).

Douglas, A. (1998) 'Motherhood and apple pie', *Community Care*, 3–9 December, p. 12.

Downey, R. (2002) 'Budget blues', *Community Care*, 16–22 May, pp. 28–30.

Drake, R. (1996) 'A critique of the role of the traditional charities', pp. 147–66 in L. Barton (ed.), *Disability and Society: Emerging Issues and Insights* (Harlow: Longman).

Drewett, A. (1999) 'Social rights and disability: the language of "rights" in community care policies', *Disability and Society*, vol. 14, no. 1, pp. 115–28.

Ellis, J (2001) 'What older people say', *Housing, Care and Support*, vol. 4, no. 2, pp. 9–11.

Emerson, E. and Hatton, C. (1996) *Moving Out: The Impact of Relocation from Hospital to Community on the Quality of Life of People with Learning Disabilities* (London: HMSO).

Esping-Andersen, G. (1990) *The Three Worlds of Welfare Capitalism* (Cambridge: Polity Press).

Estes, C.L. (1979) *The Aging Enterprise* (San Francisco: Jossey-Bass).

Estes, C.L. and Binney, E.A. (1989) 'The biomedicalisation of aging: dangers and dilemmas', *The Gerontologist*, vol. 29, no. 5, pp. 587–96.

Eurobarometer Survey (1993) *Age and Attitudes: Main Results from a Eurobarometer Survey* (Brussels: Commission of the European Communities, Directorate-General V, Employment, Industrial Relations and Social Affairs).

European Commission (1993) *European Social Policy: Options for the Union* (Luxembourg: Office for Official Publications of the European Communities).

European Commission (1994) *European Social Policy: A Way Forward for the Union* (Luxembourg: Office for Official Publications of the European Communities).

European Commission (1996) *Equality of Opportunity for People with Disabilities: A New European Community Disability Strategy* (Luxembourg: Office for Official Publications of the European Communities).

European Commission (1997) *Proposal for Guidelines for Member States Employment Policies* (Luxembourg: Office for Official Publications of the European Communities).

European Commission (1999) *Towards a Europe of All Ages* (Luxembourg: Office for Official Publications of the European Communities).

European Commission (2000) *Towards a Barrier-Free Europe for People with Disabilities* (Luxembourg: Office for Official Publications of the European Communities).

Eurostat (2000) *The Social Situation in the European Union* (Luxembourg: Office for Official Publications of the European Communities).

Evers, A. and Olk, T. (1991) 'The mix of care provisions for the frail elderly in the Federal Republic of Germany', pp. 59–100 in A. Evers and I. Svetlik (eds), *New Welfare Mixes in Care for the Elderly, Vol. 3, Canada, France, Germany, Italy, United Kingdom* (Vienna: European Centre for Social Welfare Policy and Research).

Evers, A. and Sachsse, C. (2003) 'The pattern of social services in Germany: the care of children and older people', pp. 55–79 in A. Anttonen, J. Baldock and J. Sipilä (eds), *The Young, the Old and the State: Social Care Systems in Five Industrial Nations* (Cheltenham: Edward Elgar).

Eyden, J. (1965) 'The physically handicapped', pp. 161–74 in D. Marsh (ed.), *An Introduction to the Study of Social Administration* (London: Routledge & Kegan Paul).

Fargion, V. (2001) 'Italy: moving from the southern model', pp. 183–202 in P. Alcock and G. Craig (eds), *International Social Policy* (Basingstoke: Palgrave Macmillan).

Ferlie, E., Ashburner, L., Fitzgerald, L. and Pettigrew, A. (1996) *The New Public Management in Action* (Oxford: Oxford University Press).

Finch, J. and Groves, D. (eds) (1983) *A Labour of Love: Women, Work and Caring* (London: Routledge & Kegan Paul).

Finkelstein, V.G. (1993) 'Disability: a social challenge or an administrative responsibility?', pp. 34–43 in J. Swain, V. Finkelstein, S. French and M. Oliver (eds), *Disabling Barriers – Enabling Environments* (London: Sage).

Fisher, M. (1990–1) 'Defining the practice content of care management', *Social Work and Social Services Review*, vol. 24, no. 6, pp. 659–80.

Fisher, M. (1994) 'Man-made care: community care and older male carers', *British Journal of Social Work*, vol. 24, no. 6, pp. 659–80.

Foord, M. and Simic, P. (2001) 'A sustainable approach to planning housing and social care: if not now, when?', *Health and Social Care in the Community*, vol. 9, no. 3, pp. 168–76.

Forder, J., Knapp, M. and Wistow, G. (1996) 'Competition in the mixed economy of care', *Journal of Social Policy*, vol. 25, part 2, pp. 201–22.

Forrest, R., Kennett, P. and Leather, P. (1994) *Home Owners with Negative Equity* (Bristol: SAUS Publications).

Foucault, M. (1967) *Madness and Civilisation* (London: Tavistock).

Foucault, M. (1979) *Discipline and Punish: The Birth of the Prison* (Harmondsworth: Penguin).

Frazer, R. and Glick, G. (2000) *Out of Services: A Survey of Social Services Provision for Elderly and Disabled People in England* (London: Needs Must).

Friend, J., Power, J. and Yewlett, C. (1974) *Public Planning: The Intercorporate Dimension* (London: Tavistock).

Gates, B. (2001) 'Valuing People: long awaited strategy for people with learning disabilities for the twenty-first century in England', *Journal of Learning Disabilities*, vol. 5, no. 3, pp. 203–7.

George, S. and Bache, I. (2001) *Politics in the European Union* (Oxford: Oxford University Press).

George, V. (1996) 'The demand for welfare', pp. 177–98 in V. George and P. Taylor-Gooby (eds), *European Welfare Policies: Squaring the Welfare Circle* (Basingstoke: Macmillan).

Geyer, R. (2000) *Exploring European Social Policy* (Cambridge: Polity Press).

Giarchi, G. (1996) *Caring for Older Europeans: Comparative Studies in 29 Countries* (Aldershot: Arena).

Gibbons, J. (1988) 'Residential care for mentally ill adults', pp. 157–97 in I. Sinclair (ed.), *Residential Care: The Research Reviewed* (London: HMSO).

Gilleard, C. and Higgs, P. (2000) *Cultures of Ageing: Self, Citizen and the Body* (Harlow: Prentice-Hall).

Gilroy, P. (2001) 'Cross channel care', *Community Care*, 24–30 May, pp. 21–2.

Gladstone, D. (1996) 'The changing dynamic of institutional care', pp. 134–61 in D. Wright and A. Digby (eds), *From Idiocy to Mental Deficiency* (London: Routledge).

Gladstone, D. (1999) *The Twentieth-Century Welfare State* (Basingstoke: Macmillan).

Glasby, J. and Littlechild, R. (2002) *Social Work and Direct Payments* (Bristol: The Policy Press).

Glen, A. (1993) 'Methods and themes in community practice', pp. 22–40 in H. Butcher, A. Glen, P. Henderson and J. Smith (eds), *Community and Public Policy* (London: Pluto Press).

Glendinning, C. (2002) 'A charge too far', *Community Care*, 11–17 July, pp. 34–5.

Glendinning, C. and Means, R. (2002) 'Rearranging the deckchairs on the Titanic of long-term care? Integrating health and social services for older people in England', paper presented at the Social Policy Association conference, University of Teesside, 17–19 July.

Glendinning, C., Coleman, A. and Rummery, K. (2002a) 'Partnerships, performance and primary care: developing integrated services for older people in England', *Ageing and Society*, vol. 22, no. 2, pp. 185–208.

Glendinning, C., Powell, M. and Rummery, K. (eds) (2002b) *Partnerships, New Labour and the Governance of Welfare* (Bristol: The Policy Press).

Glennerster, H. (2002) *British Social Policy since 1945* (Oxford: Blackwell).

Godlove, C. and Mann, A. (1980) 'Thirty years of the welfare state; current issues in British social policy for the aged', *Aged Care and Services Review*, vol. 2, no. 1, pp. 1–12.

Godsell, M. (2002) 'The social context of service provision for people with learning disabilities: continuity and change in the professional task', unpublished PhD thesis, University of Bristol.

Goffman, E. (1968) *Asylums: Essays on the Social Situation of Mental Patients and Other Inmates* (Harmondsworth: Penguin).

Goodwin, S. (1990) *Community Care and the Future of Mental Health Service Provision* (Aldershot: Avebury).

Gori, C. (1999) 'Care allowances for the elderly in Italy: new features and challenges', paper to July 1999 conference of the Social Policy Association, London.

Gorman, H. (2000) 'Winning hearts and minds? – emotional labour and learning for care management work', *Journal of Social Work Practice*, vol. 14, no. 2, pp. 149–58.

Greenwood, J., Strangward, L. and Stancich, L. (1999) 'The capacities of Euro groups in the integration process', *Political Studies*, vol. 8, no. 2, April, pp. 227–46.

Grieg, R. (2001) 'The real challenges in *Valuing People*', *Managing Community Care*, vol. 9, no. 3, pp. 3–6.

Griffiths Report (1988) *Community Care: An Agenda for Action* (London: HMSO).

Griffiths, S. (1997a) 'Bringing the house down', *Community Care*, 29 May–4 June, pp. 22–3.

Griffiths, S. (1997b) *Housing Benefit and Supported Housing: The Implications of Recent Changes* (York: Joseph Rowntree Foundation).

Griffiths, S. (2000) *Supporting People All the Way: An Overview of the 'Supporting People' Programme* (York: York Publishing Services).

Gurney, C. (1990) *The Meaning of Home in the Decade of Owner Occupation* (Bristol: School for Advanced Urban Studies).

Haber, C. (1983) *Beyond Sixty-Five: The Dilemma of Old Age in America's Past* (Cambridge: Cambridge University Press).

Hadley, R. and Clough, R. (1996) *Care in Chaos: Frustration and Challenge in Community Care* (London: Cassell).

Handley. P. (2000) 'Trouble in paradise – a disabled person's right to the satisfaction of a self-defined need: some conceptual and practical problems', *Disability and Society*, vol. 16, no. 2, pp. 313–25.

Hansen, E. (2002) 'Europe can help reduce vacancies', *Community Care*, 3–9 October, p. 24.

Hantrais, L. (2000) *Social Policy in the European Union*, 2nd edn (Basingstoke: Macmillan).

Hardy, B., Young, R. and Wistow, G. (1999) 'Dimensions of choice in the assessment and care management process: the views of older people, carers and care managers', *Health and Social Care in the Community*, vol. 7, no. 6, pp. 482–91.

Harris, A. (1961) *Meals on Wheels for Old People* (London: National Corporation for the Care of Old People).

Harrison, F. (1986) *The Young Disabled Adult: The Use of Residential Homes and Hospital Units for the Age Group 16–64* (London: Royal College of Physicians).

Hayes, D. (2002) 'Milburn announces major reforms and investment for older people', *Community Care*, 25–31 July, p. 6.

Health Advisory Service (1983) *The Rising Tide: Developing Services for Mental Illness in Old Age* (London: HMSO).

Help the Aged (2002) *Nothing Personal: Rationing Social Care for Older People* (London: Help the Aged).

Hendey, N. and Pascall, G. (2002) *Disability and Transition to Adulthood: Achieving Independent Living* (Brighton: Pavilion).

Henwood, M. (1994) *Hospital Discharge Workbook: A Manual on Hospital Discharge* (London: Department of Health).

Henwood, M. (2001) *Future Imperfect? Report of the King's Fund Care and Support Inquiry* (London: King's Fund).

Henwood, M., Lewis, H. and Waddington, E. (1998) *Listening to Users of Domiciliary Care Services: Developing and Monitoring Quality Standards* (Leeds: Nuffield Institute for Health).

Heywood, F. (2001) *Money Well Spent: The Effectiveness and Value of Housing Adaptations* (Bristol: The Policy Press).

Heywood, F., Oldman, C. and Means, R. (2002) *Housing and Home in Later Life* (Buckingham: Open University Press).

Heywood, F., Pate, A., Means, R. and Galvin, J. (1999) *Housing Options for Older People (HOOP): A Developmental Project to Refine a Housing Option Appraisal Tool for Use by Older People* (London: Elderly Accommodation Counsel).

Higgins, J. (1989) 'Defining community care: realities and myths', *Social Policy and Administration*, vol. 23, no. 1, pp. 3–16.

Hill, M. (ed.) (1991) *Social Work and The European Community: The Social Policy and Practice Context*, Research Highlights in Social Work 23 (London: Jessica Kingsley).

Hill, M. (1996) *Social Policy: A Comparative Analysis* (London: Prentice-Hall/Harvester Wheatsheaf).

Hill, M. (2000a) 'Organisation within local authorities', pp. 158–78 in M. Hill (ed.), *Local Authority Social Services: An Introduction* (Oxford: Blackwell).

Hill, M. (2000b) 'The central and local government framework', pp. 139–57 in M. Hill (ed.), *Local Authority Social Services: An Introduction* (Oxford: Blackwell).

Hill, M. and Hupe, P. (2002) *Implementing Public Policy* (London: Sage).

Hofman, A., Rocca, W. and Brayne, C. (1991) 'The prevalence of dementia in Europe: a collaborative study of 1980–1990 findings', *International Journal of Epidemiology*, vol. 20, no. 3, pp. 736–8.

Hoggett, P. (1996) 'New modes of control in the public sector', *Public Administration*, vol. 74, no. 1, Spring, pp. 9–32.

Hoggett, P. (2001) 'Agency, rationality and social policy', *Journal of Social Policy*, vol. 30, part 1, pp. 37–56.

Holden, C. (2003) 'Globalisation and welfare: a meso-level analysis', pp. 107–22 in R. Sykes, C. Bochel and N. Ellison (eds), *Social Policy Review No. 14: Developments and Debates 2001–2002* (Bristol: The Policy Press).

Holland, C. and Peace, S. (2001) 'Inclusive housing', pp. 235–60 in S. Peace and C. Holland (eds), *Inclusive Housing in an Ageing Society* (Bristol: The Policy Press).

Hood, C., James, O. and Scott, C. (2000) 'Regulation of government: has it increased, is it increasing, should it be diminished?' *Public Administration*, vol. 78, no. 2, pp. 283–304.

House of Lords Library (1995) *Community Care (Direct Payments) Bill: Library Notes* (London: House of Lords).

Hoyes, L. and Means, R. (1993) 'Quasi-markets and the reform of community care', pp. 93–124 in J. Le Grand and W. Bartlett (eds), *Quasi-Markets and Social Policy* (Basingstoke: Macmillan).

Hoyes, L. and Means, R. with Hawes, D., Smart, G. and Smith, R. (1996) *Supported Housing and Community Care* (London: Housing Corporation).

Hoyes, L., Lart, R., Means, R. and Taylor, M. (1994) *Community Care in Transition* (York: Joseph Rowntree Foundation/London: Community Care).

Hudson, B. (1987) 'Collaboration in social welfare: a framework for analysis', *Policy and Politics*, vol. 15, no. 3, pp. 175–82.

Hudson, B. (1992) 'All dressed up – but nowhere to go?', *Health Services Journal*, 22 October, pp. 22–4.

Hudson, B. (ed.) (2000) *The Changing Role of Social Care* (London: Jessica Kingsley).

Hudson, B. (2002) 'Interprofessionality in health and social care: the Achilles' heel of partnership?', *Journal of Interprofessional Care*, vol. 16, no. 1, pp. 7–17.

Hugman, R. (1994) 'Social work and case management in the UK: models of professionalism and elderly people', *Ageing and Society*, vol. 14, no. 2, pp. 237–53.

Hunt, M. (2001) *The Human Rights Act: What are the Implications for Older People?* (London: Help the Aged).

Hunter, M. (1998) 'Jam tomorrow', *Community Care*, 10–16 December, pp. 8–9.

Huws Jones, R. (1952) 'Old people's welfare – successes and failures', *Social Services Quarterly*, vol. 26, no. 1, pp. 19–22.

Huxham, C. (ed.) (1996) *Creating Collaborative Advantage* (London: Sage).

Interdepartmental Review of Funding for Supported Accommodation (1998) *Supporting People: A New Policy and Funding Framework for Support Services* (London: Department of Social Security).

Jamieson, A. (1991) 'Community care for older people', pp. 107–26 in G. Room (ed.), *Towards a European Welfare State?* SAUS Study 6 (Bristol: SAUS Publications).

Jamieson, A., Harper, S. and Victor, C. (eds) (1997) *Critical Approaches to Ageing and Later Life* (Buckingham: Open University Press).

Jerrom, C. (2002) 'Scotland blazes a trail on free personal care for older people', *Community Care*, 27 June–3 July, pp. 18–19.

JM Consulting Ltd (1999a) *Review of the Diploma in Social Work* (London: Department of Health).

JM Consulting Ltd (1999b) *Review of the Delivery of the Diploma in Social Work in England* (London: Department of Health).

Joffe, J. and Lipsey, D. (1999) 'Note of dissent', pp. 113–43 in Sutherland Report, *With Respect to Old Age: A Report by the Royal Commission on Long Term Care* (London: The Stationery Office).

Johnson, M. (1990) 'Dependency and interdependency', pp. 209–28 in J. Bond and P. Coleman (eds), *Ageing in Society: An Introduction to Social Gerontology* (London: Sage).

Johnson, N. (1987) *The Welfare State in Transition: The Theory and Practice of Welfare Pluralism* (Brighton: Wheatsheaf).

Johnson, P. (1987) *Structural Dependency of the Elderly: A Critical Note* (London: Centre for Economic Policy Research).

Jones, C. (2001) 'Voices from the front line: state social workers and new labour', *British Journal of Social Work*, vol. 31, no. 4, pp. 547–62.

Jones, K. (1972) *A History of the Mental Health Services* (London: Routledge & Kegan Paul).

Jones, K. (1993) *Asylums and After* (London: The Athlone Press).

Jones, K. and Fowles, A. (1984) *Ideas on Institutions* (London: Routledge & Kegan Paul).

Joseph Rowntree Foundation (2002) *Britain's Housing in 2022: More Shortages and Homelessness* (York: Joseph Rowntree Foundation).

Kaufman, S.R. (1994) 'The social construction of frailty: an anthropological perspective', *Journal of Aging Studies*, vol. 8, no. 1, pp. 45–58.

240   *References*

Kelly, M. (2001) 'Lifetime homes', pp. 55–76 in S. Peace and C. Holland (eds), *Inclusive Housing in an Ageing Society* (Bristol: The Policy Press).

Kendall, L. and Harker, L. (eds) (2002) *From Welfare to Wellbeing: The Future of Social Care* (London: Institute for Public Policy Research).

Kennett, P. (2001) *Comparative Social Policy* (Buckingham: Open University Press).

Kleinman, M. (2002) *A European Welfare State? European Union Social Policy in Context* (Basingstoke: Palgrave Macmillan).

Knapp, M., Hardy, B. and Forder, J. (2001) 'Commissioning for quality: ten years of social care markets in England', *Journal of Social Policy*, vol. 30, part 2, pp. 283–306.

Knapp, M., Wistow, G. and Jones, N. (1992) 'Smart moves', *Health Services Journal*, 29 October, pp. 28–30.

Knapp, M., Wistow, G., Forder, J. and Hardy, B. (1993) *Markets for Social Care: Opportunities, Barriers and Implications*, PSSRU Discussion Paper 919 (Canterbury: Personal Social Services Research Unit, University of Kent).

Kondratowitz, H.-J. von, Tesch-Römer, C. and Motel-Klingebiel, A. (2002) 'Establishing systems of care in Germany: a long and winding road', mimeo, pp. 19.

Labour Party (1997) *New Labour: Because Britain Deserves Better* (London: The Labour Party).

Laing, W. and Saper, P. (1999) 'Promoting the development of a flourishing independent sector alongside good quality public services', pp. 87–102 in Part One of *Community Care and Informal Care*, Research Volume 3, The Royal Commission on Long Term Care (London: The Stationery Office).

Langan, J., Means, R. and Rolfe, S. (1996) *Maintaining Independence in Later Life: Older People Speaking* (Oxford: Anchor Trust).

Langton-Lockton, S. (1998) 'Centre forward: extending Part M to new housing', *Access by Design*, no. 75, January/April, p. 5.

Lart, R. (1997) *Crossing Boundaries: Accessing Community Mental Health Services for Prisoners on Release* (Bristol: The Policy Press).

Lawson, R. (1996) 'Germany: maintaining the middle way', pp. 31–50 in V. George and P. Taylor-Gooby (eds), *European Welfare Policy: Squaring the Welfare Circle* (Basingstoke: Macmillan).

Leach, S. and Wilson, D. (2000) *Local Political Leadership* (Bristol: The Policy Press).

Leason, K. (2002) 'About-turn on minimum care home standards sparks anger on all sides', *Community Care*, 22–28 August, p. 8.

Leat, D. (1988) 'Residential care for younger physically disabled adults', pp. 199–239 in I. Sinclair (ed.), *Residential Care: The Research Reviewed* (London: HMSO).

Leather, P. (2000) *Crumbling Castles? Helping Owners to Repair and Maintain their Homes* (York: Joseph Rowntree Foundation).

Le Grand, J. and Bartlett, W. (eds) (1993) *Quasi-Markets and Social Policy* (Basingstoke: Macmillan).

Leira, A. (1992) *Welfare States and Working Mothers* (Cambridge: Cambridge University Press).

Leisering, L. (2001) 'Germany: reform from within', pp. 161–82 in P. Alcock and G. Craig (eds), *International Social Policy* (Basingstoke: Palgrave Macmillan).

Lewis, J. (2001) 'Social services departments and the health/social care boundary: players or pawns?', pp. 23–39 in I. Allen (ed.), *Social Care and Health: A New Deal?* (London: Policy Studies Institute).

Lewis, J. and Glennerster, H. (1996) *Implementing the New Community Care* (Buckingham: Open University Press).

Lipsky, M. (1980) *Street Level Bureaucracy* (New York: Russell Sage).

Livesey, B. (2002) 'Delays in mental health tribunal hearings breach human rights', *Community Care Legal Updates*, 20 May, www.community-care.co.uk.

Lloyd, L. (2000) 'Caring about carers: only half the picture?', *Critical Social Policy*, vol. 20, no. 1, pp. 136–50.

Lloyd, M. (2000) 'Where has all the care management gone? The challenge of Parkinson's disease to the health and social care interface', *British Journal of Social Work*, vol. 30, no. 6, pp. 737–54.

Lloyd, M. (2001) 'The politics of disability and feminism: discord or synthesis?', *Sociology*, vol. 35, no. 3, pp. 715–28.

Local Government Association (2001) *An Inspector Calls: A Survey of Local Authorities on the Impact of Inspection* (London: Local Government Association).

Lovelock, R., Powell, J. with Craggs, S. (1995) *Shared Territory: Assessing the Social Support Needs of Visually Impaired People* (York: Joseph Rowntree Foundation/London: Community Care).

Lowe, R. (1999) *The Welfare State in Britain since 1945* (Basingstoke: Macmillan).

Lukes, S. (1974) *Power: A Radical View* (London: Macmillan).

Lund, B. and Foord, M. (1997) *Housing Strategies and Community Care: Towards Integrated Living?* (Bristol: The Policy Press).

Lunt, N., Mannion, R. and Smith, P. (1996) 'The finance of community care', pp. 78–96 in N. Lunt and D. Coyle (eds), *Welfare and Policy: Research Agendas and Issues* (London: Taylor & Francis).

Lymbery, M. (1998) 'Care management and professional autonomy: the impact of community care legislation on social work with older people', *British Journal of Social Work*, vol. 28, no. 6, pp. 863–78.

McClatchey, T. (2002) 'Dementia and demography: development of a predictive model of the demand for, location and cost of care', PhD thesis, Bristol: University of the West of England.

McClatchey, T., Means, R. and Morbey, H. (2001) *Housing Adaptations and Improvements for People with Dementia* (Bristol: University of the West of England).

McEwan, P. and Laverty, S. (1949) *The Chronic Sick and Elderly in Hospital* (Bradford: Bradford (B) Hospital Management Committee).

Maher, J. and Green, H. (2002) *Carers 2000: Results from the Carers Module of the General Household Survey 2000* (London: The Stationery Office).

Malin, N., Rose, D. and Jones, G. (1980) *Services for the Mentally Handicapped in Britain* (London: Croom Helm).

Malin, N., Manthorpe, J., Rose, D. and Wilmot, S. (1999) *Community Care for Nurses and the Caring Professions* (Buckingham: Open University Press).

Marinakou, M. (1998) 'Welfare states in the European periphery: the case of Greece', pp. 231–47 in R. Sykes and P. Alcock (eds), *Developments in European Social Policy: Convergence and Diversity* (Bristol: The Policy Press).

Marks, D. (1999) *Disability: Controversial Debates and Psychosocial Perspectives* (London: Routledge).

Marks, G., Haesly, R. and Mbaye, H. (2002) 'What do subnational offices think they are doing in Brussels?', *Regional and Federal Studies*, vol. 12, no. 3, pp. 1–23.

Marsh, A., Gordon, D., Heslop, P. and Pantazis, C. (2000) 'Housing deprivation and health: a longitudinal analysis', *Housing Studies*, vol. 15, no. 3, pp. 411–28.

Marshall, M. (1989) 'The sound of silence: who cares about the quality of social work with older people?', pp. 109–22 in C. Rojek, G. Peacock and S. Collins (eds), *The Haunt of Misery: Critical Essays in Social Work and Helping* (London: Routledge).

Martin, B. (2002) 'The money programme', *Community Care*, 8–14 August, pp. 30–1.

Martin, F. (2001) 'Evidence is the key to promise of intermediate care', *Community Care*, 26 July–1 August, pp. 18–19.

Martin, J., Meltzer, H. and Elliot, D. (1988) *The Prevalence of Disability Among Adults*, OPCS Surveys (London: HMSO).

Martin, M. (1995) 'Medical knowledge and medical practice: geriatric knowledge in the 1950s', *Social History of Medicine*, vol. 7, no. 3, pp. 443–61.

Martin, S. and Davis, H. (2001) 'What works and for whom? The competing rationalities of Best Value', *Policy and Politics*, vol. 29, no. 4, pp. 465–75.

Matarasso, F. (1997) *Use or Ornament? The Social Impact of Participation in the Arts* (Stroud: Comedia).

Matthews, O. (undated) *Housing the Infirm*, published by the author and originally distributed through W.H. Smith & Son.

Means, R. (1986) 'The development of social services for elderly people: historical perspectives', pp. 87–109 in C. Phillipson and A. Walker (eds), *Ageing and Social Policy: A Critical Assessment* (Aldershot: Gower).

Means, R. (1996) 'From "special needs" housing to independent living?', *Housing Studies*, vol. 11, no. 2, pp. 207–31.

Means, R. (1997a) 'Home, independence and community care: time for a wider vision?', *Policy and Politics*, vol. 25, no. 4, pp. 409–19.

Means, R. (1997b) 'Housing options in 2020: a suitable home for all', pp. 142–64 in M. Evandrou (ed.), *Baby Boomers: Ageing in the 21st Century* (London: Age Concern England).

Means, R. (1999) 'Housing and housing organisations: a review of their contribution to alternative models of care for elderly people', Appendix Three (pp. 299–324) in Tinker *et al.* (eds), *Alternative Models of Care for Older People*, Research Volume 2, The Royal Commission on Long Term Care (London: The Stationery Office).

Means, R. (2001) 'Lessons from the history of long-term care for older people', pp. 9–28 in J. Robinson (ed.), *Towards a New Social Compact for Care in Old Age* (London: King's Fund).

Means, R. and Smith, R. (1998a) *Community Care: Policy and Practice* (Basingstoke: Macmillan).

Means, R. and Smith, R. (1998b) *From Poor Law to Community Care: The Development of Welfare Services for Elderly People, 1939–1971* (Bristol: The Policy Press).

Means, R., Morbey, H. and Smith, R. (2002) *From Community Care to Market Care: The Development of Welfare Services for Older People* (Bristol: The Policy Press).

Means, R., Brenton, M., Harrison, L. and Heywood, F. (1997) *Making Partnerships Work in Community Care: A Guide for Practitioners in Housing, Health and Social Services* (Bristol: The Policy Press).

Means, R., Anderson, L., Greener, I., Griffiths, N., Hek, G., Pollock, J. and Powell, J. (2001) *Establishing an Evaluation and Research Framework for a Community Rehabilitation Service* (Bristol: University of the West of England).

Mencap (2002) *The Housing Timebomb: The Housing Crisis Facing People with a Learning Disability and Their Older Parents* (London: Mencap).

Mental Health Foundation (1994) *Creating Community Care: Report of the Mental Health Foundation Inquiry into Community Care for People with Severe Mental Illness* (London: Mental Health Foundation).

Mental Health Foundation (1995) *Mental Health in Black and Minority Ethnic People. The Fundamental Facts. The Report of a Seminar on Race and Mental Health, 'Towards a Strategy'* (London: Mental Health Foundation).

Mental Health Foundation (1996) *Building Expectations: Opportunities and Services for People with a Learning Disability* (London: Mental Health Foundation).

Milburn, A. (2002) Speech to the 2002 Annual Social Services Conference, Cardiff, www.community-care.co.uk.

Millar, J. and Warman, A. (1996) *Family Obligations in Europe* (London: Family Policy Studies Centre).

Miller, C., Freeman, M. and Ross, N. (2001) *Interprofessional Practice in Health and Social Care* (London: Arnold).

Miller, E. and Gwynne, G. (1972) *A Life Apart* (London: Tavistock).

Milner, J. and Madigan, R. (2001) 'The politics of accessible housing in the UK', pp. 77–100 in S. Peace and C. Holland (eds), *Inclusive Housing in an Ageing Society* (Bristol: The Policy Press).

Mind (2002) *Briefing on Draft Mental Health Bill* (London: Mind).

Ministry of Health (1957) *Local Authority Services for the Chronic Sick and Infirm*, Circular 14/57 (London: Ministry of Health).

Ministry of Health (1965) *The Care of the Elderly in Hospitals and Residential Homes*, Circular 18/65 (London: Ministry of Health).

Mitchell, S. (2000) 'Modernising social services: the management challenge of the 1998 social services White Paper', pp. 179–201 in M. Hill (ed.), *Local Authority Social Services* (Oxford: Blackwell).

Mordaunt, E. (2000) 'The emergence of multi-inspectorate inspections: going it alone is not an option', *Public Administration*, vol. 78, no. 4, pp. 751–69.

Moroney, R. (1976) *The Family and the State* (London: Longman).

Morris, C. (1940) 'Public health during the first three months of war', *Social Work* (London), January, pp. 186–96.

Morris, J. (1990) 'Women and disability', *Social Work Today*, 8 November, p. 22.

Morris, J. (1991) *Pride Against Prejudice: Transforming Attitudes to Disability* (London: The Women's Press).

Morris, J. (1993) *Community Care or Independent Living* (York: Joseph Rowntree Foundation/London: Community Care).

Morris, J. (2002) *Young Disabled People Moving into Adulthood* (York: Joseph Rowntree Foundation).

Morris, P. (1969) *Put Away: A Sociological Study of Institutions for the Mentally Retarded* (London: Routledge & Kegan Paul).

Munday, B. (1996) 'Social care in the member states of the European Union: contexts and overview', pp. 21–66 in B. Munday and P. Ely (eds), *Social Care in Europe* (Hemel Hempstead: Prentice-Hall).

Munday, B. (2002) 'Europe's largesse', *Community Care*, 25 April–1 May, pp. 38–40.

Murphy, E. (1991) *After the Asylums: Community Care for People with Mental Illness* (London: Faber & Faber).

Murray, P. (2002a) 'Lessons of leisure', *Community Care*, 25–31 July, pp. 42–3.

Murray, P. (2002b) *Hello! Are You Listening? Disabled Teenagers' Experience of Access to Inclusive Leisure* (York: York Publishing Services).

National Pensioners Convention (2000) *The Future of Care*, NPC Briefing No. 17 (London: National Pensioners Convention).

Neill, J. and Williams, J. (1992) *Leaving Hospital: Elderly People and their Discharge to Community Care* (London: HMSO).

Nicoll, W. and Salmon, T. (2001) *Understanding the European Union* (Harlow: Longman).

Nocon, A. and Baldwin, S. (1998) *Trends in Rehabilitation Policy: A Review of the Literature* (London: Audit Commission/King's Fund).

Nolan, M. and Caldock, K. (1996) 'Assessment: identifying the barriers to good practice', *Health and Social Care in the Community*, vol. 4, no. 2, pp. 77–85.

Nolan, M., Grant, G. and Keady, J. (1996) *Understanding Family Care* (Buckingham: Open University Press).

Nuffield Provincial Hospitals Trust (1946) *The Hospital Surveys: The Domesday Book of the Hospital Services* (Oxford: Oxford University Press).

Nugent, N. (1999) *The Government and Politics of the European Union*, 4th edn (Basingstoke: Macmillan).

Nugent, N. (2001) *The European Commission* (Basingstoke: Palgrave Macmillan).

Office for National Statistics (1997) *Social Trends 27* (London: HMSO).

Office of the Deputy Prime Minister (2002) *Best Value Performance Indicators 2002/2003* (London: Office of the Deputy Prime Minister).

Oldman, C. (2000) *Blurring the Boundaries: A Fresh Look at Housing Provision and Care for Older People* (Brighton: Pavilion).

Oliver, M. (1990) *The Politics of Disablement* (Basingstoke: Macmillan).

Oliver, M. (1996) *Understanding Disability: From Theory to Practice* (Basingstoke: Macmillan).

Orme, J. (2001a) 'Regulation or fragmentation? Directions for social work under New Labour', *British Journal of Social Work*, vol. 31, no. 4, pp. 611–24.

Orme, J. (2001b) *Gender and Community Care: Social Work and Social Care Perspectives* (Basingstoke: Palgrave Macmillan).

Ovretreit, J. (1993) *Co-ordinating Community Care: Multi-disciplinary Teams and Care Management in Health and Social Services* (Buckingham: Open University Press).

Owens, P., Carrier, J. and Horder, J. (eds) (1995) *Interprofessional Issues in Community and Primary Health Care* (Basingstoke: Macmillan).

Pacolet, J., Bouten, R., Lauoye, H. and Verseick, K. (1999) *Social Protection for Dependency in Old Age in the Fifteen Member States and Norway: Synthesis Report Commissioned by the European Commission and the Belgian Minister of Social Affairs* (Luxembourg: Office of Official Publications of the European Communities).

Pannell, J., Morbey, H. and Means, R. (2002) *'Surviving at the Margins': Older Homeless People and the Organisations That Support Them* (London: Help the Aged).

Parker, G. and Clarke, H. (2002) 'Making the ends meet: do carers and disabled people have a common agenda?', *Policy and Politics*, vol. 30, no. 3, pp. 347–59.

Parker, J. (1965) *Local Health and Welfare Services* (London: Allen & Unwin).

Parker, R. (1988) 'An historical background', pp. 1–38 in I. Sinclair (ed.), *Residential Care: The Research Reviewed* (London: HMSO).

Parton, N. (1991) *Governing the Family* (Basingstoke: Macmillan).

Payne, M. (1995) *Social Work and Community Care* (Basingstoke: Macmillan).

Payne, S. (1999) 'Outside the walls of the asylum? Psychiatric treatment in the 1980s and 1990s', pp. 245–65 in P. Bartlett and D. Wright (eds), *Outside the Walls of the Asylum: The History of Care in the Community, 1750–2000* (London: The Athlone Press).

Peace, S. and Holland, C. (eds) (2001) *Inclusive Housing in an Ageing Society* (Bristol: The Policy Press).

Peace, S., Kellaher, L. and Willcocks, D. (1997) *Re-evaluating Residential Care* (Buckingham: Open University Press).

Pearce, J. (2001) 'Small print', *Community Care*, 2–8 August, pp. 10–11.

Peck, E., Gulliver, P. and Towell, D. (2002) *Modernising Partnerships: An Evaluation of Somerset's Innovations in the Commissioning and Organisation of Mental Health Services* (London: King's College).

Pedersen, L. (1998) 'Health and social care for older people in Denmark: a public solution under threat?', pp. 83–103 in C. Glendinning (ed.), *Rights and Realities: Comparing New Developments in Long Term Care for Older People* (Bristol: The Policy Press).

Perkins, R. (2001) 'Danger and incompetence: mental health and New Labour', *Critical Social Policy*, vol. 21, no. 4, pp. 536–39.

Peters, T. and Waterman, R. (1982) *In Search of Excellence* (New York: Harper & Row).

Peterson, J. and Shackleton, M. (2002) *The Institutions of the European Union* (Oxford: Oxford University Press).

Petmesidou, M. (1996) 'Social protection in Greece: a brief glimpse of a welfare state', *Social Policy and Administration*, vol. 30, no. 4, pp. 324–47.

Phillipson, C. (1982) *Capitalism and the Construction of Old Age* (Basingstoke: Macmillan).

Phillipson, C. (1998) *Reconstructing Old Age: New Agendas in Social Theory and Social Policy* (London: Sage).

Phillipson, C. and Walker, A. (eds) (1986) *Ageing and Social Policy: A Critical Assessment* (Aldershot: Gower).

Phillipson, C., Bernard, M., Phillips, J. and Ogg, J. (2001) *The Family and Community Life of Older People: Social Networks and Social Support in Three Urban Areas* (London: Routledge).

Philp, I. (ed.) (2001) *Family Care of Older People in Europe* (Amsterdam: IOF Press).

Pickard, L. (1999) 'Policy options for informal carers of elderly people', pp. 1–99 in Part Two of *Community Care and Informal Care*, Research Volume 3, The Royal Commission on Long Term Care (London: The Stationery Office).

Pieda plc (1996) *An Evaluation of the Disabled Facilities Grant* (London: HMSO).

Plank, D. (2000) 'Performance for the people or virtual reality? Social services and modernising local government', *Managing Community Care*, vol. 8, no. 1, pp. 13–21.

Platt, D. (2002) 'Why stars are underrated', *Community Care*, 27 June–3 July, pp. 36–8.

Player, S. and Pollock, A. (2001) 'Long term care: from public responsibility to private good', *Critical Social Policy*, vol. 21 no. 2, pp. 231–55.

Postle, K. (2001a) 'The social work side is disappearing. It started with us being called care managers', *Practice*, vol. 13, no. 1, pp. 13–26.

Postle, K. (2001b) 'Things fall apart; the centre cannot hold: deconstructing and reconstructing social work with older people for the 21st century', *Issues in Social Work Education*, vol. 19, no. 2, pp. 23–43.

Postle, K. (2002) 'Working "Between the idea and the reality": ambiguities and tensions in care managers' work', *British Journal of Social Work*, vol. 32, no. 3, pp. 335–51.

Powell, M. (ed.) (1999) *New Labour, New Welfare State?* (Bristol: The Policy Press).

Powell, M. (2000) 'New labour and the third way in the British welfare state: a new and distinctive approach?' *Critical Social Policy*, vol. 20, no. 1, pp. 39–60.

Powell, M. and Hewitt, M. (2002) *Welfare State and Welfare Change* (Buckingham: Open University Press).

Power, M. (1997) *The Audit Society: Rituals of Verification* (Oxford: Oxford University Press).

Poxton, R. (ed.) (1999) *Working Across the Boundaries: Experiences of Primary Health and Social Care Partnerships in Practice* (London: King's Fund).

Pressman, J. and Wildavsky, A. (1973) *Implementation* (Berkeley: University of California Press).

Price Waterhouse/Department of Health (1991) *Implementing Community Care: Purchaser, Commissioner and Provider Roles* (London: HMSO).

Priestley, M. and Rabiee, P. (2001) *Building Bridges: Disability and Old Age* (University of Leeds: Centre for Disability Studies).

Purdue, D., Razzaque, K., Hambleton, R., Stewart, M. with Huxham, C. and Vangen, S. (2000) *Community Leadership in Area Regeneration* (Bristol: The Policy Press).

Pynos, J. and Liebig, P. (eds) (1995) *Housing Frail Elders: International Policies, Perspectives and Prospects* (Baltimore, Md: Johns Hopkins University Press).

Quilgars, D. (1998) *A Life in the Community: Home-Link: Supporting People with Mental Health Problems in Ordinary Housing* (Bristol: The Policy Press).

Qureshi, H. and Henwood, M. (2000) *Older People's Definitions of Quality Services* (York: Joseph Rowntree Foundation).

Rao, N. (2000) *Reviving Local Democracy: New London, New Politics?* (Bristol: The Policy Press).

Rapaport, A. (1995) 'An initial look at the concept of "home",' pp. 25–52 in D. Benjamin and D. Stea (eds), *The Home Words: Interpretation, Meanings and Environments* (Aldershot: Avebury).

Raynes, N., Temple, B., Glenister, C. and Coulthard, L. (2001) *Quality at Home for Older People: Involving Service Users in Defining Home Care Specifications* (Bristol: The Policy Press).

Revans, L. (2001a) 'Hutton unveils new care standards', *Community Care*, 8–14 March, pp. 2–3.

Revans, L. (2001b) 'People with learning difficulties in from the cold', *Community Care*, 29 March–4 April, pp. 10–11.

Revans, L. (2001c) 'Funds needed now', *Community Care*, 12–18 July, p. 6.

Revans, L. (2001d) 'Party politics', *Community Care*, 27 September–3 October, pp. 34–5.

Revans, L. (2002a) 'Social services take on wider role as councils combine departments', *Community Care*, 15–21 August, p. 6.

Revans, L. (2002b) 'Star mapping', *Community Care*, 27 June–3 July, pp. 32–4.

Revans, L. (2002c) 'Human Rights Act fails to protect residents in private care home', *Community Care*, 28 March–3 April, p. 8.

Richards, S. (1994) 'Making sense of needs assessment', *Research Policy and Planning*, vol. 12, no. 1, pp. 5–9.

Richards, S. (1996) 'Defining and assessing need: an ethnographic study of the community care needs assessment of older people', PhD thesis, University of Southampton.

Richards, S. (2000) 'Bridging the divide: elders and the assessment process', *British Journal of Social Work*, vol. 30, no. 1, pp. 37–49.

Richardson, J. (ed.) (2001) *European Union: Power and Policy Making*, 2nd edn (London: Routledge).

Rickford, F. (2001) 'Solid foundations', *Community Care*, 8–14 March, pp. 18–19.

Riseborough, M. (2000) *Overlooked and Excluded: Older People and Regeneration* (London: Age Concern England).

Ritchie, J., Dick, D. and Lingham, R. (1994) *Report of the Inquiry into the Care and Treatment of Christopher Clunis* (London: HMSO).

Robb, B. (1967) *Sans Everything: A Case to Answer* (London: Allen & Unwin).

Roberts, G. (1992) 'Legal aspects of community care', paper delivered to the Law Society Conference, 'Community Care: A Challenge to the Legal Profession', 20 November.

Roberts, N. (1970) *Our Future Selves* (London: Allen & Unwin).

Rodger, J. (2000) *From a Welfare State to a Welfare Society: The Changing Context of Social Policy in a Postmodern Era* (Basingstoke: Macmillan).

Roebuck, J. (1979) 'When does old age begin? The evolution of the English definition', *Journal of Social History*, vol. 12, no. 3, pp. 416–28.

Room, G. (1991) 'Towards a European welfare state?', pp. 1–14 in G. Room (ed.), *Towards a European Welfare State?*, SAUS Study 6 (Bristol: SAUS Publications).

Rossell, T. and Rimbau, C. (1989) 'Spain – social services in the post-Franco democracy', pp. 105–33 in B. Munday (ed.), *The Crisis in Welfare: An International Perspective on Social Services and Social Work* (Hemel Hempstead: Harvester Wheatsheaf).

Rowlings, C. (1981) *Social Work with Elderly People* (London: Allen & Unwin).

Rowntree Report (1980) *Old People: Report of a Survey Committee on the Problems of Ageing and the Care of Old People* (New York: Arno Press).

Rudd, T. (1958) 'Basic problems in the social welfare of the elderly', *The Almoner*, vol. 10, no. 10, pp. 348–9.

Rummery, K. (2002) *Disability, Citizenship and Community Care: A Case for Welfare Rights?* (Aldershot: Ashgate).

Rummery, K. and Glendinning, C. (1999) 'Negotiating needs, access and gatekeeping: developments in health and community care policies in the UK and the rights of disabled and older citizens', *Critical Social Policy*, vol. 19, no. 3, pp. 335–51.

Rummery, K. and Glendinning, C. (2000) *Primary Care and Social Services: Developing New Partnerships for Older People* (Abingdon: Radcliffe Medical Press).

Ryan, J. with Thomas, F. (1980) *The Politics of Mental Handicap* (Harmondsworth: Penguin).

Sainsbury Centre for Mental Health (2002) *Breaking the Circles of Fear: A Review of the Relationship between Mental Health Services and African and Caribbean Communities* (London: Sainsbury Centre for Mental Health).

Salvage, A. (1995) *Who Will Care? Future Prospects for Family Care of Older People in the European Union* (Dublin: European Foundation for the Improvement of Living and Working Conditions).

Samson, E. (1944) *Old Age in the New World* (London: Pilot Press).

Sapey, B. (1995) 'Disabling homes: a study of the housing needs of disabled people in Cornwall', *Disability and Society*, vol. 10, no. 1, pp. 71–86.

Saunders, P. (1990) *A Nation of Home Owners* (London: Unwin Hyman).

Schneider, U. (1999) 'Germany's long-term care insurance: design, implementation and evaluation', *International Social Security Review*, vol. 52, no. 2, pp. 31–74.

Schunk, M. (1998) 'The social insurance model of care for older people in Germany', pp. 29–46 in C. Glendinning (ed.), *Rights and Realities: Comparing New Developments in Long Term Care for Older People* (Bristol: The Policy Press).

Scull, A. (1993) *The Most Solitary of Afflictions: Madness and Society in Britain, 1700–1900* (New Haven, Conn.: Yale University Press).

Seebohm Report (1968) *Report of the Committee on Local Authority and Allied Personal Services* (London: HMSO).

Sennett, R. (1998) *The Concession of Character: The Personal Consequences of Work in the New Capitalism* (New York: Norton & Co.).

Servian, R. (1996) *Theorising Empowerment: Individual Power and Community Care* (Bristol: The Policy Press).

Service Working Group for Personal Social Services (2002) *Expenditure Report 2003/4 to 2005/6* (London: Local Government Association).

Shakespeare, T. (1996) 'Power and prejudice: issues of gender, sexuality and disability', pp. 191–214 in L. Barton (ed.), *Disability and Society: Emerging Issues and Insights* (Harlow: Longman).

Shanas, E., Townsend, P., Wedderburn, D., Friis, H., Milhof, P. and Stehouwer, J. (1968) *Old People in Three Industrialised Societies* (London: Routledge & Kegan Paul).

Shaw, I. (2000) 'Mental health', pp. 105–18 in M. Hill (ed.), *Local Authority Social Services: An Introduction* (Oxford: Blackwell).

Sheldon, J. (1948) *The Social Medicine of Old Age* (Oxford: Oxford University Press).

Sheppard, M. (1995) *Care Management and the New Social Work: A Critical Analysis* (London: Whiting & Birch).

Sidell, M. (1995) *Health in Old Age: Myth, Mystery and Management* (Buckingham: Open University Press).

Simons, K. (1997) 'Residential care or housing and support', *British Journal of Learning Disabilities*, vol. 25, pp. 2–6.

Simons, K. (2000) *Pushing Open the Door: Housing Options: The Impact of a 'Housing and Support' Advisory Service* (Bristol: The Policy Press).

Smart, G. and Means, R. (1997) *Housing and Community Care: Exploring the Role of Home Improvement Agencies* (Oxford: Anchor Trust).

Social Exclusion Unit (1998) *Rough Sleeping* (London: Social Exclusion Unit).

Social Policy Ageing Information Network (2001) *The Underfunding of Social Care and its Consequences for Older People* (London: Social Policy Ageing Information Network).

Social Services Inspectorate and Audit Commission (2002) *Tracking the Changes in Social Services in England, Joint Review Team Sixth Annual Report 2001/2* (London: Social Services Inspectorate and Audit Commission).

Sopp, L. and Wood, L. (2001) *Living in a Lifetime Home: A Survey of Residents' and Developers' Views* (York: York Publishing Services).

Starkey, F., Taylor, P. and Means, R. (2001) 'Coming to terms with primary care trusts: the views of PCG Board members', *Managing Community Care*, vol. 9, issue 2, pp. 22–9.

Stathopoulos, P. (1996) 'Greece: what future the welfare state', pp. 136–54 in V. George and P. Taylor-Gooby (eds), *European Welfare Policy: Squaring the Welfare Circle* (Basingstoke: Macmillan).

Steiner, A. (2001) 'Intermediate care – a good thing', *Age and Ageing*, vol. 30, supp. 3, pp. 33–9.

Steinfield, E. (1981) 'The place of old age: the meaning of housing for old people', pp. 198–246 in J. Duncan (ed.), *Housing and Identity: Cross Cultural Perspectives* (London: Croom Helm).

Sullivan, H. and Skelcher, C. (2002) *Working Across Boundaries: Collaboration in Public Services* (Basingstoke: Palgrave).

Sumner, G. and Smith, R. (1969) *Planning Local Authority Services for the Elderly* (London: Allen & Unwin).

Sutherland Report (1999a) *With Respect to Old Age: A Report by the Royal Commission on Long Term Care* (London: The Stationery Office).

Sutherland Report (1999b) *With Respect to Old Age*, Research Volume 1, The Royal Commission on Long Term Care (London: The Stationery Office).

Sutherland Report (1999c) *With Respect to Old Age*, Research Volume 3, The Royal Commission on Long Term Care (London: The Stationery Office).

Swithinbank, A. (1996) 'The European Union and social care', pp. 67–95 in B. Munday and P. Ely (eds), *Social Care in Europe* (Hemel Hempstead: Prentice-Hall).

Sykes, R., Palier, B. and Prior, P. (eds) (2001) *Globalization and European Welfare States: Challenges and Change* (Basingstoke: Palgrave Macmillan).

Symeonidou, H. (1997a) 'Welfare state and informal networks in contemporary Greece', pp. 337–62 in B. Palier (ed.), *Comparing Social Welfare Systems in Southern Europe, Vol. 3, France, Southern Europe* (Paris: MIRE).

Symeonidou, H. (1997b) 'Social protection in contemporary Greece', pp. 67–86 in M. Rhodes (ed.), *Southern European Welfare States: Between Crisis and Reform* (London: Frank Cass).

Taylor, M. (2003) *Public Policy in the Community* (Basingstoke: Palgrave Macmillan).

Taylor, M., Langan, J. and Hoggett, P. (1995) *Encouraging Diversity: Voluntary and Private Organisations in Community Care* (Aldershot: Arena).

Taylor-Gooby, P. (1996) 'The response of government: fragile convergence?', pp. 199–218 in V. George and P. Taylor-Gooby (eds), *European Welfare Policy: Squaring the Welfare Circle* (Basingstoke: Macmillan).

Tester, S. (1996) *Community Care for Older People: A Comparative Perspective* (Basingstoke: Macmillan – now Palgrave Macmillan).

Tester, S. (1999a) 'Comparative approaches to long-term care for adults', pp. 136–58 in J. Clasen (ed.), *Comparative Social Policy: Concepts, Themes and Methods* (Oxford: Blackwell).

Tester, S. (1999b) *The Quality Challenge: Caring for People with Dementia in Residential Institutions in Europe – A Transnational Study* (Edinburgh: Alzheimer Scotland).

Thomas, C. (1999) *Female Forms: Experiencing and Understanding Disability* (Buckingham: Open University Press).

Thomas, D. and Means, R. (2000) 'Getting started: early research findings on a community rehabilitation service', *Managing Community Care*, vol. 8, issue 6, pp. 41–4.

Thomas, F. (1980) 'Everyday life on the ward', pp. 30–46 in J. Ryan with F. Thomas (eds), *The Politics of Mental Handicap* (Harmondsworth: Penguin).

Thompson, A. (1949) 'Problems of ageing and chronic sickness', *British Medical Journal*, 30 July, pp. 250–1.

Thompson, A. (1997) 'Working to a new rule', *Community Care*, 10–16 July, pp. 20–1.

Timmins, N. (1996) 'The politicians take over the asylum', *The Independent*, 21 February, p. 17.

Tinker, A., Wright, F. and Zeilig, H. (1995) *Difficult to Let Sheltered Housing* (London: HMSO).

Titmuss, R. (1968) *Commitment to Welfare* (London: Allen & Unwin).

Titmuss, R. (1976) *Problems of Social Policy* (London: HMSO).

Topliss, E. (1979) *Provision for the Disabled* (Oxford: Basil Blackwell).

Townsend, P. (1957) *The Family Life of Old People* (London: Routledge & Kegan Paul).

Townsend, P. (1964) *The Last Refuge* (London: Routledge & Kegan Paul).

Townsend, P. (1981) 'The structural dependency of the elderly: the creation of social policy in the twentieth century?', *Ageing and Society*, vol. 1, no. 1, pp. 5–28.

Townsend, P. (1986) 'Ageing and social policy', pp. 15–44 in C. Phillipson and A. Walker (eds), *Ageing and Social Policy: A Critical Assessment* (Aldershot: Gower).

Tredgold, A. (1952) *A Textbook on Mental Deficiency* (London: Baillière, Tindall & Cox).

Tregaskis, C. (2002) 'Social model theory: the story so far ...', *Disability and Society*, vol. 17, no. 4, pp. 457–70.

Triantafillou, J. (2002) *The Greek Open Community Centres for Older People (KAPI) as Promoters of Integrated Health and Social Care*, CARMEN Working Group 2: The Interface between Primary and Secondary Care, Final Report, May. www.carmen-network.com.

Triantafillou, J. and Mestheneos, E. (2001) 'Greece (September 1998)', pp. 75–95 in I. Philp (ed.), *Family Care of Older People in Europe* (Amsterdam: IOS Press).

Trivedi, P. (2002) 'Racism, social exclusion and mental health: a Black user's perspective', pp. 71–82 in K. Bhui (ed.), *Racism and Mental Health* (London: Jessica Kingsley).

Tulle, E. and Mooney, E. (2002) 'Moving to "age-appropriate" housing: government and self in later life,' *Sociology*, vol. 36, no. 3, pp. 685–702.

Ungerson, C. (1987) *Policy is Personal: Sex, Gender and Informal Care* (London: Tavistock).

Valios, N. (1999) 'Charities say charter's "fine words" will need funding', *Community Care*, 3–9 June, p. 23.

Valios, N. (2000) 'Appeal court broadens definition of disability', *Community Care*, 22–28 June, p. 11.

Vernon, A. (1996) 'Fighting two different battles: unity is preferable to enmity', *Disability and Society*, vol. 11, no. 2, pp. 285–90.

Vernon, A. (1999) 'The dialectics of multiple identities and the disabled people's movement', *Disability and Society*, vol. 14, no. 3, pp. 385–98.

Vernon, A. and Qureshi, H. (2000) 'Community care and independence: self-sufficiency or empowerment?', *Critical Social Policy*, vol. 20, no. 2, pp. 255–76.

Wagner Committee (1988) *Residential Care: A Positive Choice* (London: HMSO).

Walker, A. (1992) 'Integration, social policy and elderly citizens: towards a European agenda on ageing?', *Generations Review*, vol. 2, no. 4, pp. 2–8.

Walker, A. (1993) 'Introduction', pp. 7–17 in A. Walker, J. Alber and A.-M. Guillemard (eds), *Older People in Europe: Social and Economic Policies – the 1993 Report of the European Observatory* (Brussels: Commission of the European Communities).

Walker, A. and Maltby, T. (1997) *Ageing Europe* (Buckingham: Open University Press).

Walker, C., Ryan, T. and Walker, A. (1996) *Fair Shares for All?* (Brighton: Pavilion).

Wallace, H. and Wallace, W. (eds) (2000) *Policy-Making in the European Union*, 4th edn (Oxford: Oxford University Press).

Warburton, R. and McCracken, J. (1999) 'An evidence-based perspective from the Department of Health on the impact of the 1993 reforms on the care of frail, elderly people', pp. 25–36 in Part One of *Community Care and Informal Care*, Research Volume 3, the Royal Commission on Long Term Care (London: The Stationery Office).

Ware, P., Matosevic, T., Forder, J., Hardy, B., Kendall, J., Knapp, M. and Wistow, G. (2001) 'Movement and change: independent sector domiciliary care providers between 1995 and 1999', *Health and Social Care in the Community*, vol. 9, no. 6, pp. 334–40.

Watters, C. (1996) 'Representations and realities: black people, community care and mental illness', pp. 105–23 in W. Ahmad and K. Atkin (eds), *Race and Community Care* (Buckingham: Open University Press).

Webb, A. (1991) 'Co-ordination: a problem in public sector management', *Policy and Politics*, vol. 19, no. 4, pp. 229–41.

Wellard, S. (2000) 'Are indicators effective at weighing-up services?', *Community Care*, 26 October–1 November, pp. 10–11.

Welshman, J. (1999) 'Rhetoric and reality: community care in England and Wales, 1948–74', pp. 204–25 in P. Bartlett and D. Wright (eds), *Outside the Walls of the*

Asylum: The History of Care in the Community, 1750–2000 (London: The Athlone Press).

Wendon, B. (1999) 'The Commission and European Union social policy', pp. 55–73 in R. Sykes and P. Alcock (eds), *Developments in European Social Policy: Convergence and Diversity* (Bristol: The Policy Press).

Wilcox, S. (1997) *Housing Finance Review, 1997–98* (York: Joseph Rowntree Foundation).

Wild, C., Duff, P., Arber, S. and Davidson, K. (2002) 'Stress and strain of moving', *Community Care*, 18–24 April, pp. 36–7.

Wilkinson, P., Armstrong, B., Landon, M. with colleagues (2001) *Cold Comfort: The Social and Environmental Determinants of Excess Winter Deaths in England, 1986–96* (Bristol: The Policy Press).

Willcocks, D., Peace, S. and Kellaher, L. (1987) *Private Lives in Public Places* (London: Tavistock).

Williams, R. (1976) *Keywords* (Glasgow: Fontana).

Willmott, P. and Young, M. (1960) *Family and Class in a London Suburb* (London: Routledge & Kegan Paul).

Wilson, G. (1991) 'Models of ageing and their relation to policy formation and service provision', *Policy and Politics*, vol. 19, no. 1, pp. 37–47.

Winchester, R. (2001a) 'Can residents stop the great homes sell-off?', *Community Care*, 1–7 March, pp. 10–11.

Winchester, R. (2001b) 'Moved to tears', *Community Care*, 28 June–4 July, p. 26.

Winchester, R. (2002) 'Cheque's in the post', *Community Care*, 14–20 February, pp. 34–5.

Wistow, G. (1995) 'Aspirations and realities: community care at the crossroads', *Health and Social Care in the Community*, vol. 3, no. 4, pp. 227–40.

Wistow, G., Knapp, M., Hardy, B. and Allen, C. (1992) 'From providing to enabling: local authorities and the mixed economy of social care', *Public Administration*, vol. 70, no. 1, pp. 25–46.

Wistow, G., Knapp, M., Hardy, B. and Allen, C. (1994) *Social Care in a Mixed Economy* (Buckingham: Open University Press).

Wistow, G., Knapp, M., Hardy, B., Forder, J., Kendall, J. and Manning, R. (1996) *Social Care Markets: Progress and Prospects* (Buckingham: Open University Press).

Wyld, C., Duff, P., Arber, S. and Davidson, K. (2002) 'Stress and strain of moving' *Community Care*, 18–24 April, pp. 36–7.

Yeates, N. (2001) *Globalisation and Social Policy* (London: Sage).

Young, D. and Quibell, R. (2000) 'Why rights are never enough: rights, intellectual disability and understanding', *Disability and Society*, vol. 15, no. 5, pp. 747–64.

Young, M. and Willmott, P. (1957) *Family and Kinship in East London* (London: Routledge & Kegan Paul).

Young, R. and Wistow, G. (1996) 'Development of independent home care in 1995 UKHCA survey', pp. 14–15 in *The Mixed Economy of Care*, Bulletin No. 4 (Canterbury: Personal Social Services Research Unit, University of Kent and Leeds: Nuffield Institute for Health, University of Leeds).

Index

public assistance institutions (PAIs) 18–22
public expenditure 24, 34, 47–8, 97
 see also cost
purchaser–provider splits 13, 45, 52, 57–60

qualifications, professional 197
quality of life 218–20
Quality Strategy for Social Care, A 88–90
Quibell, R. 167–8
Quilgars, D. 138
Qureshi, H. 65–6

Rabiee, P. 169–70
racism 170–5
Raine, J. 98–9
rationing 70
Regional Directors of Health and Social Care 217
regulation 73
 improving standards and protection 78–87
rehabilitation 128
relocation 133–5, 163–4
renovation grants 145
rented accommodation 135, 142–3
resettlement 135–6
residential care
 boundary between health and social care 103–5
 for disabled people 25–6
 feelings and moving into 134–5
 mixed economy of social care 63–4
 for older people 5–6, 22
 rights of residents 163–4
 see also institutions/institutional care
Residents Action Group for the Elderly (RAGE) 164
residual welfare state 200
reticulists 116
retirement migration 191–2
retirement pensions 17, 33–4, 35, 188
retreat, home as 132–3

Revans, L. 122
revenue support grant 45, 70
'revolving door' syndrome 31
Richards, S. 56, 69, 70, 179
'right to buy' 141
rights *see* disability rights movement
Rights Now 161
risk 55–6
Robb, B. 31–2
Roberts, G. 165
Roberts, N. 18
Roebuck, J. 17
Room, G. 191
Rous, John 111
Rowlings, C. 40
Rowntree Report 21–2
Royal Commission on the Care and Control of the Feeble-Minded 28
Royal Commission on Long Term Care 9, 11, 117–20, 123, 162, 163, 204
Royal Commission on Mental Illness and Mental Deficiency 31
Royal National Institute for the Blind 159
Rudd, T. 37–8
rudimentary welfare state 200–11
Ryan, J. 28, 29

Sachsse, C. 204
Sainsbury Centre for Mental Health 172–3
Salvage, A. 204–5
Saper, P. 64
Saunders, P. 132, 136
Scull, A. 26, 27, 33
Second World War 19–20, 21, 34, 42
Seebohm Report 180, 222
self-defined needs 166–7
Servian, R. 176
service users *see* users
sexism 170–5
Shaw, I. 57
Sheldon, J. 37
sheltered housing 134, 139–40